For my parents
Ken Ferris

For Anne and Celia
Mark Jones

THE
REUTER GUIDE
TO
OFFICIAL
INTEREST RATES

Ken Ferris & Mark Jones

REUTERS

Probus Publishing Company

Cambridge, England
Chicago, Illinois

First published in 1994 by
Probus Europe, 11 Millers Yard, Mill Lane, Cambridge CB2 1RQ, England

Designed, illustrated and typeset by Nick Battley, London, England

ISBN 1 55738 815 6

Printed in the United Kingdom

Acknowledgements

Austria
Austrian National Bank

Belgium
Marie-Henriette Lambert & Vincent Périlleux
Head of Research Department & Economist (respectively)
Banque Nationale de Belgique

Denmark
Danmarks Nationalbank

Finland
Harri Lahdenperä
Acting Head, Planning Office
Suomen Pankki Finlands Bank

Germany
Manfred Körber
Head of Press & Information
Deutsche Bundesbank

Ireland
Central Bank of Ireland

New Zealand
Peter Katz
Manager, Operations, Financial Markets Department
Reserve Bank of New Zealand

Portugal
Banco de Portugal

Sweden
Richard Grottheim
Deputy Head, Foreign Exchange & Monetary Policy Dept.
Sveriges Riksbank

Switzerland
Werner Abegg
Assistant Director, Press Relations
Swiss National Bank.

United States
Ann-Marie Meulendyke
Assistant Vice President, Open Market Area
Federal Reserve Bank of New York

The authors would also like to thank other central bank officials who kindly provided guidance and suggestions, but prefer to remain anonymous.

For assistance on France, the authors would like to thank Esther Baroudy, *Economist, Crédit Lyonnais, Paris.*

The *Reuter Guide to Official Interest Rates* is also based on material contributed by the following Reuter bureaux:

Australia
Gary West

Austria
Douglas Busvine

Belgium
Geert de Clerq

Canada
Mike Ellis

Denmark
Adam Hannestad

Finland
Fredrik Dahl

France
Alastair Macdonald & John Chalmers

Germany
Janet Northcote

Ireland
Jane O'Sullivan

Italy
Yann Tessier

Japan
Yoshiko Mori

Netherlands
Kristin Kranenberg

New Zealand
Simon Louisson

Norway
Stella Bugge

Portugal
Robert Powell

Spain
Keith Grant

Sweden
Andrew Huddart

Switzerland
Andy Long

United Kingdom
Joe Ortiz

United States
Jacqueline Hurlock

The authors are also indebted to the production editor of *The Reuter Guide to Official Interest Rates*, Nick Battley.

Contents

x

Preface

Over the past few years we have been fielding an increasing number of questions about the significance of short-term interest rates set by central banks around the world.

It started with the Bundesbank and generalized confusion among non-finance specialists about how you could have three 'key' interest rates.

But then it became apparent that among the professionals themselves there was a lack of understanding about official interest rates outside their home country.

This perhaps reached a peak during the prolonged European currency crisis from Summer 1992 until Summer 1993 when a series of countries constructed an elaborate web of official interest rate defences against currency speculators.

The significance of Norway's overnight lending and credit rates was perhaps not fully appreciated until it was too late. Hikes in Sweden's marginal lending rate also grabbed the headlines on the way up, and on the way down. And Britain's minimum lending rate was resurrected for only the third time since it had been 'abolished' in 1981.

The *Reuter Guide to Official Interest Rates* represents our attempt to provide an easy-to-read primer for those looking for rapid answers to interest rate questions. It has been written for financial market traders, fund managers, economists, students and all those who need to know just what changes in official interest rates really mean.

The twenty countries we have covered have been chosen according to the amount of interest shown in their official interest rate policy. All previous and surviving members of the European exchange rate mechanism are there along with the other members of the Group of Seven largest industrialized nations. The remainder are countries with highly developed financial markets and actively-traded currencies.

London, May 1994   *Ken Ferris & Mark Jones* xii

Introduction

How do the money markets work?

The players and their objectives

There are two key players in the money market—the central bank and the commercial banking sector. The central bank acts as the repository for all government receipts (mostly tax payments) and all expenditure. The commercial banking sector acts as both a payments and a credit-creating system whereby money deposited with it generates much larger increases in loans.

The central bank's role in such a system is broadly three-fold:

a) To ensure the smooth running of the money market by ironing out the large fluctuations in interest rates that could result from mismatches between payments into and out of its coffers;

b) To control the creation of credit by the commercial banks by influencing interest rates and/or the availability of reserves to back commercial loans;

c) To finance the budget deficits (the difference between tax payments and public expenditure) typically run by modern governments.

This book is principally concerned with objectives (a) and (b). But first we need to look at objective (c) to show the limits to what a central bank can achieve.

Since most modern economies operate with the government's finances in deficit the central bank is at the centre of the deficit-financing process. If the deficit is to be financed without increasing the money supply (and, probably, inflation) then government bonds need to be sold to cover the gap. This is generally the objective of governments.

However, the interest rates which the government has to pay for such borrowing are largely beyond the control of the central bank. Such rates are predominantly determined by investors' expectations for inflation in the economy and what kind of return they need to compensate them for the declining value of their capital investment.

But when it comes to short-term interest rates, the central bank or government has far more influence. With its ability to restrict or expand the amount of money flowing around the money market (generally known as 'liquidity') it can force up or down the cost of borrowing.

How do central banks influence the money markets?

The ability of a central bank to influence short-term interest rates arises from its ultimate position as the sole provider of the cash reserves which form the basis of modern banking systems. The importance of that role stems from the fact that each central bank acts to keep commercial banks short of reserves so they are forced to borrow on terms set by the central bank—basically an interest rate of the central bank's choosing.

Overnight interest rates are merely the price which equates the supply of reserves from the central bank with the demand for reserves by commercial banks. But like any other monopolist, the central bank is not a price-taker but has a degree of control over the market price—in this case the rate of interest.

To see the practical consequences of this, consider a typical day in a money market.

First, flows between the central bank and the rest of the banking system. These are chiefly, though not exclusively (see the determinants of shortages below), due to the daily mismatch between government receipts from tax and payments in the form of public spending. In the case of tax payments, money is being paid out of taxpayers' accounts at commercial banks into the government's account at the central bank. In the case of public expenditure the money is paid out of the government's account at the central bank and into accounts in the commercial banking system. On a daily basis there may be more being paid out from the central bank than is received, or vice versa.

Second, flows between the commercial banks and the private sector. Each day firms are crediting their workers' bank accounts with wages and salary payments, shopkeepers are depositing their takings, cheques are written and cash is withdrawn by companies and individuals to pay for goods and services, and, finally, bank managers are authorizing loans to companies and individuals.

While the number of transactions each day is huge, to a central banker or money market analyst the system can be boiled down to one key statistic—that summarizing how much more the commercial banks as a group are paying out than they are taking in after netting out payments to and from government, and deposits and withdrawals by customers. If this is positive, i.e. the commercial banking sector is in deficit, the banks as a whole will be running down their reserves, while, if it is negative the commercial banks will be building up reserves.

The role of reserves is pivotal in modern banking systems. Commercial banks like to keep cash reserves, or assets that can quickly become cash, in case there is an abnormally large number of withdrawals. But in almost all modern banking systems they also have to keep a certain amount of cash at the central bank. It is this ability to provide reserves which gives the central bank its power to influence short-term interest rates.

If there is a general cash shortage in the banking system, then commercial banks will find they are losing reserves. Eventually, they will be unable to meet their reserve requirement at the central bank. This has to be observed at all times and there is always a mechanism by which the central bank will allow an individual commercial bank to borrow reserves on a temporary basis. But such reserves are usually only made available at a penal rate.

Thus, if there is a generalized liquidity shortage, with all commercial banks short of reserves, the central bank has the power to dictate what the level of short-term interest rates will be. The key to understanding how the central bank controls short-term interest rates is the fact that it has the power to *guarantee* there will be a liquidity shortage.

How do central banks keep the money markets short of liquidity?

The central bank acts regularly to smooth out volatile interest rates due to the mismatch between government spending and tax receipts. It does so by lending money to the commercial banks or borrowing it back from them. In particular, the central bank uses the sale and purchase of short-term bills or IOUs to relieve money market shortages or to take out surpluses.

As an example, consider the case of a very large cash surplus in the commercial banking sector. If the central bank does nothing, the surplus would put downward pressure on interbank interest rates. But most central banks would deem it sensible to take out some of the surplus by selling short-term bills—the commercial banks get a piece of paper which entitles them to an attractive interest rate and the central bank reduces the volatility of short-term rates by reducing the amount of cash in the system.

If the central bank continually sells its bills to the commercial banks, cash surpluses will become rare and commercial banks will find themselves more and more frequently having to go cap in hand to the central bank to ask for emergency assistance so they can meet their reserve requirements at the central bank. Of course, the commercial banks do not have to buy the bills, but as more and more are sold, and the quantity increases, the interest rate they pay will generally rise making bills difficult to resist.

This is the essence of how most central banks achieve some kind of leverage over commercial banks and the setting of very short-term interest rates. However, the means by which the control is exerted are extremely varied.

The determinants of money market shortages

Although the central bank is ultimately the sole provider of bank reserves, it does not have complete control over the supply of reserves on a daily basis. The key determinants of supply are:

1) Budget deficits
If public spending exceeds revenue on any particular day there will be a net payment from the government to the commercial banking sector. This will increase the supply of reserves, and vice-versa for budget surpluses.

2) Deficit-financing
Most governments aim to finance their budget deficits by selling bonds. On any particular day there may be a net inflow of reserves from the commercial banking sector to the central bank if it is selling bonds, or an outflow if it is redeeming them.

3) Currency intervention
Any foreign currency intervention in support of the domestic currency (i.e. purchases of local currency in return for the sale of foreign reserves) will reduce the supply of banking reserves to the commercial banking system and vice versa for sales of local currency. Such transactions are extremely important in smaller open economies and are, in fact, the main method through which the money market is managed.

The central bank's toolbag

When it comes to the supply of reserves the central bank actually controls, the main distinction is between: (1) straightforward lending and borrowing through various 'windows'; and (2) 'open market operations' (OMOs) which increase or reduce the liquidity of the banking system according to whether the central bank buys or sells short-term bills. A third, though rarely used, option is to change the amount of reserves the commercial banking system must keep at the central bank.

1) Direct lending
In many systems, there is a facility through which banks can borrow emergency funds from the central bank at a preset penalty interest rate. Sometimes there are limits on how much can be borrowed at such a rate to prevent over-use during emergencies like currency crises. There are also interest rates the central bank will guarantee on deposits if commercial banks can find no better use for their money.

Since emergency borrowing facilities are only used when there is not a cheaper alternative, they tend to act as the ceiling for money market rates. Similarly, since guaranteed deposit rates are only used when no-one else will accept the money at a better rate, they tend to act as a floor for market rates.

In some systems, for example that in Germany, the central bank will also guarantee to lend money by rediscounting bills at a preset rate which is well below the market rate. The rationale for offering such a facility is that it compensates commercial banks for the low, or zero, rate of interest their compulsory central bank reserves attract. In such systems, this discount rate sets the floor for money market rates since there would be no point in the central bank making the facility available unless it was lower than alternative commercial rates.

2) Open market operations (OMOs)

While direct lending through various 'windows' or rediscount facilities at the central bank may set a kind of corridor for interest rate fluctuations, the precise level of market rates is usually set by regular open market operations (OMOs). Any central bank transaction with the commercial banking sector involving the sale or repurchase of official bills can be considered an OMO.

OMOs tend to be more significant than direct lending rates due to the frequency with which they are used to manage the supply of reserves to the banking system (daily operations are typical). There are two varieties of OMO—those which supply reserves at a fixed interest rate according to how much is demanded at that price, and those that supply all the reserves required but at a variable rate of interest.

3) Reserve requirements

The least-frequently used option is a change in the central bank's reserve requirements. If a central bank wishes to increase the demand for reserves all it need do is to raise the reserve ratio (proportion of liabilities deposited at the central bank). Other things being equal, this will push up interest rates.

How to use this book

The book has been designed as an easy reference manual. Each country is treated in a separate chapter with the explanation of generic terms left to a separate glossary towards the back of the book.

Each chapter has been divided into a set of menu headings to allow the busy reader to access the required information as quickly as possible:

The rates to watch
    - gives an at-a-glance guide to the most important official interest rates in the form of a series of bullet points together with a fuller explanation of their significance for short-term money market rates.

How does the central bank influence the money market?
    - lists all the main methods by which the central bank manages the supply of banking reserves and the tone of short-term money market rates. Instruments are generally broken down into 'windows' or 'open market operations' and an assessment is made of whether the particular lever is usually used to signal major changes in monetary policy or whether it is part of the central bank's fine-tuning of the money markets.

Who controls the interest rate levers?
    - assesses whether the central bank or Ministry of Finance (Treasury) has ultimate control over interest rate decisions and tackles the key issue of who has responsibility over currency policy (which can neuter the most independent of central banks).

What drives interest rate policy?
    - provides a guide to the indicators that inform a central bank's decision-making on interest rates. The guide lists a series of targets: the operational target refers to day-to-day money market management; the intermediate to monetary policy over the medium term (usually an objective for money supply or the currency); and the final target the long-term objective of monetary policy (usually an inflation target, though sometimes supplemented by targets for growth in the economy).

How do official rates affect commercial ones?
  - tackles the issue of what impact changes in short-term official interest rates actually have on the real economy. The key measure is the proportion of mortgage and company loans that are at fixed rates of interest as opposed to floating interest rates—the greater the proportion that are fixed the less impact any given change in interest rates has on the real economy. This section also gives an idea of which official rates have the biggest effect on loans at floating rates of interest.

Timing
  - gives the frequency of regular central bank open market operations and the precise time of day when any announcements are made on the supply of liquidity or on official interest rates.

Key Reuter pages
  - shows you where to find the most up-to-date information on the money market.

Chapter 1

Australia

The rates to watch

- 'Unofficial' overnight cash rate
  - *indicates the underlying tone for money market rates*

The key money market rate is the **'unofficial' overnight cash rate** paid on unsecured overnight loans and on overnight repos. It is the key influence on the prime lending rates set by banks.

The RBA announces changes in monetary policy. These announcements are accompanied by a statement from the governor informing the market of the desired level for the overnight cash rate and the underlying reasons for the change.

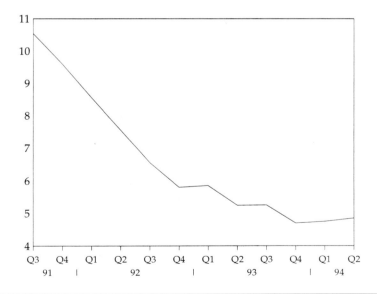

Figure 1.1   Australia: Unofficial overnight cash rate

Source: Datastream

How does the central bank influence the money market?

Open market operations

The RBA influences money market rates through open market operations. Each day at 09.30 local time, the RBA announces the liquidity position of the banking system [RBAU] and the Bank's dealing intentions that day. It also indicates the amount of Treasury notes or bonds not yet purchased from the last tender. The Bank conducts these operations with 10 'authorized' dealers.

■ Repurchase agreements
The RBA deals in short-term government paper and short-dated repurchase agreements with authorized dealers.

■ Outright purchases of government bonds
The RBA also deals outright in the purchase and sale of longer-term commonwealth government securities. These deals can be authorized dealers, banks or any other members of RITS, the Reserve Bank settlement system.

■ Swaps
Sometimes the RBA undertakes foreign currency swaps in US dollars with banks to sterilize the impact on domestic liquidity of foreign currency intervention.

■ Discount rate
The RBA also offers a rediscount facility under which it will buy Treasury notes with a remaining maturity of up to three months at market rates plus a penalty margin. The rediscount facility is seldom used.

Who controls the interest rate levers?

Under the Reserve Bank Act, responsibility for monetary policy resides with the Board of the Bank which is made up of the governor (chairman), deputy governors, the secretary to the Treasury and seven independent directors. In the event of any disagreement, the government has the power to instruct the Bank. This has never happened but if it does the details of the disagreement, including the Bank's views, must be tabled in Parliament. The RBA describes the relationship as one of "independence with consultation".

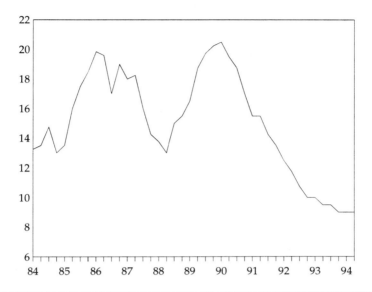

Figure 1.2   Australia: Discount rate
Source: Datastream

What drives interest rate policy?

Targets:

■ Operational
The RBA has a desired level for the overnight cash rate.

■ Intermediate
Under a deregulated financial system, the central bank has found adherence to a monetary target impossible.

■ Final
Price stability. There is an informal inflation target of two to three per cent.

How do official rates affect commercial ones?

Corporate

Most companies use bank loans. About two-thirds of such loans are variable rate. The benchmark is the Australian lending (prime) rate which tends to track movements in the overnight cash rate.

Mortgages

Nearly all mortgages are variable rate. However, interest rate changes are frequently absorbed in the maturity of the loan so limiting the impact of short-term changes in official interest rates on the household sector.

Timing

The RBA Board decides whether there should be a policy change at its meeting on the first Tuesday of each month, but it generally leaves the exact timing to the Bank's discretion.

In keeping with its overall policy of monetary stability, the Bank tends to avoid changes on the same day as major statistical releases, financial futures close-outs, etc. The most likely time for a rate change is the week after an RBA board meeting or shortly after the next important statistical release following the meeting.

There is no set time for changing the official cash rate, but since the RBA started easing monetary policy in January 1990, it has usually made an announcement at 09.30 local time saying it will act in the money market that day to change the official rate. The RBA stresses that it is free to make an announcement and change rates at any time. (Before 1990, no announcements were made.) After the announcement, the Bank conducts open market operations to change the official rate, though the announcement itself sometimes achieves this.

Unlike in some countries, there is no set timetable for repos.

Key Reuter pages

Monitor

Reserve Bank of Australia pages:

RBAA-Z	Full range
RBAA-D	Announcements of changes in monetary policy
RBAH	Repos
RBAU	Daily market cash position
RBAY	Treasury note tender announcements
RBAZ	Treasury bond tender announcements

Other pages:

YLDS	Key interest rates from overnight to 30 years

News 2000

MMT <F9> Topic code

Chapter 2

Austria

The rates to watch

- Gomex rate
  - *sets the tone for money market rates*

- Discount rate
  - *sets the floor for money market rates*

- Lombard rate
  - *sets the ceiling for money market rates*

Austria's monetary policy is similar to Germany's to the extent that the **discount rate** and **lombard rate** set the *official* floor and ceiling for money market rates. However, the **Gomex** money market intervention rate is the *effective* floor for money market rates, while lombard loans do not account for any routine bank refinancing. (Note the Austria's lombard rate is charged on short-term loans of up to three month's maturity, whereas Germany's lombard rate applies to overnight loans.)

How does the central bank influence the money market?

Stabilizing the schilling against the mark is the prime objective of Austrian monetary policy—everything else follows from this. In the first instance, schilling stability is achieved through currency market intervention—this affects money market liquidity and that affects the tone of money market rates. Thus, fluctuations in money market liquidity, as a result of central bank purchases and sales of foreign exchange through the official currency fixing, are the driving force behind domestic interest rate trends. It tends to be over longer periods that *official* interest rates are more important.

The central bank manages money market liquidity using foreign exchange operations (*see* 'Open market operations'), loans at the Gomex and discount rates, and fine-tuning instruments including variable-rate repurchase agreements and minimum reserve policy.

There is a limit to the amount each bank can borrow from the central bank without giving a reason. Part of the limit can be used up at the discount rate, which is always the lowest official rate, and the rest at the

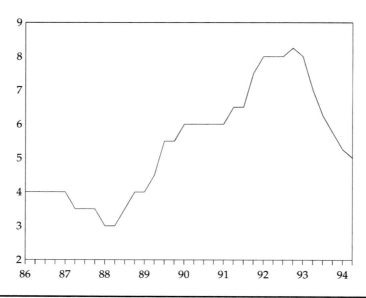

Figure 2.1   Austria: Discount rate
Source: Datastream

Gomex rate which is the cheapest money banks can get because it is usually just below the interbank rate.

Refinancing activities

■ Gomex
The Gomex rate is the money market intervention rate which the central bank tries to keep very close to the market. It is a flexible instrument which is the cheapest alternative to discount borrowing that banks can get and therefore operates as the effective floor for short-term money market rates.

About two-thirds of bank refinancing is executed at the Gomex rate. Banks can deposit approved securities—most listed securities—at the central bank and borrow at the Gomex rate.

■ Discount rate
The discount rate is the lowest of the three leading rates and applies for about a third of bank refinancing. It is the interest rate charged by the central bank on purchases of bills of exchange or securities. The bills, which must be presented by the banks, have to be payable in Austria within three months, bear at least two reputable signatures and be based on a genuine

trade transaction. The central bank can refuse to purchase bills without giving a reason.

■ Lombard rate

The lombard rate is the least important of the three leading rates and loans at this rate do not account for any routine bank refinancing. It is charged on short-term loans of up to three months' maturity granted against collateral. The central bank can refuse to grant lombard loans without giving a reason. The lombard rate has historically been about two percentage points above the discount rate.

■ Refinancing ceilings

The central bank sets a ceiling on the total amount of Gomex, discount and lombard loans granted based on banks' balance sheets. These ceilings are frequently raised/lowered to ease/tighten monetary policy.

■ Somali

The central bank can lend extra money to banks under a tender operation called the Somali (special open market line) at any time. The Somali is used to provide funds when banks have reached their refinancing ceilings at the Gomex, discount and lombard rates. This is used once or twice a year.

Open market operations

■ Foreign exchange operations

The central bank can increase/reduce commercial bank liquidity by buying/selling foreign currency for Austrian schillings on either the spot or forward markets. Forward transactions oblige the central bank to resell (repurchase) foreign currency to (from) the banking sector after a given period at a predetermined rate. Such operations are used frequently to influence money market rates.

■ Repurchase agreements

The central bank can buy or sell securities with an agreement to repurchase them at a fixed future date at a fixed amount. This is the most common open market operation.

■ Outright purchases and sales of securities

The central bank can also buy or sell open market paper and its own cash certificates outright to affect money market liquidity. However, transactions usually take the form of repurchase agreements.

■ Minimum reserve policy

Commercial banks may be forced to hold a percentage of their liabilities as non-interest-bearing deposits at the central bank. The minimum reserve requirement must be met on average each month. The central bank may change the overall minimum reserve requirement in line with its monetary policy and can set different minimum reserve ratios on different banks according to their size and the type of liabilities. An increase in the minimum reserve requirement reduces liquidity and vice versa.

Who controls the interest rate levers?

The Austrian National Bank sets monetary policy. The National Bank Act states that the government should not adopt policies which contradict those of the central bank and that no government employee can sit on the central bank's policy-making Governing Board.

What drives interest rate policy?

The National Bank Act requires the central bank to preserve both the schilling's internal value (in other words, inflation) and its external value. For a generation, this has been interpreted by the National Bank as stabilizing the Austrian currency against the mark.

How do official rates affect commercial ones?

Corporate

Only about 10-20 per cent of corporate bank loans are at a fixed rate. The precise percentage varies according to fashion, with fixed deals more popular when interest rates are low. Variable-rate loans are generally related to the Austrian prime rate which has no fixed relationship to official rates but is changed in line with money market rates.

Mortgages

The structure of Austria's mortgage market is similar to that in Germany with *bausparkassen* (similar to building societies or savings & loans) the main source of fixed rate finance for periods over 15 years or so. However, top-up loans from commercial banks are necessary to meet the full purchase price of property and these are more likely to be floating-rate or fixed for a much shorter period (3-5 years). The mortgage market is therefore largely insulated from changes in short-term official rates.

Timing

The National Bank board meets every Thursday to decide whether to adjust its lombard and discount rates. The Gomex rate can be changed at any time.

Key Reuter pages

Monitor

National Bank of Austria pages:

ECOE-J	Full range
ECOE-G	Weekly central bank reserves figures. The key figure is *Devisen und Valuten* foreign exchange reserves
QQHH	Vienna interbank money market contributed quotes
VIBO	Average interbank quotes

News 2000

MMT <F9> Topic code

Chapter 3

Belgium

The rates to watch

- Central rate
  - *sets the tone for money market rates*

- End-of-day (overdraft) rate
  - *sets the ceiling for money market rates*

- Emergency lending (special overdraft) rate
  - *highest official rate*

- Discount rate
  - *lowest official lending rate*

- Tender rate
  - *usually the same as the central rate*

- Special deposit rate
  - *sets the floor for money market rates*

The key rate is the **central rate** at which the 15 primary dealers in govern-ment debt can borrow (or deposit) funds overnight in limited amounts from the central bank. It is usually equal to the tender rate (see below) and is thus similar to the Bundesbank's repo rate, but for a shorter maturity.

The **end-of-day, or overdraft, rate** is an overnight lending rate for all financial institutions established in the Belgo-Luxembourg Economic Union (BLEU) and is also subject to a volume limit set by so-called current account credit lines. It is equal to the central rate plus a margin. Both rates usually change at the same time. Under normal circumstances, the end-of-day rate sets the ceiling for money market rates, though the emergency lending rate (see below) is the highest official rate.

The **emergency lending, or special overdraft, rate** is an overnight rate charged on the part of the overdraft exceeding the credit line, for all finan-cial institutions established in the BLEU, with no volume limit provided that, as for other lending facilities, there is sufficient collateral. It is always

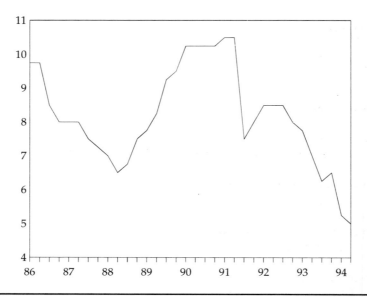

Figure 3.1   Belgium: Discount rate
Source: Datastream

higher than the end-of-day rate, sometimes by a very large margin. It is the Bank's highest rate, but is not commonly used.

The **discount rate** is a preferential rate at which financial institutions established in the BLEU can refinance commercial bills at the Rediscount and Guarantee Institute (RGI), which is then refinanced by the central bank. It is the lowest official lending rate.

The **emergency lending** and **discount rates** are not operational money market rates and thus are not used to steer money market rates. In practice, the two rates are generally not changed unilaterally, but in concert with German and/or Dutch rates.

The **tender rate**, at which the Bank supplies structural liquidity to financial institutions established in the BLEU through seven-day advances or repos, by way of an auction, is usually in line with the central rate. A change in the central rate is thus normally followed by a change in the tender rate. Changes in the rates may coincide when they fall on the day of an auction (currently Monday).

The **deposit** and the **special deposit rates** are the rates financial institutions established in the BLEU receive for placing excess funds overnight at the Rediscount and Guarantee Institute (RGI). The special deposit rate is the lowest rate paid on deposits. It sets the floor for call money and is currently the central rate minus 2.0 percentage points.

How does the central bank influence the money market?

There are various ways in which the central bank can lend to the banking system to ease a money market liquidity shortage.

When central bank lending takes the form of advances (including overdrafts) charged at the central, end-of-day, emergency lending, or tender rates, it requires collateral. This must consist of securities denominated in Belgian or Luxembourg francs which are traded on the stock exchange or on the money and capital markets. They must be issued or guaranteed by the Belgian or Luxembourg governments, or issued by regional or local Belgian or Luxembourg public authorities, or by international financial institutions of which Belgium or Luxembourg are members. Examples are Treasury certificates and linear bonds (OLOs).

■ Central rate
The central rate applies for overnight loans from (or deposits with) the central bank by primary dealers. There is a limit on overnight loans of BFr 350 million for each primary dealer, or a total of BFr 5.3 billion

■ End-of-day rate
The end-of-day rate (also known as the 'overdraft rate' or the 'rate for current account advances within credit lines') is charged on bank borrowings up to the limit of their credit facility at the central bank. (Note, however, that these credit lines are large. In 1994, they were worth more than BFr 215 billion). All financial institutions, including primary dealers, are given a facility called a current account credit line.

■ Emergency lending rate
The emergency lending rate (also called the 'special overdraft rate' or 'the rate for current account advances beyond credit lines') is a special penalty rate applied to borrowings (which can be unlimited) above the limit on each bank's credit line at the central bank.

■ Discount rate
The discount rate is the rate at which commercial banks can refinance commercial bills at the Rediscount and Guarantee Institute (RGI) against their individual limits, in the form of repurchase agreements for 15 to 60 days. The overall limit on the amount of bills which can be refinanced at the discount window is BFr 5.3 billion.

■ Tender rate

Once a week, currently on Mondays (for value two days later), the Bank supplies structural liquidity to the market through seven-day credit tenders in which all financial institutions can participate. It offers credit to banks in the form of either advances or repurchase agreements on commercial bills.

Funds are usually allocated at fixed-rate (also known as 'volume') tenders at which the tender rate is announced in advance. If the total volume of bids exceeds the amount the Bank wants to allocate, it can proportionally scale them down. The Bank sometimes limits the amount which can be requested to each institution's credit line at the central bank. The Bank applies this restriction when the tender rate is far below the one-week money market rate since, under those conditions, it is much cheaper for banks to borrow one-week funds from the central bank than from the market. In exceptional circumstances, the Bank may hold a variable-rate tender which can be either an American- or Dutch-style auction.

When the central bank wants to cut structural liquidity (for example, to offset an increase in liquidity from intervention sales of Belgian francs to support foreign currencies) it can reduce the amount of funds provided.

Structural tenders have become less important. This has resulted in an increase in the volume of daily fine-tuning operations (see 'Open market operations' below).

■ Deposit rates

The central bank can drain a surplus of liquidity in the money market through the Rediscount and Guarantee Institute (RGI).

Financial institutions can place end-of-day deposits with the RGI at various interest rates. The RGI deposits these funds with the central bank. Primary dealers are allowed to deposit their excess liquidity overnight at the RGI up to an overall limit of BFr 5.3 billion. These deposits attract the central rate.

Institutions (and primary dealers if they have exhausted the above deposit limit) can also place funds at lower rates with the RGI. The so-called 'ordinary tranche', which is limited to five per cent of their credit line at the central bank, usually attracts an interest rate one percentage point below the central rate.

Deposits above the 'ordinary tranche' attract the much lower special deposit rate, which is usually two percentage points below the central rate. This is the effective floor for call money rates.

Open market operations

Besides the allocations of structural liquidity provided by the credit tenders, the central bank also fine-tunes money market liquidity and interest rates daily through a wide range of direct, market-orientated open market intervention techniques. This is the most important method used by the central bank to lend to or borrow from the banking system.

The Bank seems to prefer fine-tuning to the tenders through which it supplies structural liquidity because the former are more flexible.

Open market operations enable the Bank either to influence the general level of liquidity to neutralize seasonal factors, or to intervene more actively to produce or maintain shortages or surpluses of liquidity to push money market rates in the desired direction.

■ Repurchase agreements
The most common form of fine-tuning is through repurchase agreements (repos).

The Bank deals daily with the primary dealers of government debt which are invited to participate in an American-style auction. However, the central bank hardly ever comments publicly on repo transactions. Primary dealers only get an indication of the repo rate when they have effectively completed a transaction with the Bank.

The repos are generally for value the next day and the normal expiration date of central bank repos is two to three business days later. Repos with longer maturities are possible but, since repos are used for short-term fine-tuning, this is unusual.

■ Outright purchases and sales of Treasury bills
The Bank's fine-tuning includes outright purchases and sales of treasury bills or other government securities and lending and borrowing operations in the interbank market. Both types of transaction are conducted only with primary dealers.

■ Foreign exchange operations
When the Bank wants to influence the franc's exchange rate directly, it will buy or sell the currency on the spot market, but this is not part of its day-to-day money market management. When there is a large foreign currency inflow/outflow, the Bank can offset it via currency swaps with commercial banks.

■ Reserve requirements
Since 1988, the Bank has gained the authority to impose reserve requirements on Belgian banks with no time limit. This authority is only intended to be used in a European context, however, and banks are not currently obliged to meet reserve requirements.

Who controls the interest rate levers?

The National Bank of Belgium sets interest rate policy. The central bank has statutory independence from the government. The bank's policy-making body—the Regency Council, or *Conseil de Régence*—has responsibility for setting interest rates. The council includes the governor, the bank's directors and 10 other members, of which five must belong to Belgium's economic federations representing employers and unions. In practice, most interest rate changes are decided by the Board of Directors.

However, the government's policy of shadowing the German mark within the exchange rate mechanism of the ERM has left the National Bank with little practical independence.

What drives interest rate policy?

Targets:

■ Operational
Money market rates.

■ Intermediate
Since the launch of the ERM in 1979, the overriding objective of monetary policy has been to ensure the stability of the Belgian franc in the system. In June 1990, this objective was made more ambitious by pegging the franc to the mark. Before the European currency crisis in the summer of 1993, the financial markets' perception was that the National Bank would like the franc's fluctuation bands to be ¼ per cent either side of its central ERM rate against the mark.

■ Final
Price stability.

How do official rates affect commercial ones?

Corporate

The lending practices of Belgian banks are similar to those of banks in the Netherlands and Germany. Thus, the majority of corporate loans are at fixed rates. Short-term finance, mainly overdrafts, are based on the prime rate which itself tracks the 'central rate'.

Mortgages

Until 1992, fixed-rate mortgages were the only type available. A change in the law has allowed variable-rate mortgages to be introduced, but the products launched so far have tended to be based on rates that are reviewed every three or five years. To all intents and purposes, mortgage interest rates are divorced from short-term movements in official rates.

Timing

The central, end-of-day and emergency lending rates valid for the day are announced in principle at about 10.30 local time. Once announced, the rate for the day will not change, although the Bank has the right to change it.

However, the Bank will sometimes announce, later in the day, the rates effective for the next day. This happens, for instance, when the National Bank follows the Dutch central bank by changing rates in the afternoon.

The Bank normally enters the market after updating its central rate for the day. In principle, the Bank trades every day.

The central bank gives an indication of its money market management in a weekly statement released every Wednesday at 11.00 local time. But the statement, basically a weekly update of its balance sheet, refers to Monday figures, gives only net on-balance changes and lumps several categories of transactions together, making it hard to interpret. The Bank does, however, release a comment which gives some explanation.

In principle, the discount rate [NBBY] is changed only on Wednesdays, when the Bank's Regency Council meets. But the Bank's board of directors has a mandate to change the rate on other days within the limits set by the Regency Council. A change will usually coincide with other rate changes.

The Bank gives seven-day advances at its tenders held on Mondays. The rate for a volume tender is announced at about 10.30 local time [NBVA] and the results at about 13.00 [NBVC].

Key Reuter pages

Monitor

Reuters reports:
MBE1   Regular money market report
MBE3   Weekly money market liquidity

National Bank of Belgium pages
NBBC-Z   Full range
NBBN   National Bank index page

Cont.

(cont.)

NBBC	Clearing - stripped OLOs
NBBG-J	General money market information
NBBO-R	Announcement of volume repo tender rate (Dutch)
NBBQ-R	Repo tender auction results
NBBS	Renten Fonds-Fonds des Rentes
NBBU-V	Indicative rates for T-bills and OLOs
NBBW	Indicative rates for government securities
NBBX	Indicative exchange rates
NBBY	Central, end-of-day and emergency lending rates valid for the day. Changes in the discount rate
NBVA-B	Announcement of volume repo tender rate (French)
NBVC-D	Repo tender auction results
NBVE-G	Secondary market in Treasury bills/OLOs

Other pages:

RTAL	Discount rate and date of most recent change

News 2000

MMT <F9> Topic code

Chapter 4

Canada

The rates to watch

- Overnight rate
  - *sets the tone for money market rates*

- Three-month Treasury bill rate
  - *operational target for Bank of Canada money market intervention*

- Bank rate
  - *Bank of Canada's minimum lending rate which acts as a benchmark for money market rates*

- SPRA rate (rate on special purchase and resale agreements)
  - *sets the ceiling for money market rates in special circumstances*

- SRA rate (rate on sale and repurchase agreements)
  - *sets the floor for money market rates in special circumstances*

The Bank of Canada uses the **overnight rate** to influence yields on three-month Treasury bills. This, in turn, determines the **Bank rate** which is set 0.25 of a percentage point above the average tender rate on three-month Treasury bills. The Bank rate, is set on Tuesdays, the same day as T-bill auctions, and is the rate at which the Bank of Canada relieves regular money market shortages.

The intervention rate at which the central bank buys or sells three-month T-bills compared with the previous three-month auction average gives an idea of the next move in Bank rate. Bank of Canada watchers are particularly interested in when the central bank conducts operations and where the 'when-issued' three-month T-bill was trading when the intervention took place.

The first time the Bank intervenes in the money market after Tuesday's T-bill auction indicates the maximum amount it wishes the Bank rate to change at the following week's setting. Intervention after that is used to reinforce this policy goal.

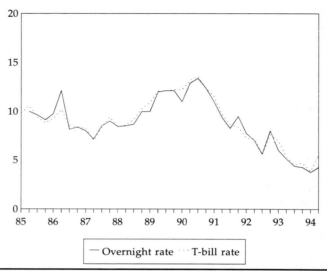

Figure 4.1   Canada: Overnight rate & T-bill rate
Source: Datastream

Figure 4.2   Canada: Bank rate
Source: Datastream

The Bank can therefore be expected to regularly intervene by buying/selling T-bills at a certain level if it bought/sold them there earlier in the week following the auction unless policy considerations or market conditions change significantly.

Intervention before 10.00 EDT is unusual and would therefore be taken as a strong statement.

SPRAs are used by the Bank of Canada to relieve temporarily undesired upward pressure on overnight rates. The rate at which the Bank of Canada chooses to purchase securities under special purchase and resale agreements is generally viewed as a ceiling for money market rates.

SRAs are used to offset undesired downward pressure on overnight rates. The rate at which the Bank of Canada chooses to sell securities under sale and repurchase agreements is generally viewed as a floor for money market rates.

How does the central bank influence the money market?

■ Bank rate

The Bank rate is the minimum rate at which the Bank of Canada lends overnight funds to the directly-clearing members of the Canadian Payments Association (CPA) including chartered banks. The Bank rate applies to the pricing of regular purchase and resale agreements (PRAs - see below) with dealer jobbers. Analysis of money market intervention therefore comes down to how it affects the Bank rate, which is set at 0.25 of a percentage point above the average rate at the weekly Treasury bill auction.

■ Weekly Treasury bill auction

The weekly Treasury bill tender rate is a weighted average of the yields on successful bids for the new three-month T-bill sold by tender each Tuesday. Investment dealers and banks (primary distributors) and the Bank of Canada submit tenders to the Department of Finance for the three-month bills to be issued that week.

■ Adjustment of settlement balances

This is the main technique used to influence money market liquidity and, in turn, interest rates and cash management. It involves the daily adjustment of settlement balances that direct clearers must hold at the Bank of Canada. By changing the amount of settlement balances available to the banking system, the Bank can influence the level of short-term rates.

For example, if the Bank wants higher money market rates, it provides fewer balances than demanded by the direct clearers. They will try to adjust their positions by various means: for example, higher bids for overnight deposits, calling back special call loans or selling liquid assets such as Treasury bills or bankers' acceptances. The upward pressure on the overnight rate that follows will eventually put upward pressure on most other interest rates. This is due partly to the fact that money market inventories are generally financed with overnight funds.

On the other hand, a fall in rates will occur when the bank sets settlement balances above the level demanded by the direct clearers. In this case, financial institutions will tend to react by lowering the rates they are prepared to pay for deposits or, perhaps, by either buying Treasury bills and bankers' acceptances or lending call money.

Drawdown/redeposit mechanism

The mechanism through which the Bank alters settlement balances is the so-called 'drawdown/redeposit' technique. This involves the transfer of deposits between the government's account at the Bank of Canada and its accounts at the direct clearers. A drawdown refers to the transfer of deposits to the Bank from the direct clearers, effectively draining the supply of available cash balances. A redeposit is the opposite, a transfer from the Bank to the direct clearers; in other words, an injection of balances.

The Bank adjusts the level of balances daily, making drawdown and redeposit decisions soon after 17.00 local time each business day. Each clearer is informed of direct transfers at 08.30 local time the following business day.

From the monetary policy perspective, each direct clearer will compare the actual system drawdown or redeposit to its forecast and make a judgement as to whether there might have been a shift in the Bank of Canada's short-run policy stance.

The drawdown/redeposit, in one daily transaction, does two things. First, it neutralizes the net flow of government transactions. Second, it serves as the basic mechanism through which the Bank adjusts the level of settlement balances in the system in line with its interest rate objectives. The direct clearers try to sort out these two components and they devote a considerable amount of time and energy to forecasting government flows to ensure as clear a reading of monetary policy intentions as possible. For example, on a day when tax receipts are projected to total, say, C$1 billion, an offsetting redeposit to the system of C$1 billion would be expected, setting aside any monetary policy component. Market participants sometimes misinterpret the total dollar amount of the drawdown/redeposit; inferring a policy move when the Bank had not intended one. A large drawdown or redeposit can simply be the result of a large volume of government transactions and may not have a monetary policy component. A much better guide to policy intentions is the morning's fluctuations in the overnight rate.

Open market operations

The drawdown/redeposit mechanism is the preferred method of implementing monetary policy since it relies heavily on market forces to achieve the desired money market conditions. There are occasions, however, when the desired impact on rates is not achieved and the Bank will then tend to use its reinforcing or supporting instruments which come under the heading of 'open market operations'. These instruments are not used to adjust the level of cash in the system, quite the contrary. When the Bank wants to have a specific impact on the rate structure at a specific term, it intervenes in the market directly to influence either the overnight rate or the three-month T-bill rate. Any unwanted rise or fall in the level of cash in the system as a result of these transactions is subsequently neutralized through the drawdown/redeposit.

■ Purchase and resale agreements (PRAs)
These are regular repos which involve Bank of Canada purchases of short-term government debt that designated investment dealers, called jobbers, can buy back at any time from the next business day up to two weeks ahead. Dealers that have technical lines of credit with the Bank of Canada are allowed to obtain funds from the Bank through PRAs if call money is above the Bank rate.

The Bank also occasionally intervenes with special and reverse repos when the overnight rate differs from its target, thereby indirectly influencing T-bill rates.

■ Special purchase and resale agreements (SPRAs)
SPRAs are used by the Bank of Canada to relieve temporarily undesired upward pressure on overnight rates. In a repo-type operation, the Bank offers to buy short-term securities from money market jobbers, with an agreement to resell them on the next business day, thereby reducing the amount that must be financed in the market. The rate, set at the discretion of the Bank of Canada, is the focus of market participants. They use it in their general assessment of the Bank's monetary policy objectives.

■ Sale and repurchase agreements (SRAs)
A reverse repo-type operation, SRAs are used to offset undesired downward pressure on overnight rates. The Bank of Canada offers to sell securi-

ties to banks, under an agreement to repurchase them on the next business day. The rate chosen by the Bank is the focus of considerable market attention, and is generally viewed as a floor for money market rates. The offer itself is often sufficient to eliminate downward pressure on the overnight rate and, partly as a result, the amount of SRAs dealt tends to be quite small relative to SPRAs.

■ Outright purchases or sales of Treasury bills
The final tool under open market operations involves outright sales or purchases of Treasury bills. This instrument is generally used to influence the three-month T-bill rate directly. Since the Bank's bill portfolio represents less than 10 per cent of the outstanding stock of bills, the Bank's ability to influence the market through supply has been reduced. Nevertheless, bill market transactions tend to have a strong signal effect, partly because of market expectations that open market operations will be reinforced in the days to come with cash management operations.

The Bank may occasionally switch the maturities of the bills it trades. For example, it may buy three-month T-bills and sell shorter maturities, such as those in the one-month area, to reduce upward pressure on the three-month rate. Similarly, the Bank at times may switch maturities in the market for portfolio adjustment purposes.

Who controls the interest rate levers?

The Bank of Canada sets monetary policy. More precisely, it is set by the governor after consultation with other members of the Bank's management committee. At regular weekly meetings, the Bank's management committee decides an appropriate target range for that week's Bank rate.

While the Bank of Canada is one of the most independent central banks, it is still subject to some restraints. For example, there is a statutory requirement for regular, in practice weekly, meetings between the governor and the finance minister. The minister has the authority to direct the governor, though this has never happened.

What drives interest rate policy?

Targets:

■ Operational
The Bank of Canada uses the overnight rate as the short-term tool to meet its inflation-reduction targets.

■ Intermediate
The principal intermediate guide is M2+, a slightly broader version of M2.

■ Final

Since February 1991, the Bank of Canada and the minister of finance have jointly set explicit inflation targets. In December 1993, the target band for inflation (CPI) was set at 1-3 per cent from the end of 1995 to 1998.

How do official interest rates affect commercial ones?

Corporate

Much corporate borrowing attracts the prime rate used by commercial banks for loans to their best customers. Prime loosely tracks official rates, but is not changed very often. Some 40 per cent of the Bank of Canada's measure of business credit consists of short-term credits, most of which are based on prime or other short-term rates.

Mortgages

The interest rate on most mortgages is fixed, though typically only for 1-5 years. Mortgages are thus largely insulated from immediate changes in short-term official rates.

Timing (local time)

08.30
- Clearers are informed of direct transfers of settlement balances between the Bank and the direct clearers, which can then determine their final deposit balances.

08.40
- Daily changes in policy stance can be seen at this time when the overnight rate opens for the day.

10.00
- Bank intervention before this time is usually interpreted as a strong statement by the Bank of Canada.

14.00
- The key Bank rate is set at this time each Tuesday.

17.00
- The Bank adjusts the level of balances daily, making drawdown and redeposit decisions soon after this time each business day. Each clearer is informed of direct transfers at 08.30 EDT the following business day (see above).

Key Reuter pages

Monitor

Reuters reports:
MCC1   Regular money market report covering money market intervention and the overnight rate

Bank of Canada pages:
TBIL   Canadian Treasury bill auction results available each Tuesday at 14.00 EDT
BOFC-D   Indicative exchange rates
CDMN   Canadian money market composite interest rate page
CFIX-Z   Bank of Canada composite money market fixings

Other pages:
RTAL   Three-month T-bill rate and date of last change
YLDS   Key interest rates from overnight to 30 years

News 2000

MMT <F9> Topic code

Chapter 5

Denmark

The rates to watch

- Certificate of deposit (CD) rate
  - *sets the tone for money market rates*

- Repo rate
  - *equal to the CD rate and therefore also sets the tone for money market rates*

- Deposit rate
  - *shadows the discount rate and sets the floor for very short-term money market rates*

- Discount rate
  - *a useful confirmation signal on official interest rate changes and sets the tone for commercial banks' corporate lending rates*

The Danish National Bank (Danmarks Nationalbank) has four main interest rates.

The 14-day **certificate of deposit rate** and the **repo rate** are by far the most important because they are the main instruments through which the central bank manages the money market. The 14-day CD rate is more volatile than the deposit or discount rates. Along with the repo rate, it sets the tone for money market rates.

The Bank conducts operations in both CDs and repos because CDs are settled on the same day, while repos can only be settled the day after a transaction. Thus, if the Bank needs to inject or drain liquidity today it uses CDs.

The **deposit rate** (*foliorente*) is the rate the central bank pays on commercial banks' current account deposits. Only a limited amount of funds can be placed in such deposits. The deposit rate shadows the discount rate and sets the floor for very short-term money market rates.

The **discount rate** (*diskonto*) is used as the benchmark for domestic bank base rates. It is no longer significant for money market rates but is still very important because it is regarded as a useful confirmation signal for a general change in interest rates.

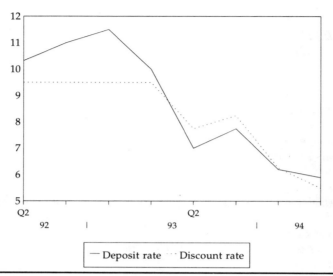

Figure 5.1   Denmark: Deposit rate and discount rate
Source: Datastream

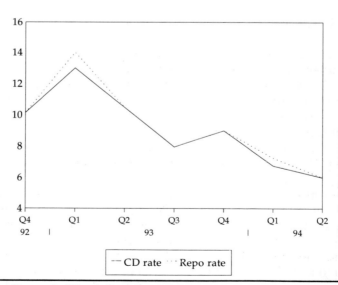

Figure 5.2   Denmark: CD rate & repo rate
Source: Datastream

Usually, there is a spread of 25-50 basis points between the deposit/discount rates, on the one hand, and the CD/repo rates on the other. In times of crisis, like currency unrest, this can widen significantly and it has reached 550 basis points.

There is no equivalent to the Bundesbank's lombard rate in setting a ceiling for Danish money market rates.

How does the central bank influence the money market?

The key instruments for steering money market rates and liquidity are purchases and sales of 14-day CDs and state paper repurchase deals (repos).

■ Certificates of deposit (CDs)
The central bank has a weekly sale of 14-day certificates of deposit (CDs) to help banks manage their liquidity needs. The CDs are traded between banks and with the central bank, which redeems them at par on expiry.

The Bank drains liquidity by selling CDs. They are issued once a week, on Fridays, so far always at a fixed rate announced at 10.00 local time. Banks buy CDs at this rate, with the total volume issued announced at 16.00. The CDs are well suited to liquidity management because the trading and settlement day is the same and deals therefore have an impact on the same day. The CDs expire two weeks later when they are replaced by a new series and there are thus always two series outstanding.

The Bank can add liquidity by buying back CDs from the banks before they expire. The procedure is similar to the weekly CD sale but can happen any day, even Friday. The Bank makes an announcement at 10.00. The rate is usually fixed, but a variable-rate auction can be called.

The rate at which the central bank buys back CDs includes a special added buy-back fee, usually 0.10 per cent. (For example, if the Bank has issued CDs at 9.5 per cent, any subsequent offer to buy them back will be at 9.6 per cent any other level would signify a rate change.)

The Bank announces the buy-back rate as the CDs rate plus the special buy-back charge. However, Reuters does not add the special buy-back charge in its reports.

At times of market turmoil the buy-back fee may be removed so that the Bank buys back and sells CDs at the same rate.

■ State paper repurchase agreements
The central bank also uses 14-day repos based on state (domestic government) paper, denominated in kroner and issued from 1975, as collateral. Prices are fixed by the Nationalbank.

Usually there is no limit to the amount that may be requested by the banks and then supplied to them by the central bank. But if there is pressure on the Danish crown, for instance, a limit is set to keep liquidity tight, normally as a certain percentage of a bank's capital.

Repos almost always mature in two weeks but may be conducted for other periods if large liquidity fluctuations occur due to, say, outflows caused by tax payments. Repos are then often combined with an offer to buy back CDs as these are the two ways the Bank can affect liquidity. The market usually knows this in advance and such action therefore has little or no impact on rates.

■ Deposit rate

The maximum amount of funds banks can hold in interest-bearing overnight current account deposits (*foliorente*) at the central bank is set according to the size of the bank. However, these limits are rarely reached. Current account deposits attract the deposit rate. This shadows the discount rate and sets the floor for very short-term (overnight and tomorrow/next) money market rates.

■ Discount rate

There is no discount window where banks can borrow funds at the discount rate. However, the discount rate still plays an important role because it is used to signal a general change in interest rates.

Who controls the interest rate levers?

The central bank is authorized to set interest rate policy, while the government decides on the exchange rate regime. There is broad agreement between the government and central bank on the objective of exchange rate stability. The exchange rate is thus the key to monetary policy.

What drives interest rate policy?

Targets:

■ Operational
Fourteen-day CD rates.

■ Intermediate
Crown stability against the core EMS currencies.

■ Final
Price stability.

How do official interest rates affect commercial ones?

Corporate

Corporate loans are usually priced off the discount rate, or linked to money market rates. A change in the discount rate of at least a ¼ point is usually necessary before base rates are changed.

Mortgages

Most mortgages are fixed-rate for terms of 20-30 years. Mortgage institutions only provide up to 80 per cent of the purchase price of a property. The rest is provided by banks, usually at variable rates.

Timing (local time)

10.00
- [DKNB] shows if the central bank has an offer to the money market. Since the Bank almost always uses a fixed rate, this is where rate changes occur.
Note, however, that in September 1993 the central bank surprised everyone by cutting rates at 09.00 instead of at its regular 10.00 operations.
On Thursdays (state paper repos) and Fridays (CD sale) there is virtually always an offer to the markets.

16.00
- If an offer has been made the same morning [DKND] shows the result (repo volume, how many CDs have been sold, bought back etc.). This is where liquidity is affected. (Reuters only reports the result of fixed-rate money market operations on international news services if it is significant or unusual.)
The timing of deposit and discount rate changes is harder to pinpoint. The most likely time for a rate change is 16.00 [DKNJ], but rates have also been changed at 10.00 when the Bank also announces its money market actions.

In special cases, where there is some urgency for the central bank to act (for example, during a currency crisis), rates have been changed at 09.00 and 17.00.

If the Bundesbank changes key rates, the timing of a Danish rate change is unpredictable and may come as soon as 10 minutes after a German move.

The only factors previously to have upset the standard times of 10.00 and 16.00 have been a German rate change, pressure on the crown and the outcome of Denmark's Maastricht vote in May 1993.

Key Reuter pages

Monitor

Reuters reports:
MDD1   Reuters money market report

Danmarks Nationalbank pages:
DKNA-X, DKMA-B   Full range
DKNA   Danmarks Nationalbank index page
DKNB   Central bank offers to supply funds via state paper repos and CDs or to drain funds through buy-backs of CDs
DKND   The result of central bank operations (repo volume, how many CDs have been sold, bought back etc.)
DKNJ   Deposit and discount rate changes
DKNX   Hot news

News 2000

MMT <F9> Topic code

Chapter 6

Finland

The rates to watch

- One-month tender rate
  - *sets the trend for money market rates*

- Call money deposit rate
  - *sets the floor for money market rates*

- Liquidity credit rate
  - *sets the ceiling for money market rates*

- Base rate
  - *signals monetary policy changes but have no direct impact on money market rates*

- Three-month certificate of deposit (CD) rate
  - *sets the tone for money market rates; sometimes used to signal major official rate changes*

The structure of official interest rates in Finland resembles a channel. The call money deposit rate sets the floor for money market rates, the liquidity credit rate sets the ceiling, and the tender rate is the axis around which all other rates turn.

The tone of money market rates is also affected by the Bank of Finland's daily open market operations in Treasury bills and certificates of deposit. The Bank sometimes operates in three-month CDs to signal major shifts in interest rate policy.

The **tender rate** set at Bank of Finland auctions of one-month paper is the key interest rate. The tender is usually variable-rate, but can be fixed.

Both the **call money deposit rate**, at which banks can deposit overnight funds at the central bank, and the **liquidity credit rate**, at which banks can borrow overnight funds from the central bank, are tied with a spread to the tender rate.

The importance of tender rate changes for the market varies: sometimes they only reflect money market conditions, at other times they are used to push money market rates up or down. The Bank says it uses the auctions mainly for liquidity reasons.

The tender rate is decisive for the level of one- and two-month CDs and also for the cost of overnight funds. Longer maturities are less influenced by the tender rate.

Changes in the administratively-set **base rate** attract wide media attention compared to the publicity given to the tender rate, but its importance has declined in line with the liberalization of the markets and it now mostly follows money market rates.

The Bank also watches the **three-month certificate of deposit (CD) rate** and often operates in that maturity when it wants to give a signal on interest rates.

How does the central bank influence the money market?

The Bank of Finland controls the money market through a wide range of rates and instruments. It uses open market operations (mainly purchases and sales of three-month paper), tender rate auctions, normal repo auctions and weekly repo-rate auctions (though the latter are not seen as a monetary policy tool but used more to foster trade in government securities). However, the central bank mainly influences money market liquidity through repos.

■ Tender rate

The tender rate is set through Bank of Finland auctions of one-month paper, that is, the weighted average of all the latest accepted bids for central bank funds or certificates (its own certificates of deposit (CDs), commercial bank CDs or, increasingly, Treasury bills) offered for sale in the money market.

Usually, tenders are conducted at a variable rate. Banks are asked to put forward bids or offers in terms of both prices and amounts for a given maturity, normally one month. The central bank can reject offers if bids are too low. However, the Bank can also set a fixed-rate tender (common before the markka was floated on 8 September 1992) at which banks make bids in terms of amounts only.

Auctions are not held at fixed intervals and their frequency varies greatly (usually from a few times a week to a few times a month). The Bank can ask for offers at any time during the day but normally does so in early trade. At the auctions, the Bank either adds funds to, or drains them from, the market.

■ Call money deposit rate/liquidity credit rate

Both the call money deposit rate and the liquidity credit rate are tied with a variable spread to the tender rate. Typically, the call money deposit rate is two to three percentage points below the tender rate, while the liquidity credit rate is one to two percentage points above the tender rate. The terms (maturity and margin) for liquidity credit can be changed according to market conditions and maturities can be one, seven, 14 or 28 days.

■ Base rate
The base rate signals monetary policy changes. It is set by the Parliamentary Supervisory Board and is levied on old loans and tax-free deposits. There are a large number of these so the rate remains important, but the central bank has not granted any new credit linked to the base rate for a number of years. The base rate tends to move in line with the tender rate but is not changed as frequently.

Open market operations

Although the Bank mainly affects liquidity through the tender rate, it also uses open market operations involving outright purchases and sales of CDs or T-bills or repurchase agreements. Banks are asked to quote two-way prices with the standard amount for outright CD deals being around 20 million markka.

The Bank intervenes frequently since the market is generally thin due to the small number of market-makers.

Intervention is normally in one- to three-month maturities, but may cover others. The Bank says it looks especially closely at the three-month certificate of deposit (CD) rate and that it also often operates in that maturity when it wants to give a signal on interest rates. The Bank does not usually comment on such intervention.

■ Weekly repurchase agreements
The Bank also holds weekly repo auctions in one-week maturities, a measure announced in June 1993 as part of a package to foster trade in government securities.

Although not really a monetary policy tool, the weekly repo affects money market liquidity. It is used to fund the bond portfolios of the primary dealers (at present the five biggest banks, plus one brokerage firm).

■ Reserve requirements
The Bank also guides credit growth, interest rates and money supply through a reserve system imposed on banks.

Under the minimum reserve system banks are required to hold a percentage of their liabilities as non-interest-bearing deposits at the Bank. This may be changed if economic or monetary conditions require. The percentage varies between banks according to their balance sheet structures, but may be up to five per cent of their liabilities. At present, banks are required to deposit one per cent of M3, 1.5 per cent of M2 and two per cent of M1 liabilities at the Bank.

If banks fall short of their reserve requirement, they have to borrow from the central bank at a penalty interest rate set five percentage points above the highest rate payable on central bank credit at that time (that is, the liquidity credit rate).

The present system was introduced on 1 July 1993 to boost the effectiveness of monetary policy and to control the money supply. (However, unlike the Bundesbank, the Bank of Finland does not publish a target for money supply growth.)

Who controls the interest rate levers?

The central bank sets monetary policy. The Parliamentary Supervisory Board, made up of nine Members of Parliament (MPs), only decides on base rate changes, leaving the Bank of Finland to set all other interest rates.

What drives interest rate policy?

Targets:

■ Operational
There is none.

Intermediate

Until the extreme currency volatility of September 1992, the markka was held within a narrow fluctuation band against the European currency unit (Ecu). Since 8 September 1992, the markka has been floating. No alternative intermediate target has been set, but the Bank of Finland uses several variables as indicators for its monetary policy (the exchange rate, monetary aggregates, credit aggregates, long-term interest rates).

■ Final
The Bank of Finland sets an inflation target.

How do official rates affect commercial ones?

Corporate

Most corporate loans are variable-rate. They are based on the three-month Helsinki interbank offered rate (Helibor) which, in turn, tracks the one-month tender rate used by the central bank to set the trend for money market rates. The prime rate, which is set by the biggest banks and only changes about two to three times a year, moves in line with longer-term rates (typically 12 months). Prime is mainly used for consumer loans.

Mortgages

Most mortgages are based on the prime rate or are at fixed rates reviewed once every three years or so. Mortgage rates are thus sensitive to changes in official rates over the medium term, but are relatively immune from short-term changes in market rates.

Timing

Tender auctions are not held at fixed intervals and their frequency varies greatly (usually from a few times a week to a few times a month). The Bank can ask for offers at any time during the day, but normally does so in early trade.

Key Reuter pages

Monitor

Bank of Finland pages:

SPFB-K	Full range
SPFB	Tender, call money deposit and liquidity credit rates
SPFC	Assets and liabilities, updated once a week
SPFD	Other announcements, such as base rate changes, major currency announcements, such as the floating of the markka etc.
SPFG	Underlying inflation, consumer prices, monetary aggregates (M1, M2, M3), markka deposits & lending, total lending.
SPFH	Items affecting money market liquidity
SPFI	Government benchmark bonds
SPFJ	Interest rates: markka lending, new lending, deposits
HELX	Indicative exchange rates

News 2000
MMT <F9> Topic code

Chapter 7

France

<hr>

The rates to watch

- Intervention rate
  - *sets the floor for money market rates*

- Five-to-10-day lending rate
  - *sets the ceiling for money market rates*

The **intervention rate** at which the Bank of France allocates funds on securities repurchase agreements usually acts as the floor for short-term money market rates, while the five-to-10-day emergency facility rate sets the ceiling. The intervention rate is generally seen as the most powerfully symbolic of the Bank's rates.

The **five-to-10 day lending rate** is typically about 75 to 100 basis points above the intervention rate.

Bank of France instruments

	Interest rate levers	**Liquidity levers**
Major signals	Intervention rate 5-10 day lending rate	Direct intervention
Fine-tuning	Overnight rate	

How does the central bank influence the money market?

■ Repurchase agreements
The use of repurchase agreements is the main way the Bank of France influences money market liquidity and, hence, is the key monetary policy instrument.

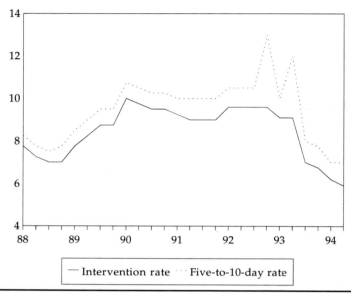

Figure 7.1   France: Intervention rate & five-to-10-day lending rate
Source: Datastream

The Bank of France lends to banks on a regular basis at its discretion to inject liquidity into the banking system at money market securities repurchase tenders (*opérations sur appel d'offre*). The tenders usually take place once or twice a week, though when purchases of francs through foreign exchange intervention have reduced liquidity twice weekly tenders are common.

The rate at which funds are allocated at these tenders is the intervention rate, also known as the 'call for tender' rate. This is usually the cheapest central bank money banks can get and sets a notional floor on short-term money market rates.

Apart from adjusting the intervention rate, the central bank also uses the tenders to regulate market liquidity by making net injections or withdrawals of funds.

The Bank of France invites primary dealers to submit bids, for themselves and on behalf of the other banks, specifying the amount of securities and the interest rates they are willing to pay. They can only bid at rates pitched at or above the intervention rate.

In the morning, banks present a range of bids saying how much they want to borrow at each of a series of possible intervention rates. The Bank of France then decides the rate it will use, adds up all the offers it has at that rate and above, and satisfies them pro rata according to how much it wants to inject or drain in total. Although it asks for a range of bids, it invariably allocates funds at the established intervention rate.

The Bank can also announce the intervention rate to apply early in the morning of the tender or a day or two before. On these occasions the intervention rate may be cut by any amount. For example, on 22 October 1993 the Bank said its intervention rate would be cut by 0.30 of a percentage point.

The securities which can be used as collateral are Treasury bills, certain commercial paper, and certain short-term credits (not exceeding two years) denominated in French francs.

The maturity of new repo pacts is mostly mechanically determined by the calendar of tenders and so is rarely taken as a policy signal. Repos almost always have maturities of about a week.

The Bank of France has recently split bids for its tenders into two. Banks bidding for funds must distinguish between bids using Treasury bills as collateral and a separate bid backed by private paper. Typically, the Bank might satisfy a varying percentage of bids backed by T-bills and a higher percentage of bids offering private bills as collateral.

The change was introduced during a period of very high rates and tight liquidity to allow the central bank to allocate more of the cheap funds it gives at the tender to banks using private paper as collateral. This, in turn, was supposed to hold down the interest rates private companies could borrow at by making their commercial paper more valuable to banks than T-bills.

■ Five-to-10 day lending window
The second most important tool for the Bank of France is its five-to-10-day lending window (*pensions de 5 à 10 jours*) which is a repurchase agreement credit institutions can use at their discretion via principal market operators (*opérateurs principaux de marché* - OPMs).

In contrast to the intervention rate, the five-to-10-day window is an emergency facility always available to commercial banks (with one exception, *see* 'Exceptional measures' below) which can draw funds in unlimited amounts at a penalty rate as a last resort. Institutions choose a maturity of between five and 10 days.

Borrowing is conducted, as at money market tenders, through securities repurchase agreements, or repos. Banks which want to use the five-to-10-day window usually telephone an OPM which calls the money market room at the Bank of France giving both the amount and type of security to be used as collateral. Treasury bills, commercial paper and short-term credits can also be used as collateral for these loans.

Since banks can always borrow at the five-to-10-day rate (sometimes called the 'official repurchase facility' rate), it sets a notional ceiling on overnight money market rates.

Usually, the five-to-10 day lending rate is about 75 to 100 basis points above the intervention rate, although this gap has risen sharply during foreign exchange crises. That premium means the five-to-10-day lending window is not used that often since call money would have to trade above the five-to-10-day rate for the latter to be attractive for banks. The only time banks would borrow overnight funds at a rate above the five-to-10-day repo rate is if they expected the overnight rate to fall below the repo rate quite soon.

The call money, or overnight, rate tends to move within the channel set by the five-to-10-day and intervention rates but can slip outside according to market liquidity and expectations. This can also happen when there are occasional shortages of the eligible bills needed as collateral to borrow at the five-to-10-day rate, or at the intervention rate during tenders.

If call money consistently trades close to the intervention or five-to-10-day lending rates it could indicate that there may be an imminent policy change.

The five-to-10-day and intervention rates are not changed very often and may be changed independently or together.

Alternatively, a weekly tender at an unchanged intervention rate firmly underlines the intention of the Bank of France to maintain its current monetary policy stance.

■ Direct intervention

The Bank of France can also use a range of measures to reduce short-term pressure on money market rates by adding or draining liquidity as it sees fit at any rate it determines through securities repurchase agreements or reverse repurchase agreements.

These repos are overnight or two-day operations usually at rates close to those in the money market at that time.

The most common action would be an offer of overnight funds through a repurchase agreement at a rate somewhere below the five-to-10-day rate if, say, the Bank felt market rates were being unnecessarily squeezed up by a shortage of liquidity at a time when no tender was scheduled.

In the opposite case, the Bank of France may offer a reverse repurchase agreement to drain funds at a rate somewhere above the intervention rate.

These repos can either be conducted with a small number of banks in secret or made public depending on the reasons why the Bank of France wants to inject or withdraw liquidity.

■ Reserve requirements

The fourth main Bank of France instrument is the setting of the level of interest-free reserves commercial banks must have in their accounts at the central bank. Banknotes are included in reserves.

Banks must maintain reserves in proportion to the different types of liability they hold. The maintenance period runs from the 16th of each month to the 15th of the following month.

Changes in reserve requirements can be used to offset the impact on liquidity of a change in money market rates caused by a change in official intervention rates.

This is particularly suited to situations where rates have been changed for external reasons, such as defending the franc, when a cut in reserve ratios gives a signal to banks either to reduce or not raise their base lending rates.

In May 1992, for example, the Bank cut reserve requirements to allow the commercial banks to cut their base lending rates. But the most celebrated case was in November 1991 when reserve ratios were cut with the explicit aim of avoiding a rise in bank base rates after an increase in key official rates.

"I wanted... to avoid this increase (in official rates) pushing up the cost of financing of companies, particularly small firms and the self-employed, for whom borrowings are still to a large extent indexed to bank base rates," said the then Finance Minister Pierre Bérégovoy.

Sharp cuts in reserve requirements over the last two years (the last cut was in May 1992) have left them very low and greatly reduced their significance. Banks now have to hold as reserves 1.0 per cent of sight deposits and 0.5 per cent of time deposits and CDs under one year. The reserve ratio for time deposits of more than one year is currently zero.

The Bank of France has reduced the requirements to insulate domestic monetary conditions from interest rate changes made for external reasons and to stop high reserve ratios from driving money market flows away from Paris to other markets, for example Luxembourg. This may deter the Bank of France from raising reserve requirements in the future.

■ Exceptional measures

Three currency crises in 1992 and 1993 forced the Bank to come up with other exceptional measures based on the four basic instruments, usually to force interest rates up while indicating it is only doing so for a very short time.

One such measure has been the suspension of the five-to-10-day lending rate. Since the Bank of France must always stand as the lender of last resort to banks, it has on occasion replaced the five-to-10-day rate with an emergency 24-hour facility. This makes it harder for banks to borrow cheaply from the central bank and sell francs on the foreign exchange market. Another way of looking at it is to say the maturity available on last-resort funds has been shortened from 10 days to overnight.

For example, at the end of July 1993, during the European currency crisis, the Bank introduced the 24-hour facility to help defend the French franc. Once members of the European exchange rate mechanism (ERM) abandoned their attempts to defend the tight bands within which their currencies had been allowed to fluctuate, the Bank of France began to steadily lower the emergency rate but left the five-to-10 day and intervention rates unchanged. The Bank's aim was to reduce banks' borrowing costs by lowering the 24-hour rate while continuing to support the franc by keeping its headline floor and ceiling rates unchanged.

The Bank of France has also, on occasion, shortened the five-to-10-day facility to a five-day facility.

Since the currency crisis of September 1992, the Bank has tended to raise the last-resort or ceiling rate whether it is for five-to-10-days, five days or 24 hours quite steeply. But, in general, it has not raised the intervention rate to insulate domestic banks against a rise in the cost of funds. As a result, the gap between the intervention and ceiling rates has been as wide as four percentage points.

■ Other open market operations
The Bank of France may also smooth money market rates by buying or selling Treasury bills at market prices.

Who controls the interest rate levers?

The Bank of France's nine-member Monetary Policy Council sets interest rates. It is forbidden by law to "solicit or accept" external instructions on the conduct of monetary policy.

What drives interest rate policy?

The ultimate aim of the Bank of France's monetary policy is price stability, defined as annual price rises of no more than two per cent over the medium term. In order to achieve this, it refers to two intermediate targets: stability of the franc within the exchange rate mechanism; and medium-term growth in M3 of five per cent per annum. However, it also takes into account other variables including long-term interest rates and the balance of payments.

How do official official rates affect commercial ones?

Corporate

Large borrowers increasingly have their loans linked directly to money market rates. Small businesses have about a third of their borrowings in overdrafts linked to money market rates and a quarter in short-term loans which are also affected by movements in official rates. The Bank of France estimates that about 60 per cent of total corporate borrowing is at floating rates.

Mortgages

Banks dominate the mortgage market in France and, while floating rate loans are becoming more popular, the overwhelming majority of mortgages are provided at a fixed rate.

Interest rate expectations

The price of the three-month Pibor (Paris interbank offered rate) contract traded on Matif (Marché à Terme International de France), the futures exchange, provides information on market expectations for interest rates. The contract is cash settled on the second business day before the third Wednesday of the relevant month at 11.00 local time. It is expressed as 100 minus the Paris interbank offered rate to be delivered. Thus, an expected interest rate of six per cent gives a contract price of 94.00. For example, if the December contract was trading at 94.00 and Pibor was currently six per cent it would imply that the futures market expects no change in Pibor by December. Alternatively, if the December contract was trading at 92.00 that would imply that the futures market expects a two percentage point rise in Pibor to eight per cent by the end of the year.

Timing

Since gaining its independence in January 1994, the Bank of France has held meetings of its Monetary Policy Council on alternate Thursdays (not coinciding with the Bundesbank). Thus, the intervention rate is given at the same time as the amount of the net drain or injection of funds.

Sometimes, however, if the market is particularly jittery, the Bank will announce the intervention rate to apply early in the morning of the tender (usually around 08.30 local time) or even, very exceptionally, a day or two before it.

Tenders are nearly always held on Mondays and Thursdays with funds under the new pact being injected the following day. Occasionally, for example, when the day before the expiry of an old repo is a holiday, a tender will be held on the same day as the funds are injected into the market.

Details of the maturity of the new repo pact offered and confirmation of the amount of the old pact falling due are published [BDFB-D] at around 08.30 local time on the day of the tender.

If, as is usual, the funds are not to be injected until the following day, the Bank announces the results of the tender (the amount allocated and the rate) at 1315 local time. The results of same-day tenders are usually announced at 11.30 local time.

The five-to-10-day rate, or any other rate being used as a ceiling, has nothing to do with the money market tender and so its terms and conditions can be changed by the Bank at any time. It often announces changes early in the morning, by about 08.30 local, but there is no hard and fast rule.

Key Reuter pages

Monitor

Reuters reports:

MFR1	Money market allocation report
MFR3	Full money market report

Bank of France pages

BDFA-J, BFFX-Z, SVTF-H	Full range
BDFA	Bank of France index page
BDFB	The Bank of France usually posts brief messages on changes to the five-to-10-day lending rate, or any other rate being used as a ceiling, on this page, where the terms and conditions of the ceiling rate are permanently displayed
BDFB-D	Details of the maturity of the new repo pact offered and confirmation of the amount of the old pact falling due on the day of the tender
BDFC-D	As a result of the central bank's decision to split bids for its repurchase tenders into two, both the percentage of bids backed by Treasury bills that were satisfied [BDFC] and the percentage backed by private paper [BDFD] are announced

Cont.

(cont.)
BDFE-F   Fuller Bank of France announcements on changes to the ceiling rate when available. Occasionally the Bank of France will telephone or fax news agencies with important announcements first but not always

BDFI-J   Information on Bank of France reserves

Other pages
YLDS   Key interest rates from overnight to 30 years

News 2000

MMT <F9> Topic code

Chapter 8

Germany

The rates to watch

- Repo rate
  - *sets the tone for money market rates*

- Discount rate
  - *sets the floor for money market rates*

- Lombard rate
  - *sets the ceiling for money market rates*

The **repo rate** is now the main tool for guiding the overnight money market rate. Repos enable the Bundesbank to adjust monetary policy without changing its headline rates.

A change from a fixed- to a variable-rate repo (or vice versa) may indicate a policy change. But while higher rates at a variable-rate repo reflect higher bids for funds by banks, they do not necessarily point to tighter policy in the short term (and vice versa).

The **discount rate** normally sets the floor for money market rates, while the **lombard rate** usually sets the ceiling. Thus, the discount rate is more important when interest rates are falling whilst the lombard rate is the key rate when interest rates are rising.

Bundesbank instruments

	Interest rate levers	Liquidity levers
Major signals	Discount rate Lombard rate	Rediscount quotas Lombard ceilings Minimum reserve ratios
Fine-tuning	Repo rate Currency intervention	Repo terms Liquidity paper

How does the central bank influence the money market?

The Bundesbank's main instruments are either designed for long-run major policy changes or to fine-tune the money market.

Refinancing activities

■ Rediscount policy
Section 19 of the Bundesbank Act allows the central bank to buy (and sell) trade bills from commercial banks at the discount rate. Banks can obtain funds from the Bundesbank by discounting bills backed by three solvent parties and which mature in three months or less.

The discount rate has a more limited and indirect impact on market rates than the lombard and repo rates, since it only applies to trade bills and banks can only borrow up to the credit limit set by the Bundesbank for each institution. The discount rate is still important because it is usually below market rates and sets a floor for one- to three-month money. However, there are exceptions to the role of the discount rate in setting the floor for short-term money market rates.

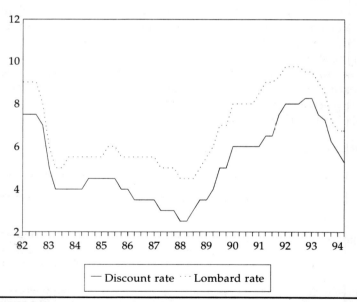

Figure 8.1   Germany: Discount & lombard rates
Source: Datastream

For example, during the ERM crisis of July 1993 which resulted in the currency fluctuation bands being widened, from 2 ¼ per cent for most countries to 15 per cent for all members, the Bundesbank said it would not prevent market rates falling below the discount rate, then 6.75 per cent, and the fixed repo rate of 6.95 per cent. Call money subsequently fell from 7.0 to 6.50 per cent as large sums of cash—the result of the previous week's central bank currency market intervention to defend the ERM—stayed in circulation.

If the money market is very liquid and the overnight rate falls below the discount rate, banks do not use their rediscount quotas since they can obtain funds at lower rates in the money market. When this happens the Bundesbank usually gives banks the option to invest in federal Treasury bills (usually of three days' maturity) at an interest rate which then becomes the floor for the overnight rate instead of the discount rate. Recently, the interest rate on these short-term Treasury bills has been around ¼ of a point below the prevailing repo rate.

However, under normal circumstances, when the discount rate is below the overnight rate, banks usually use up their full rediscount quota since rediscount credit is normally the cheapest way of obtaining funds from the central bank.

The discount rate was cut to a record low 2.5 per cent in December 1987 as the Bundesbank added liquidity to the banking system after the October 1987 world stock market crash. It was raised to a record 8.75 per cent in July 1992.

■ Rediscount quotas
The Bundesbank can vary the total amount of rediscount credit available at the discount rate available to banks through rediscount quotas. Individual banks' access to the overall quota is based on their capital liabilities and business structure.

A cut in rediscount quotas is a tightening of monetary policy and tends to lead to higher money market rates. Raising the quotas is a relaxation of monetary policy and tends to lead to lower rates. However, the quotas are changed only rarely.

■ Lombard policy
Section 19 of the Bundesbank Act also allows the central bank to grant loans to the banking system at the lombard rate for a period not exceeding three months against collateral, including specific securities (such as certain bills of exchange, Treasury bills, Treasury discount paper etc.) and Debt Register claims (such as federal government bonds). These financing lines are known as lombard loans.

The lombard rate, or emergency funding rate, usually sets the ceiling for short-term money market rates because lombard loans are intended to be used temporarily in special circumstances, such as when liquidity is tight. However, if there is excess demand for funds and a large volume of lombard loans has already been granted, money market rates for periods of less than a week may exceed the lombard rate.

Since 1985, when the Bundesbank stepped up its use of repos to reduce excessive reliance by banks on lombard loans, the demand for such loans (and, incidentally, use of the discount window as well) has fallen. Nevertheless, lombard borrowing still tends to be high on the last day of the month if banks need funds to meet their monthly reserve requirements.

Lombard loans are granted in accordance with general monetary policy conditions and in keeping with the particular circumstances of the institutions requesting the loan. In principle, a lombard loan should be granted only for the short-term bridging of a temporary liquidity need and only if the borrowing seems to be appropriate and acceptable in terms of its size and duration.

The Bundesbank reserves the right to restrict general access to the lombard window or to discontinue lombard loans altogether for monetary policy reasons. For example, during the 1970s and early 1980s, the Bundesbank repeatedly stopped granting lombard loans to underline that their use should be restricted to special circumstances. Instead, when it became necessary to add liquidity, the Bundesbank offered special lombard loans.

■ Special lombard loans

The special lombard facility can also be suspended at any time, in which case the loan has to be repaid the following day. It is characterized by a special lombard rate which can be changed daily. As an example, in February 1981, the 'normal' lombard facility (then at 9.0 per cent) was suspended until further notice, and banks were only provided with special lombard loans, initially at 12 per cent. Even this special facility was suspended for a brief period in 1981. From September 1979 to February 1980, the Bundesbank limited lombard loans to a proportion of banks' rediscount quotas.

The lombard rate of 9.75 per cent in mid-1992 was the highest on record, not taking into account the rate set on the special facility. The lombard rate is always above the discount rate.

■ Reserve requirements

The Bundesbank uses its minimum reserve policy for two main purposes: to control the demand for central bank balances and to neutralize the effects of foreign exchange market intervention.

Firstly, according to the Bundesbank, minimum reserves are the 'lever' through which money creation by banks is controlled. Increasing the mini-

mum reserve ratio raises the demand for central bank balances to meet the requirements.

Second, changes in the ratio are an alternative to open market operations in sterilizing the monetary impact of currency market intervention. Thus, Bundesbank sales of marks for foreign exchange can be neutralized in terms of their impact on the money supply through a rise in the minimum reserve ratio.

Minimum reserve policy requires banks to hold a specific percentage of their liabilities to non-banks sight, time and savings deposits and other short- to medium-term borrowing as balances on giro accounts at the central bank. The ratios cannot exceed 30 per cent for sight, 20 per cent for time and 10 per cent for savings deposits; the Bundesbank may, however, set a percentage of up to 100 per cent for liabilities to non-residents. Within the limits, the Bundesbank may set different percentages for different types of banks in the light of general monetary policy considerations.

Failure to meet the reserve requirement is subject to a stiff penalty interest rate on the amount overdue of up to three percentage points above the lombard rate for 30 days. In practice, institutions rarely fall short of the minimum reserve ratio. Since the Bundesbank pays no interest on minimum reserve balances, institutions do not hold significant excess reserves.

Changes to minimum reserves initially affect the amount of liquidity in the banking system. But they also affect interest rates. In the case of a rise in minimum reserve ratios, banks will try to pass on the costs they incur, by having more funds in non-interest-bearing central bank accounts, to their customers via increased lending rates.

A rise in minimum reserve ratios represents a tightening of monetary policy and a fall represents a relaxation. However, in practice, changes in reserve requirements are rarely used as a monetary policy tool. They were last changed when the Bundesbank cut them to two per cent for time liabilities and savings deposits effective 1 March 1993.

Open market operations

■ Repurchase agreements
The Bundesbank may buy and sell securities such as rediscount bills, public sector paper, Debt Register claims and other officially-listed bonds, to affect money market liquidity and interest rates.

The central bank first conducted such operations in 1955. They fell out of favour in the 1960s, but returned to prominence in 1979 when today's repos were introduced. They are mainly used to provide banks with funds for a limited period.

Unlike refinancing activities, repos leave the initiative in the hands of the Bundesbank. This is because it always has control of the amount of funds allocated at both fixed- and variable-rate repos. The Bundesbank conditions the money market so banks have to bid at rates close to its target, since otherwise they may not get the funds they need. If that happened, the banks would then have to borrow at higher rates in the money market.

In the past decade, repos have been the Bundesbank's key policy instrument for reserve injections and interest rate adjustments.

The Bundesbank steers money market liquidity via weekly tenders for securities repurchase funds (repos). It announces on Tuesdays (*see* 'Timing') whether the following day's repo will be at a fixed or variable rate.

The Bundesbank now mainly holds 14-day (two-week) repos, sometimes with a 28-day (one-month) pact alongside. However, when the repo tender is set each Tuesday, the Bundesbank has discretion over whether one, two or, theoretically, more repos are conducted and at what maturities. At month-end, the Bundesbank occasionally does not hold a tender to avoid adding or withdrawing funds from the market on the last day of the month when banks have to square their books.

Repos often dominate rediscount borrowing as the main source of liquidity from the Bundesbank.

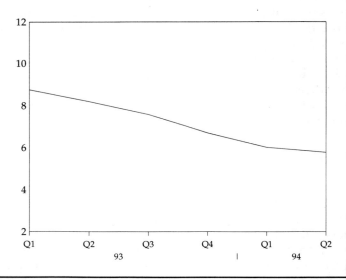

Figure 8.2   Germany: Two-week repo rate
Source: Datastream

- Variable-rate tenders

At variable-rate tenders, banks bid in terms of both the amount of funds they require and the rates they are prepared to pay. Allotments are made at individual bidding rates under an American-style auction at which no fixed minimum rate is set. (The Dutch-style, under which a minimum rate is set, was last used in September 1988.)

The Bundesbank decides what volume of bids to accept, and which of the bids it will accept in full. Bids above the lowest accepted rate, which is called the 'marginal rate', are allocated in full, while bids at the lowest accepted rate may receive a lower proportion of funds.

The Bundesbank does not give details of all the interest rates at which funds have been allocated, but stipulates the lowest accepted rate and the rate at which most funds have been granted. Repo rates are usually offered at a discount to the lombard rate

The Bundesbank can influence policy by determining the lowest accepted rate and by the amount of money it chooses to allocate overall. It may choose not to allocate any funds if bids are too low. But banks will tend to bid at rates close to those prevailing in the money markets for fear of being left without an allocation of funds and having to borrow at higher rates in the money market.

- Fixed-rate tenders

If the Bundesbank wants to keep a firm grip on repo rates and give the market clear guidance, it can offer banks repo funds at fixed-rate tenders (also called 'volume repos'). It has often done this in recent years to guide money market rates after a change in the key lombard and/or discount rates.

Under fixed-rate tenders, the Bundesbank sets the repo rate and banks submit bids for the amounts they want at the fixed rate. The Bundesbank then accepts a total amount consistent with its liquidity objective and allocates funds on a pro rata basis among the bidders. This often involves a scaling down of the original bids.

The fixed rate can also be used when the Bundesbank wants to reassert its control over market rates, such as when such rates diverge significantly from the Bundesbank's target. This allows the Bundesbank to signal preferred money market rates. For example, it cut the minimum repo rate for 14-day funds by 15 basis points to 6.80 per cent on 3 August 1993 in an attempt to regain control over the money market. Technically, the rate cut aimed to ensure that week's repo was appealing enough to banks to make the Bundesbank's open market operations effective. The central bank would have got almost no bids in that week's fixed rate 14-day repo if it had left the rate at the previously announced 6.95 per cent since call money was trading at only 6.40/50 per cent.

- Ad hoc repurchase tenders

At times of extraordinary liquidity needs, the Bundesbank can fine-tune the money market by offering ad hoc repos with shorter maturities in what it calls fast tenders, also known as 'quick securities tenders'. Such repos are offered only to banks operating in the money market for same-day settlement. The Bundesbank will tell banks it is offering repo funds to the market at a specific interest rate, usually for between two and 10 days.

- Repo cancellations

Regular repos can also be cancelled. In 1992, when the money market was flooded with funds after massive foreign currency intervention, the Bundesbank used a combination of measures to drain liquidity, including the sale of Treasury bills and the cancellation of regular repo tenders.

Foreign exchange operations

The Bundesbank can also manage liquidity through currency swaps or outright foreign exchange operations.

Under a currency swap, it adds liquidity by buying foreign exchange from banks spot and, at the same time, selling it back forward, usually for a few days. Conversely, the Bundesbank can drain liquidity by selling foreign exchange spot and buying it back forward.

The swap rate is equal to the interest rate charged on the extra liquidity injected into the market. Such transactions are conducted at rates close to those prevailing in the market and usually do not affect the external value of the mark.

The Bundesbank can also use foreign exchange repos to fine-tune the money market. In these transactions, the central bank transfers claims to the delivery of specific foreign assets it holds to the banks for a limited period. This has the same impact on liquidity as a swap. However, a swap which lowers the monetary base also reduces the central bank's foreign assets, while under a foreign exchange repo these assets remain the property of the Bundesbank, leaving net foreign assets unchanged.

Currency swaps and foreign exchange repos are more flexible than regular repos and are therefore more suitable instruments to use to fine-tune the money market.

Liquidity paper

In March 1993, the Bundesbank introduced a new instrument to absorb market liquidity, after cutting banks' minimum reserve requirements, when it announced the sale of 25 billion marks' worth of Bundesbank liquidity paper, known as *Bulis*.

Who controls the interest rate levers?

The Bundesbank sets monetary policy and is the most independent of the G7 central banks. It has a legal obligation to protect the external value of the Deutschemark. Without prejudice to the performance of its functions, the Bundesbank is required to support the general economic policy of the federal government. In using its powers under the Bundesbank Act, the central bank is independent of instructions from the federal government.

What drives interest rate policy?

Targets:

■ Operational
The Bundesbank seeks to control money market rates via repos.

■ Intermediate
The Bundesbank sets an annual target for broad money (M3), but is also known to watch the external value of the Deutschemark extremely closely.

■ Final
Price stability, which the Bundesbank defines as between nought and two per cent.

How do official rates affect commercial ones?

Corporate

In 1992, bank loans accounted for approximately 84 per cent of the money borrowed by companies. One-third of bank loans were short-term borrowing and two-thirds related to medium- or long-term capital market rates. Much of the other 16 per cent of company borrowing was raised from the capital markets and therefore likely to be unaffected by short-term interest rate movements. Overall, then, about two-thirds of corporate borrowing is fixed-rate.

Mortgages

Home ownership is far less important in Germany (40 per cent), than in the UK (65 per cent). German home loans are available from a wide variety of sources and most home buyers use a combination of several but the overwhelming majority is either fixed or renegotiable only at infrequent intervals (five years for mortgage banks). To all intents and purposes, fixed home loans are insulated from short-term interest rate movements.

Interest rate expectations

The price of the euromark contract traded on the London International Financial Futures & Options Exchange (LIFFE) and the Fibor (Frankfurt interbank offered rate) contract traded on the DTB (Deutsche Terminbörse), the German futures exchange, provide information on market expectations for interest rates. The LIFFE and DTB contracts are both cash settled one business day before the third Wednesday of the relevant month.

The LIFFE contract is expressed as 100 minus the three-month euromark rate. Thus, an expected rate of six per cent gives a contract price of 94.00. For example, if the December contract was trading at 94.00 and euromark rates were currently six per cent, that would imply that the futures market expects no change in euromark rates by December. Alternatively, if the December contract was trading at 92.00 that would imply that the futures market expects a two percentage point rise in euromark rates to eight per cent by the end of the year.

The DTB contract is expressed as 100 minus the Frankfurt interbank offered rate to be delivered. Thus, an expected Fibor of five per cent gives a contract price of 95.00. For example, if the December contract was trading at 95.00, and Fibor was currently five per cent, that would imply that the futures market expects no change in Fibor by December. Alternatively, if the December contract was trading at 94.00, that would imply that the futures market expects a one percentage point rise in Fibor, to six per cent, by the end of the year.

Timing

The Bundesbank announces any change to the key lombard and discount rates at a news conference after its fortnightly council meetings, usually held in Frankfurt and/or through a press release [BBKH].

The announcement of the terms on which the next regular repo will be conducted, including whether it will be at a fixed or variable rate, is normally made each Tuesday (circa 09.00 local time) when the bidding takes place. If it is a fixed-rate repo, the rate is usually announced at that time.

Note that the Bundesbank may announce a fixed rate before Tuesday's auction, often immediately after a change in the key lombard and/or discount rates, if it wants to send a clear signal to the market on where it wants short-term rates to be.

If it is a variable-rate repo, then the rate is announced along with the allocation on Wednesday (circa 10.00 local time) [BBKL].

The setting of tenders and allocation of funds is sometimes shifted to avoid a clash with holidays.

Key Reuter pages

Monitor

Reuters reports:

MMG1	Money market report covering repo tenders/allocations and special money market activities, such as injection of funds through Section 17
MMG3	Full money market report

Bundesbank pages (in German):

BBKA	Bundesbank index page
BBKE-G	Shows new German government bond/note issues and changes to conditions on *Bundesobligationen* (five-year bonds)
BBKH	Bundesbank official interest rate changes and other news announcements
BBKL	New Bundesbank regular repo tenders/allocation announcements (usually Tuesday and Wednesday)
BBKM	Other selected Bundesbank money market operations; for example the T-bills issued in July 1993
BBKT-U	List of recent Bundesbank repo tenders/allocations
BBKW	Banks' reserve holdings with the Bundesbank and details of borrowing at the lombard rate
BBKX	Rates for exchange of foreign cheques/bills

Other pages:

RTAJ	Weekly Bundesbank statement
RTAK	Bundesbank weekly reserves
RTAL	Discount rate
RTAV	Bundesbank official currency indices
YLDS	Key interest rates from overnight to 30 years

News 2000

MMT <F9> Topic code

60

Chapter 9

Ireland

The rates to watch

- Repo rate
  - *sets the tone for money market rates*

- Short-term facility rate
  - *usually sets the ceiling for money market rates*

- Overnight deposit rate
  - *sets the absolute floor for money market rates*

The day-to-day tone for money market rates is set by the Central Bank of Ireland's repo operations with commercial banks. **Repo rates** are usually in line with the market. If the repo rate is set above market rates it is a signal that rates are lower than the central bank would like.

The **short-term facility (STF) rate** is similar to the Bundesbank's lombard rate. It is quota-based and sets the ceiling for money market rates in normal circumstances.

During the foreign exchange crisis of November 1992, the central bank suspended the STF for the first time and replaced it with the more flexible secured overnight advances facility under which banks could borrow at a rate designed to deter them from selling punts for foreign currency. The STF was reintroduced in February 1993.

The central bank's **overnight deposit rate** sets the absolute floor for money market rates but is essentially an extremely unattractive rate for commercial banks. It is used only at the end of the day when a bank is left with a surplus that no other bank wishes to take.

How does the central bank influence the money market?

Refinancing activities

■ Short-term facility (STF)
Under this facility banks may borrow funds up to their individual quotas, from the central bank against approved security at an interest rate set

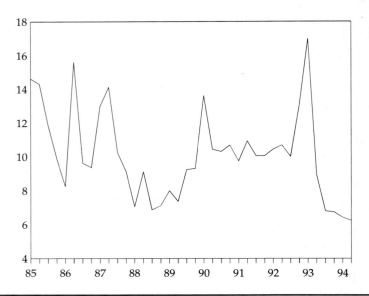

Figure 9.1   Ireland: Short-term facility rate
Source: Datastream

slightly above money market rates. Institutions usually borrow funds overnight but the term may be lengthened at the central bank's discretion.

■ Secured overnight advances
If a credit institution has used up its STF quota it can, at the central bank's
discretion, borrow additional funds through a secured overnight advance at
a penalty rate. During the exchange rate mechanism (ERM) crisis in 1992/3,
the central bank suspended the STF and replaced it with the secured overnight advances facility under which rates were set daily.

■ Reserve requirement
The central bank has a Primary Liquidity Ratio which applies to licensed
banks, building societies, and state-sponsored financial institutions. The ratio was unified at three per cent for these institutions in February 1994. It
expresses liquid assets (cash and balances with the central bank) as a percentage of liabilities used to fund Irish pound lending (so-called 'Relevant
Resources'). The interest rate paid on these reserves is below market rates.
The Bank can raise the primary ratio to withdraw market liquidity or lower
it to add liquidity. In practice, changes to the primary ratio are made infre-

quently and not as part of routine liquidity management. In this context, they have been mainly employed in the past to accommodate seasonal demand for liquidity around the end of the year.

Open market operations

Each morning the central bank estimates the liquidity position in the money market and decides whether and how to inject or drain funds. Liquidity is usually provided through repurchase agreements. If the market is in surplus, liquidity can be taken out through fixed-term deposits, usually at market rates. Leaving the market short and needing to borrow under the short-term facility would be a signal for higher rates.

■ Sale and repurchase agreements
The central bank's primary money market management tool is repurchase agreements. Repos are usually conducted bilaterally with individual institutions, but when there are large money market shortages, they may be advertised for tender. Repos are usually overnight but can be for longer periods, such as a week or a month. Allocations of funds are at the discretion of the central bank and are variable rate. Repos are usually at market rates. If the repo is set above market rates it is a signal that rates are lower than the central bank would like.

■ Fixed-term deposits
The central bank normally uses fixed-term deposits to drain excess liquidity from the market. The rates on such deposits are usually in line with the market. The maturity of term deposits ranges from overnight to one month.

■ Foreign exchange swaps
The central bank occasionally swaps foreign exchange for Irish pounds to withdraw liquidity or vice versa to add funds.

Who controls the interest rate levers?

The Central Bank of Ireland controls monetary policy. The Bank's policy-making Board normally includes the Secretary of the Department of Finance, but the Bank is nevertheless fully independent. All of the Board are members in their own right and do not attend Board meetings in their professional capacities. The secretary of the Department of Finance, or the deputy, is often later appointed as governor of the Central Bank.

What drives interest rate policy?

Targets:

■ Operational
Interbank rates.

■ Intermediate
Currency stability. There is a statutory objective to safeguard the value of the currency. Thus, interest rates are set at whatever level is necessary to safeguard the punt.

■ Final
Price stability. Interest rate policy is geared towards maintaining a firm exchange rate to underpin price stability.

How do official rates affect commercial ones?

Corporate

Nearly all corporate bank loans are at a variable rate related to the one-month interbank rate. Each week, the Central Bank of Ireland calculates a representative one-month rate for loans to small- and medium-sized businesses and personal customers. There is an agreement between the central bank and the four biggest commercial banks—Ulster, Allied Irish, National Irish and the Bank of Ireland—to charge no more than 5½ percentage points above that rate for overdrafts and term loans.

Mortgages

Traditionally, most mortgages have been at variable rates, as in the UK. However, since the 1993 exchange rate mechanism (ERM) currency crisis, half of all new mortgages have been at fixed rates for periods of 1-5 years. The majority of existing mortgages are at variable rates and so the mortgage market as a whole is still extremely sensitive to movements in interbank rates and, in turn, short-term official rates.

Timing

The central bank announces its forecast of the money market liquidity position at 08.15 GMT. Repos are normally conducted between 09.00 and 10.00

GMT. If there is a forecasting error (regarding Exchequer spending for example) the Bank can operate in the afternoon. End-month statistics show how much liquidity was provided.

Key Reuter pages

Monitor

Reuters reports:

IRMB	Bond market report
IRMF	Foreign exchange report

Central Bank of Ireland pages:

CBII	Irish punt exchange rate index
CBIS	End-month statistics (external reserves, money supply, private sector credit at banks/all credit institutions)
CBIX	Announcements of interest rate changes

News 2000

MMT <F9> Topic code

Chapter 10

Italy

The rates to watch

- Fixed-term advances rate
  - *usually sets the ceiling for money market rates*
- Repo rates
  - *sets the tone for money market rates*
- Discount rate
  - *a strong signal of the general interest rate trend*

The two most important Bank of Italy interest rates are the **fixed-term advances rate** (similar to Germany's lombard rate except that the amount advanced is at the central bank's discretion) and the **repo rate**.

The fixed-term advances rate usually sets the ceiling for repo rates. However, repos are now the main short-term liquidity management tool. They are conducted in both lire and foreign currency.

The discount rate still has a strong symbolic value and indicates where the Bank of Italy feels interest rates should be. Money market rates are usually kept above the discount rate.

Clues on the direction of monetary policy can be picked up from the amount allocated at repos and the average and marginal rates set. Also important is any change in the spread of the fixed-term advances rate over the discount rate.

How does the central bank influence the money market?

There are five main ways in which the Bank of Italy can provide liquidity to the market. They are: rediscounting, ordinary advances, fixed-term advances, repos, and outright operations in Treasury securities.

■ Discount rate

Loans (rediscounts) are granted on collateral which includes Treasury bills (BOTs) and other tradeable securities.

Rediscount borrowing is negligible these days, but the discount rate is a strong signal of general interest rate trends.

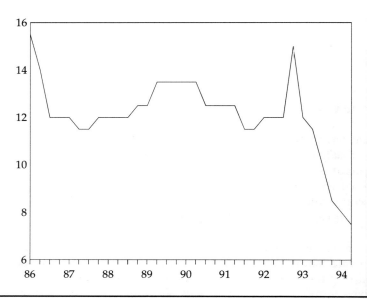

Figure 10.1   Italy: Discount rate
Source: Datastream

■ Ordinary advances (*anticipazioni ordinaire*)
These are credit lines agreed with individual lending institutions, such as banks, and guaranteed with collateral which can include state and other traded bonds.

Ordinary advances are the customary way banks borrow from the central bank for their everyday needs. The rate charged on this form of assistance credit is equal to the discount rate. Banks must also pay a fixed fee equal to 0.3 per cent of their credit line every four months.

Each bank has a maximum credit line (*linea di credito*) at the central bank but, either for technical reasons or as a precaution, leaves a certain margin undrawn which it keeps at its disposal (*margine disponibile*) as 'liquidity of last resort'.

Advances under the credit lines have a maximum maturity of four months, but the underlying contracts usually incorporate an automatic renewal clause.

According to its economic priorities, the Bank may at any time change the total amount of ordinary credit granted to the banking system through proportionate adjustments in individual credit lines. However, it must give two working days' notice.

■ Fixed-term advances (*anticipazioni a scadenza fissa*)
Fixed-term advances are a more expensive source of bank finance because of the higher rate and shorter maturity. They are, therefore, mainly used if the central bank wants to tighten credit. Under those circumstances, the Bank will drop repos in favour of fixed-term advances to make it easier to increase short-term interest rates. This is why the fixed-term advances rate sets a ceiling for repo rates.

■ Repos
In an effort to smooth monetary and interest rate targeting, the Bank of Italy sets the day-to-day level of money market rates through the repo rate. Repo maturities vary, but they are usually for less than two months.

Repos are carried out at competitive auctions in which money market operators are invited to bid on both the price (interest rate) and volume of funds.

The Bank of Italy has two types of repo:

a)   Lira-denominated repos, most of which are conducted using Treasury bills and bonds;

b)   Foreign currency repos, which aim to reduce the impact of a temporary scarcity of securities and help to rebuild official foreign currency reserves. They can be conducted in any of the major currencies but are usually in dollars or marks. The central bank adds liquidity by purchasing foreign currency spot and simultaneously fixing the maturity of the contract. The forward price is set by competitive auction. The Bank began to conduct such currency swaps with the banking system in October 1992 because it was having difficulty covering liquidity shortages through repos on government debt alone.

The Bank of Italy calls repos on an irregular basis when liquidity conditions dictate and there is no preset schedule. They are usually conducted several times a week.

The Bank holds repos or intervenes in the money market when it perceives a need to add or drain liquidity given the expected flows of reserves.

Repos are now always at a variable rate. The last reverse repo to drain liquidity was in 1990. The Bank may reject some bids below its threshold which is not announced in advance. The auction technique implies that repo interest rates change frequently according to market conditions. Since mid-1993 repo rates have fluctuated between the discount rate and the fixed-term advances rate.

■ Outright operations in Treasury securities

Recently, the Bank of Italy introduced auctions on the secondary market for T-bills as an additional method of controlling liquidity.

Other liquidity tools

■ Reserve requirements

Banks are obliged to keep a fixed proportion of domestic and foreign currency deposits as reserves with the Bank of Italy. This amounts to 17.5 per cent for deposits with a maturity of less than 18 months and 10 per cent for certificates of deposit (CDs) with a maturity of not less than 18 months. (In 1993, the central bank estimated that the average reserve ratio will be 13.7 per cent which is very high by international standards.)

Further reductions in reserve requirements are expected to follow the abolition of the Treasury overdraft. The legislation that abolishes the overdraft also gives the Bank of Italy the power to change the requirements.

Each bank can use up to seven per cent of its deposits with the central bank on any one day to meet daily liquidity needs. But it must maintain an average throughout the monthly account. So, for example, if it draws down one per cent of its reserves for one day, at some stage during the month it must have in its account the full reserve requirement plus one per cent. If a bank fails to meet reserve requirements it risks heavy penalties.

Squaring of reserve positions towards the end of the computation period (mid-month) can occasionally cause short-term interest rates to fall quite sharply due to the very low return on excess deposits (0.5 per cent).

Who controls the interest rate levers?

Since the early 1980s the Bank of Italy has been steadily distancing itself from the Treasury and now enjoys an independence similar to that of the Bundesbank. No government representatives take part in the Bank's decisions on monetary policy and those decisions do not require government approval. The governor of the Bank of Italy is chosen by the Board of the Bank of Italy and the appointment has subsequently to be confirmed by the president of the Republic. The term of office is indefinite.

What drives interest rate policy?

Targets:

■ Operational

Bank liquidity and money market interest rates, weighted according to market circumstances.

■ Intermediate
The Bank of Italy has a target for the M2 measure of money supply but also monitors the external value of the lira.

■ Final
Monetary stability.

How do official rates affect commercial ones?

Business loans

Over 60 per cent of loans to smaller Italian companies are on overdraft of are short-term loans related to short-term interest rate movements.

Home loans

More than 50 per cent of Italian mortgages are at fixed rates. A particular feature of the Italian mortgage market is that payments of interest and principal are usually only made semi-annually. There is thus a lag between changes in official rates and the impact on the cost of housing finance.

Interest rate expectations

The price of the eurolira contract traded on the London International Financial Futures & Options Exchange (LIFFE) provides information on market expectations for the three-month eurolira rate. The contract is cash settled one business day before the third Wednesday of the relevant month. It is expressed as 100 minus the three-month eurolira rate. Thus, an expected eurolira rate of 10 per cent gives a contract price of 90.00. For example, if the December contract was trading at 92.00 and the eurolira rate was currently eight per cent it would imply that the futures market expects no change in the eurolira rate by December. Alternatively, if the December contract was trading at 91.00 that would imply that the futures market expects a one percentage point rise in the eurolira rate to nine per cent by the end of the year.

Timing

Changes in the discount and/or fixed-term advances rates [BITT] are usually announced by the Bank of Italy after the bond market closes from 17.00 local time onwards.

The central bank sets lira repos [BITA] at about 08.30 and gives the results from 10.30-11.00. Foreign currency repos [FXBI-J] are announced in the evening and take effect three working days from the next working day the normal settlement period for foreign exchange transactions.

Key Reuter pages

Monitor

Reuters reports:

MMI1/2	Repos

Bank of Italy pages:

BITA-Z, IGVA-L, FXBK-M, ATIK-M	Full range
BITA-B	Lira repo announcements and results
BITE	BOT (Treasury bill) auctions
BITG-R	Secondary government securities market
BITS	Daily data on the general reserve position of the banking system as a whole. The left-hand column gives the average banks have to keep on deposit throughout the month. The right-hand column lists the cash actually deposited at the Bank of Italy
BITT	Bank of Italy rate change statements; discount rate and fixed-term advances rate
BITV-Z	Government bond auctions
FXBI-J	Foreign currency repo results announcements
IGVA-L	Bank of Italy secondary market listings
ATIK	List of recent lira repos
ATIM	List of recent foreign currency repos

Other pages:

ITLU	Snapshot of money market rates
RTAL	The discount rate and date of last change
YLDS	Key interest rates from overnight to 30 years

News 2000

MMT <F9> Topic code

Chapter 11

Japan

The rates to watch

- Uncollateralized (unsecured) overnight call rate
  - *sets the tone for money market rates*

- Official discount rate (ODR)
  - *lagging rate of psychological significance*

Japan is nearing the end of a decade-long period in which most interest rates have been deregulated. These changes mean the Bank of Japan now sets only its **official discount rate**, at which it lends to commercial banks, and the liquidity deposit rate. Other interest rates are set in the open market and the BOJ aims to influence them, indirectly, through its market operations.

The most important short-term interbank money market rate is the **uncollateralized overnight call rate**. The Bank of Japan (BOJ) closely monitors call rate movements and puts most emphasis on them when managing the market.

The BOJ appears to have an unpublished target zone for the call rate, but the market usually gets an idea of the BOJ's target range and credit stance by interpreting the signals in its daily operations.

For the past several years, the market has focused more on the amount and timing of BOJ operations. Rates set by the BOJ have rarely ruffled any market feathers, as they have been largely in line with prevailing market rates.

The weekly average call rate, and its level at intervention time, can provide signals on the BOJ's policy stance.

How does the central bank influence the money market?

■ Official discount rate
Since the BOJ prefers to signal monetary policy changes through the uncollateralized overnight call rate, the official discount rate (ODR) is now typically a lagging indicator of monetary policy. Nevertheless, the ODR still has an impact.

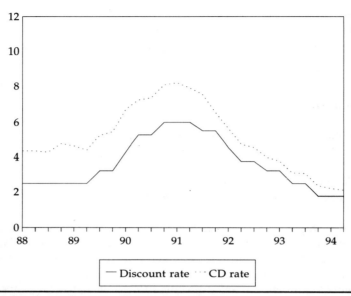

Figure 11.1   Japan: Official discount rate & certificate of deposit rate
Source: Datastream

The ODR applies to the rediscounting of commercial bills and official loans secured with Japanese government bonds (JGBs), specially-designed securities and bills corresponding to commercial bills as collateral.

If the ODR is increased, financial institutions find that the cost of raising funds is affected directly, via the higher cost of acquiring discount window loans from the BOJ, and, indirectly, through the increased money market rates that usually precede, and often trigger, an ODR change. The opposite is, of course, true for a reduction in the ODR.

■ Special lending facility
The special lending facility was introduced in March 1981 to give the BOJ another tool to help fine-tune the money markets. Under this facility, the BOJ can, temporarily and exceptionally, lend to private financial institutions at a special official lending rate set independently of the ODR. However, so far, it has never been used.

Open market operations

The BOJ controls the call rate through its money market operations. Open market operations cover securities operations, bill operations and sales of Japanese government bills.

Since March 1993, money market trading hours have been from 09.00 to 17.00 local time. The closing time can be extended to 17.30 or 18.00 occasionally, for example when afternoon activity is substantial.

All money market rates can theoretically move throughout trading hours, but most activity is concentrated in the morning 09.00 to 12.00.

The key rates also move mostly in the morning and even if they rise/fall sharply in the afternoon such movements often just represent small lot transactions in a thin market. (Reuters [BOJA-D] market commentary pages use 'most actively traded' or 'central rate' for the key rates, with a fluctuation range if necessary.)

The terms of the BOJ's regular money market operations range from one day to about a month. The rates for most operations are set through competitive bids which reflect current market conditions.

■ Regular BOJ operations

09.20

- The BOJ adds/drains funds to offset the day's shortage/surplus using the following techniques:

a) overnight repurchases of commercial bills (add, rare);
b) loans to commercial banks (add, very common);
c) recall of BOJ loans previously made (drain, common);
d) sale of Japanese government financing bills (FBs) under repurchase pacts which are mostly announced the day before (drain, common). The frequency and maturity of these agreements is often timed to fall on days when large surpluses or shortages are expected;
e) commercial paper (CP) purchase (add, rare, seen only after discount rate change and when the BOJ wants to alter significantly its target zone for the call rate);
f) purchase of Treasury bills under repurchase agreements with maturities of less than one month (add, common).

10.10

- The BOJ adds/drains funds to offset the shortage/surplus not for that day, but for the subsequent days. These operations typically settle one to three business days later, and maturities run up to a few weeks. The BOJ uses the following techniques at this time:

a) seeks offers of commercial bills (add, common). The BOJ does not set the rate, but sometimes accepts larger/smaller amounts than initially announced;

b) outright purchase of 10- or 20-year Japanese government bonds (JGBs) (permanent add, common). This is a method of permanent reserve injection, supplying base money to support economic growth. Outright purchases of JGBs are small compared with the other daily reserve adjustments;

c) purchases of 10- and 20-year bonds via repurchase agreements, or *gensaki* (add, common);

d) Ministry of Finance (MOF) Trust Fund Bureau outright bond purchases (add, once a month) or under repurchase agreements (add, a few times a month). The BOJ acts as agent for the operations and announces the details. The Trust Fund Bureau also sells bonds outright, which drains liquidity.

The repo rate can signal the BOJ's stance at the longer end of the money market.

Other times

a) At about 09.20 local time, or 16.30, the BOJ sells financing bills (FBs) to offset surpluses of liquidity in coming days. This operation is seen as purely technical and has no policy implications (drain, common);

b) MOF sinking fund bond purchases, through the BOJ as acting agent, are usually conducted after 12.00. In an attempt to dampen rises in long-term bond yields (add, common);

c) BOJ recall of loans to banks occurs when money market rates plummet after operation time (drain, rare).

Traders base their forecasts of BOJ operations on money market supply/demand conditions for the day.

The BOJ announces each day, usually at 17.20 local time, its projection of supply/demand conditions in the money market for the next day, and its revision of supply/demand conditions for the day just ending. Occasionally, the BOJ announces its projections at 17.50 or 18.20 if trading hours have been extended.

The BOJ announces a further revision of supply/demand conditions at 10.00 the following day. (Projections [BOJE], revisions [BOJF] updated soon after the BOJ announcement.)

Net shortage/surplus conditions [BOJE] and the level of commercial banks' reserves [BOJF] are equally important.

If bank reserves are more than adequate, the BOJ does not need to provide funds equivalent to the full market shortage because banks can draw down reserves at the BOJ to offset the gap.

When the BOJ provides more than the projected money market shortage, or allows a surplus to stand, it usually wants to accommodate money market rates via easier credit; warn against excessively high rates set by the market; and allow commercial banks to cover a shortfall in their reserves at the BOJ.

When the BOJ provides less than the projected money market shortage, or drains more than the net surplus, it wants to tighten market conditions so that rates rise; warn against market expectations of lower interest rates; and cancel out a surplus of commercial bank reserves.

■ Reserve requirements
Commercial banks are required to hold a certain amount of reserves, equivalent to a specified proportion of their assets, at the BOJ, at the end of each one-month reporting period and also over that period, on a cumulative basis.

Towards the end of each reserve reporting period, the shorter end of the money market usually firms and volatility increases. The BOJ often supplies ample funds to try to avoid this kind of excess volatility in the money market.

The BOJ always makes its reserve adjustment operations clear. The reserve condition of commercial banks, published daily [BOJF], indicates how much banks have to accumulate in the remaining days of the reserve period. The aggregate amount of all operations (including discount window loans) is announced the same morning or afternoon and the BOJ also publishes, twice daily, its own estimates of market factors affecting reserves.

The market is therefore relieved of the task of estimating reserve factors. Interpreting open market operations with knowledge of the BOJ's reserve estimates usually makes the central bank's interest rate intentions quite clear.

Reserve ratios have rarely been used as an adjustment tool in recent years.

Who controls the interest rate levers?

There is no hard and fast rule. Under the Bank of Japan Law (1942) the Bank's Policy Board has the authority to formulate, direct and carry out monetary policy. While ultimate control of monetary policy rests with the Ministry of Finance, the Bank of Japan Law gives the central bank sole responsibility for changing the official discount rate.

There are seven members of the Policy Board, four of whom are appointed by the cabinet and approved by both houses of the Diet (Japanese Parliament). There are four representatives from private industry, one from the Bank of Japan and two from the government. The government members, taken from the Ministry of Finance and the Economic Planning Agency, do not have voting rights.

What drives interest rate policy?

Targets:

■ Operational
The Bank of Japan has a target zone for the call rate.

■ Intermediate
There is no intermediate target.

■ Final
Price stability.

How do official rates affect commercial ones?

Corporate

Corporate debt is divided evenly between fixed- and floating-rate loans. The long-term prime rate, at which banks lend to their best customers, is linked to the yield on five-year bank debentures. However, a large proportion of corporate borrowing is through the issue of bonds, most of which are effectively fixed-rate.

Mortgages

Most mortgages are at variable rates. The Housing Loan Corporation, which is responsible for about 40 per cent of all housing finance, reviews its loans occasionally but sets a ceiling. Overall, the mortgage market is largely insulated from short-term changes in official interest rates.

Timing (local time)

Since March 1993, money market trading hours have been from 09.00 to 17.00 or 18.00. The closing time can be extended to 17.30 when afternoon activity is substantial.

All money market rates can theoretically move throughout trading hours, but most activity is concentrated in the morning 09.00 to 12.00.

Most BOJ open market operations are also conducted in the morning. Lending also usually takes place in morning but sometimes in the afternoon as well.

The BOJ's regular money market operations are at 09.20 and 10.10, but it also conducts ad hoc operations.

The BOJ announces each day, at 17.20, 17.50 or 18.20 local time, its projection of supply/demand conditions in the money market for the next day, and its revision of supply/demand conditions for the day just ending.

The BOJ announces a further revision of supply/demand conditions at 10.00 the following day. (Projections [BOJE], revisions [BOJF] updated soon after the BOJ announcement.)

Net shortage/surplus conditions [BOJE] and the level of commercial banks' reserves [BOJF] are equally important.

The BOJ lends up to 15.00 with commercial paper operations conducted at around 09.00. Activities in *tegata* (bills of exchange) and others are mostly carried out around 09.20 and 10.10.

Key Reuter pages

Monitor

Reuters reports:

BOJA-I	Full range
BOJA-D	Always updated after BOJ money market operations
	• By 03.00 GMT, Reuters reviews the BOJ's morning operations, analyses its credit stance and gives the afternoon outlook for key rates based on interviews with money traders
	• By 07.00 GMT Reuters reviews movements in market rates so far, BOJ operations and the central bank's stance
	• By 09.00 GMT Reuters files an outlook on the BOJ's monetary stance for the coming day based on projections of the demand for and supply of funds plus a short review of movements in market rates so far and the BOJ's activities
BOJE	BOJ projections of supply/demand conditions in the money market announced at 01.00 GMT the following day. Net shortage/surplus conditions can also be found on this page
BOJF	Revisions to BOJ projections of supply/demand conditions in the money market updated soon after the BOJ announcement. The level of commercial banks' reserves are also given on this page
YLDS	Key interest rates from overnight to 30 years

Cont.

(cont.)

News 2000

TANSHI <F5> Quote

There are no BOJ pages on money market rates so Reuters picks up daily rate moves by asking money traders or from pages updated by the major money market brokers Tokyo TANSHI, Yamani TANSHI, UEDA TANSHI and Nihon TANSHI

These pages show ON *mutan*, the uncollateralized overnight call rate. (*Mutan* is Japanese for uncollateralized, while *yutan* means collateralized). The pages also give the daily core rate for the overnight call rate quoted in Reuters regular money market report [BOJA-E]

NOTE: These pages are only available to Reuter clients who are approved by TANSHI companies

TANSHJ <F5> Quote
MMT <F9> Topic code

Closing money market rates and non-restricted prices

Chapter 12

The Netherlands

The rates to watch

- Special advances rate
  - *sets the tone for money market rates*

- Secured loans rate (interest rate on advances)
  - *sets the floor for money market rates*

The special advances rate is the money market intervention rate. It tends to set the tone for money market rates and is usually between 0.1 and 0.5 percentage points above the secured loans rate. It is roughly comparable to Germany's repo rate, but usually fixed rather than variable.

The secured loans rate is similar to the German discount rate, but there is no equivalent for the Bundesbank's lombard rate. It is the Nederlandsche Bank's lowest rate and is usually changed by a quarter percentage point or a multiple thereof.

The discount rate was abolished on 1 January 1994.

How does the central bank influence the money market?

The money market is most easily understood as a system of central bank windows where commercial banks can obtain funds limited by quotas. Quotas are set such that commercial banks are always short of funds and therefore need to borrow from the central bank's special advances facility.

■ Credit quota
Every three months, the Bank sets a limit, or quota, on the amount banks can borrow through its regular credit facilities at the secured loans rate. The limit is deliberately set below the banking system's expected demand for liquidity so that banks depend on supplementary lending by the central bank.

The aggregate credit line is set at about ⅔ of the estimated money market deficit. Additional liquidity is then provided through special advances and changes in minimum cash requirements (see below).

The secured loans rate sets the floor for call money since if the latter exceeds the former money market players will prefer to borrow at the se-

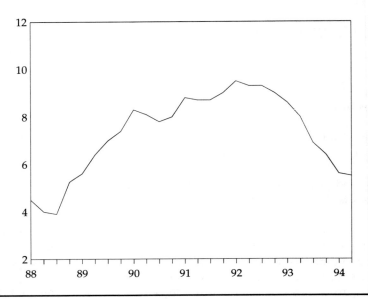

Figure 12.1   Netherlands: Special advances rate
Source: Datastream

cured loans rate. However, call money can exceed the advances rate since recourse to advances is limited by restrictions reinforced by the credit quota and surcharges.

The credit quota sets a daily average for commercial banks' borrowing at the central bank at the secured loans rate. The quota normally runs for three months.

Early each day, the Bank announces how much banks have drawn under the existing quota. This indicates how tight the money market has been so far.

Towards the expiry of a credit quota, commercial banks tend to build up savings under the scheme. This can put pressure on call money just before the credit quota expires.

■ Money market cash reserve
By setting a money market cash reserve, the Bank creates a shortage of liquidity since banks have to draw down their liquid funds to meet the cash reserve requirement. This enables the central bank to steer money market rates with special advances.

The maturity of a cash reserve usually ranges from a few days to a few weeks and is changed by the central bank in line with market conditions.

When the Bank expects the market to become very short of funds, the cash reserve requirement can be set at zero per cent for a single day or perhaps longer.

■ Nederlandsche Bank Certificates (NBCs)

NBCs are interest-bearing negotiable certificates issued to drain structural money market surpluses. They are an additional liquidity management tool used alongside the money market cash reserve.

NBCs were introduced in March 1994 in response to the strong increase in liquidity caused by the events leading up to the European currency crisis in the summer of 1993. Compulsory Nederlandsche Bank intervention sales of guilders to support other member currencies in the exchange rate mechanism between September 1992 and August 1993 led to a sharp increase in the amount of the money market cash reserve in the Netherlands. As a result, the money market cash reserve became more structural, whereas when it was introduced in 1988 it was designed to drain temporary money market surpluses and to create limited shortages.

NBCs are issued at monthly auctions and have a maturity of six months. Bidders must state the volumes (multiples of Dfl 5 million) they wish to take up at various yields (intervals of 0.01 per cent). Bids must be submitted by 11.00 local time. Allotment takes place on a discount basis through the so-called Dutch auction system whereby all bids honoured are settled at the lowest accepted price (highest yield). The Bank does not repurchase NBCs before maturity.

The auctions are open to credit institutions registered in the Netherlands and to foreign central banks.

■ Special advances

Special advances are short-term loans (effectively current account loans) offered to commercial banks against collateral, mainly Treasury paper.

The special advances rate is fixed by the central bank. Changes to the rate are in multiples of 10 basis points.

Banks are invited to tender for a special loan with a fixed term, an open amount and a fixed rate. The central bank then decides how much to allocate. The maturity of special advances is between one and four days. The Bank bases the maturity on its forecasts for money market liquidity. But at times of uncertainty, it may keep pacts particularly short so it can quickly set a new advances rate.

The Bank can offer an extra advances pact on top of a running facility. This usually happens if liquidity turns out to be lower than expected, making the existing pact insufficient for commercial banks. In turn, the Bank can also decide not to offer any advances for a day or longer if it thinks the market is liquid enough.

■ Secured loans rate
The secured loans rate is a closely-watched official rate. It applies to commercial banks' daily borrowing at the central bank under the credit quota scheme.

■ Promissory note rate
The central bank does not, in practice, conduct transactions at the promissory note rate anymore and it therefore has no direct impact on the money market. It is now only used as a base for the rates charged by commercial banks. The promissory note rate equals the secured loans rate plus 0.5 of a percentage point.

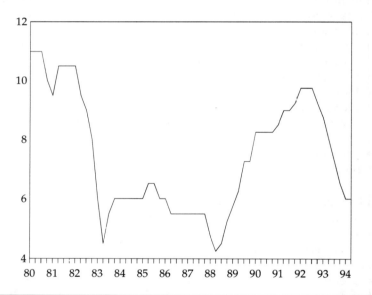

Figure 12.2   Netherlands: Promissory note rate
Source: Datastream

■ Currency swaps
Under special circumstances, the central bank can also use currency swaps, usually for dollars, to regulate liquidity. The Bank can ease/tighten credit by purchasing/selling dollars spot in exchange for guilders, with a forward agreement to resell dollars/repurchase guilders.

■ Money market intervention

If there is an undesirable rise/fall in money market rates, the central bank can ask commercial banks to lend/borrow call money in their own name but for the central bank's account. These requests are mainly designed to maintain or restore an orderly market rather than to guide the general level of interest rates.

Who controls the interest rate levers?

The Nederlandsche Bank sets monetary policy. Rate decisions are taken by the Bank's Executive Board (the governor, plus four directors). Under the central bank's statutes, the finance minister has the authority to issue a directive if this is deemed necessary to co-ordinate Bank and government policies. But such a directive has not been issued since the Bank Act of 1948. While the central bank has effective independence in setting interest rates, in practice, it has little autonomy given the objective of preserving the link between the guilder and the Deutschemark (see below).

What drives interest rate policy?

Guilder stability against the mark. An unpublished target band of 1.12-1.13 guilders per mark has existed for more than 10 years. The strength of Dutch commitment to guilder stability against the mark was underlined in the summer of 1993 when other member countries in the European exchange rate mechanism (ERM) adopted new 15 per cent fluctuation bands, while the Dutch authorities stuck to the old 2¼ per cent bands.

How do official rates affect commercial ones?

Corporate

The majority of corporate loans are fixed rate. According to central bank figures, in 1992 only a quarter of bank loans to the corporate sector had a maturity of two years or less. The rates on these short-term loans (overdrafts), most of which float, are related to money market rates. The promissory note rate is often the benchmark for overdrafts.

Mortgages

Nearly all borrowing by Dutch households is at rates fixed for a long period. To all intents and purposes, such borrowing is entirely insulated from short-term movements in official interest rates.

Timing (local time)

The Bank is free to change rates at any time, for example when the guilder is under pressure on the foreign exchange market, but normally sticks to a rigid timetable.

The central bank's Executive Board usually meets every Thursday to consider its monetary policy stance.

The Bank usually announces the rate and maturity for new advances at 16.00. Subscriptions for a new pact open the next working day between 09.00 and 09.30 and the Bank announces allocations shortly after, usually at about 10.00.

Each day, the Bank announces how much banks have drawn under the existing credit quota.

Both the credit quota and cash reserve are announced three working days before the expiry of the latest scheme, at the same time as the central bank announces details of its interest rates.

NBCs are issued at monthly auctions. The Bank announces auction, payment and maturity dates, plus the maximum amount of NBCs offered for sale, five business days before they are issued [DNBN].

Key Reuter pages

Monitor

Reuters reports:
MHL1	Advances, quotas etc.
MHL3	Full money market report

Nederlandsche Bank pages:
DNBN	Announcement of NBC auction, payment and maturity dates, plus the maximum amount offered for sale. The Bank also uses this page to announce the total amount of bids, the total amount of NBCs allotted, the highest accepted yield and the percentage allotted at that yield

Ministry of Finance pages
AGFB-Z	Full range
AGFB	Index page
AGFI-J	Money market announcements

Other pages:
AIBO	Amsterdam interbank offered rates

News 2000

MMT <F9> Topic code

Chapter 13

New Zealand

The rates to watch

In New Zealand, there are no specific official interest rates to watch as such, although monetary policy changes are effected through movements in money market rates.

The Reserve Bank of New Zealand operates a system of money market management which relies purely on regulating the amount of cash in the system and, unlike nearly every other central bank in the industrialized world, does not set rates administratively.

When the Reserve Bank wants to signal a change in interest rates, it usually announces a change in the amount of surplus cash it is targeting for the banking system as a whole or, relatively infrequently, announces changes in the penalty margin over market rates which has to be paid by banks using the Reserve Bank's discount window.

The three important short-term interest rates are: the discount rate, set by the Bank at a fixed margin above comparable market rates for Reserve Bank bills; the overnight rate, which is simply a market-determined rate; and the float tender rate, set by the Bank in line with market rates.

How does the central bank influence the money market?

■ Cash target

The Bank forecasts daily influences on settlement cash—mainly flows between the government and private sector—and uses these to determine how much to inject into, or withdraw from, the money market.

The Reserve Bank usually targets specific small positive settlement cash balances (the sum of the settlement banks' balances with the Reserve Bank at the end of each day) in the banking system. The surplus can be raised/lowered to signal a change in monetary policy:

a)   If the surplus was raised from, say, NZ$20 million to NZ$40 million, there would be far more cash in the system available to individual banks to meet their settlement obligations at the central bank. It is therefore less likely that any individual bank will have to go to the Reserve Bank's discount window for cash reserves and, therefore, banks are less likely to have to pay the discount window penalty.

This, in turn, means there is less pressure on interest rates in the system as a whole.

b)   If the Reserve Bank's targeted surplus was cut from NZ$20 million to zero, it would have the opposite effect. There would be less cash in the system and more banks would be forced to borrow at the discount window at a penalty rate. This would put upward pressure on money market rates.

■ Methods of supplying liquidity
There are four main ways in which the Reserve Bank can increase money market liquidity:

a)   Open market operations - injections of funds by way of 'secured loans' (secured against Treasury bills, government bonds, registered bank bills, TCOs, NCDs) or, less frequently, purchases of government bonds.

   If the banking system as a whole is short of settlement balances following the open market operation or as a result of a forecast error, banks have to sell (discount) Reserve Bank bills with the central bank in exchange for settlement cash (*see* 'Discount rate' below) because they are not allowed to have overdrafts on their Reserve Bank deposit accounts.

b)   Daily cash float tender - at which the Reserve Bank lends a large part of the government's daily cash receipts to the banks for one day.

   All central banks face a fundamental problem in their management of money markets: how to forecast accurately the liquidity situation for the coming day. This problem is usually caused by the difficulty of forecasting which tax payments will be made on any particular day. The Reserve Bank of New Zealand has neatly side-stepped this problem by agreeing to lend back to the system, for just one day, all the tax receipts received. The next day, when these payments are due, the Reserve Bank knows how much impact tax receipts will have on liquidity and thus has a much more accurate idea of what it needs to do to hit its cash surplus target for the banking system.

   The Reserve Bank charges the float tender rate for such loans. It is almost always set in line with the overnight rate.

c)   Discount window - the Reserve Bank can also alter monetary policy by changing the fixed margin which banks have to pay to discount Reserve Bank bills with up to 28 days to maturity.

Bills are discounted at a penalty rate set above comparable market rates for Reserve Bank bills.

The risk of incurring this penalty encourages banks to compete to maintain holdings of settlement cash, and discountable bills. The greater the cost of discounting, other things being equal, the tighter are monetary conditions.

d)   Rate on settlement cash balances - the Reserve Bank could also change interest rates on settlement cash balances held at the Reserve Bank overnight. However, since 1991, it has paid a rate set at the higher of the minimum float tender rate minus 300 basis points or zero per cent.

■ Methods of withdrawing liquidity
Open market operations - as part of the Bank's daily cash management operations, funds may be withdrawn from the banking system by way of the sale of Treasury bills in the open market.

Who controls the interest rate levers?

The Reserve Bank sets monetary policy. Under the 1989 Reserve Bank Act, once policy targets have been established by the government the Reserve Bank has complete control over how the targets are met. Under current legislation, the only target is to "achieve and maintain stability in the general level of prices". The government is allowed to override the target but if it does a directive must be tabled in Parliament. The Reserve Bank has complete operational independence.

What drives interest rate policy?

Targets:

■ Operational
Daily target for cash surplus in the banking system.

■ Intermediate
The Reserve Bank uses an eclectic check-list of inflationary indicators: the exchange rate (as measured by the trade-weighted index (TWI)); the shape of the yield curve; the level of interest rates relative to expected inflation; money and credit growth; economic growth; and asset prices. All are used as early-warning signals on inflationary trends, but the exchange rate (trade-weighted index) is regarded by the Bank as the most important.

■ Final
The government has an inflation target.

How do official rates affect commercial ones?

Corporate

Companies juggle between floating-rate loans and fixed-rate deals for any-thing up to five years. Note that there is no prime rate.

Mortgages

The majority of existing mortgages are at floating rates, but some new mortgages are being taken out at fixed rates for 6 months to 3 years.

Timing

Details of the float tender are announced at approximately 07.40 local time [RBZC], at which point bidding begins. The float tender closes 10 minutes later and the results are announced at about 08.05.

At 09.45, details of the open market operations (OMO) are announced to the market [RBZB] and bidding gets under way. The results of the OMO are published at around 10.25.

Discount rates are announced at approximately 10.45.

The Reserve Bank holds a weekly Treasury bill tender, and bond tenders are held up to every three weeks as determined by the government debt programme. However, the most important tender is the twice-weekly sale of 63-day Reserve Bank bills, since these are the passport to the discount window for emergency lending. Any reduction in the volume of these ten-ders would mean fewer discountable bills on issue, increasing the demand for, and cost of, Reserve Bank bills. Reserve Bank bill tenders are held every Monday and Thursday, and the results are published at around 14.45 [RBZD].

Key Reuter pages

Monitor

Reserve Bank of New Zealand pages:

RBZA-RBZZ,	
NZRB-Q, RBNZ	Full range
RBZZ	Reserve Bank index page
RBZA	Open market operation, liquidity flows/discount rates
RBZB	Open market operation tender details
RBZC	Float tender details
RBZD	Reserve Bank bill tender details
RBZE	Treasury bill tender details

Cont.

(cont.)

RBZF	Treasury bill tender analysis
RBZG/H	Treasury bill analysis
RBZI	Government stock tender details
RBZJ	Government stock secondary sales
RBZK-M	Projected liquidity flows
RBZN-O	Monetary and credit aggregates
RBZP/Y	Policy statements/comments
RBNZ	Trade-weighted average
NZRB-F	Outstanding government stock on issue
NZRG-H	Tender rates
NZRI-L	Repurchase tender details
NZRM-O	Bond repo results
NZRP-Q	Announcement of repo closure

News 2000

MMT <F9> Topic code

Chapter 14

Norway

The rates to watch

- Deposit rate
  - *sets the floor for money market rates*

- Overnight lending rate
  - *sets the ceiling for money market rates*

The **deposit rate** on overnight deposits at the central bank (Norges Bank) has become increasingly important. It sets the floor for money market rates since, otherwise, banks could earn more by leaving funds on deposit at the central bank than by lending in the money market.

The **overnight lending rate** usually sets the ceiling for money market rates since banks will be unwilling to pay more for loans on the open market than they need pay the central bank. Note, however, that market rates can exceed the overnight lending rate when there are expectations that banks' quotas for this form of borrowing might be too small to cover their liquidity needs.

The Bank has said it would like a two percentage point gap between the overnight lending rate and the deposit rate which it achieved on 3 August 1993.

Other central bank rates, like fixed-interest rate loans (offered to banks to avoid tight liquidity), should be within the spread of the deposit rate and the overnight lending rate. However, they may exceed the overnight rate if liquidity is tight and the central bank restricts lending.

There are no repo operations.

How does the central bank influence the money market?

The structure of the money market is best understood as a kind of channel with the deposit, or credit, rate and the overnight rate setting the floor and ceiling respectively. Day-to-day short-term money market rates usually lie between these two. Their precise level is determined by the degree to which money market shortages or surpluses are smoothed out through open market operations.

■ Bank deposits
Banks with surplus funds can deposit them at the central bank if they cannot place them at a higher interest rate anywhere else. This is why the deposit, or credit, rate sets the floor for money market rates.

■ Overnight loans (D-loans)
Loans at the overnight lending rate take place automatically through the right of commercial and savings banks to draw up to a specified amount through a borrowing facility (D-loans) on their current accounts with the central bank. (Banks with excess liquidity can also place funds in these accounts, which attract the deposit rate.) The central bank fixes the interest rate on D-loans and this can, in principle, be changed every day. The limits on D-loans—set on the 1st and 16th of every month—are based on a percentage of banks' equity and subordinated capital minus their subordinated loan capital. At present, D-loans are uncollateralized, but the central bank has announced plans to introduce a collateral requirement (no date has yet been set). At that time, the basis for the D-loans limit will be changed to a bank's total assets.

■ Fixed interest rate loans (F-loans) or deposits.
The central bank introduced the F-loan borrowing facility for private banks in 1987 to supplement the D-loan facility. It provides fixed-rate loans for up to a year, though normally they have a maturity of less than four weeks. The interest rate is set through auctions which are announced periodically. F-loans provide a more stable supply of liquidity to the banks which shelters them from sharp fluctuations in short-term rates. The limits on F-loans are set each quarter and equal a bank's equity and subordinated capital minus its subordinated loan capital.

■ Treasury certificates of deposit
These are short-term (one year or less) interest-bearing negotiable securities issued by the Treasury. The central bank is a market-maker for these securities in the secondary market. They were first issued in January 1985 and are quoted on the Oslo Stock Exchange.

Norges Bank's purchases and sales of Treasury certificates in the secondary market were intended to be an important instrument of short-term liquidity control. However, the Bank has found it difficult to ensure the build-up of sufficient holdings in the hands of the banks and the public to be able to to inject liquidity by buying certificates on the secondary market.

Nevertheless, over the medium-term, it is likely that the rising government budget deficit will boost the bond market and reduce the banks' reliance on central bank finance. This would give the central bank more leeway to use open market operations to control short-term fluctuations in liquidity.

■ Special term loans (S-loans)
Loans on special terms are not used to manage liquidity but provide banks with funds on special application. They are provided to individual banks having difficulty raising funds in the money market or through deposits from the public. S-loans are the central bank's 'lender of last resort' facility.

■ Currency swaps
Redistribution of liquidity between the largest Norwegian banks usually takes place in the currency swaps market. The eurokrone interest rates in this market are based on forward and spot exchange rates on US dollar and eurodollar interest rates. Swaps are rarely used.

■ Bank certificates of deposit
These CDs are rarely used.

Who controls the interest rate levers?

The guidelines for monetary policy are set by the government, after consultation with the central bank which has no formal independence on policy decisions. The central bank is responsible for implementing monetary policy and the governor decides on changes in official interest rates. However, according to the Norges Bank Act, matters of special importance must be submitted to the Ministry of Finance before the Bank makes any decisions.

What drives interest rate policy?

Targets:

■ Operational
There is none.

■ Intermediate
Like most other small, open European economies, Norway's priority is currency stability. Until December 1992, the krone was pegged to the European currency unit (Ecu) with exchange rate mechanism-style 2.25 per cent fluctuation bands. Now, the central bank aims for a broadly stable exchange rate.

■ Final
Price stability.

How do official rates affect commercial ones?

Corporate

Nearly all loans are at variable rates. They are affected almost immediately by changes in short-term official interest rates.

Mortgages

Nearly all mortgage loans are at fixed rates and thus, for all practical purposes, they are unaffected by changes in short-term official rates.

Timing

The directors of different central bank departments meet when interest rate changes are being considered, but there are no fixed dates and rates can be changed at any time.

Rate changes are, however, normally announced around 16.00 local time, often on Fridays.

Key Reuter pages

Monitor

Norges Bank pages:

NOCB-R, NOCV-DF	Full range
NOCB	Index page
NOCC-D	Changes in the deposit and overnight lending rates and routine central bank operations, plus hot news

News 2000

MMT <F9> Topic code

Chapter 15

Portugal

The rates to watch

- Liquidity injection rate
  - *sets an indicative ceiling for money market rates*

- Liquidity mop-up rate
  - *usually sets the floor for money market rates*

- Daily lending facility rate
  - *sets the ceiling for money market rates in normal circumstances*

The Bank of Portugal's key **intervention rates** on Treasury and central bank securities determine short-term money market rates.

The central bank announces one intervention rate at which it sells bills and certificates outright to drain liquidity (**liquidity mop-up rate**) and another at which it buys bills and certificates to inject short-term funds (**liquidity injection rate**) through securities repurchase tenders.

The mop-up rate typically sets the floor for money market rates. However, when there is a large liquidity surplus, short-term rates tend to fall below the mop-up rate. If this happens, the Bank of Portugal may announce a sale of securities.

The liquidity injection rate is usually below, but sometimes equal to, the daily lending facility rate. It typically sets the ceiling for money market rates but when there is a large liquidity shortage, overnight rates tend to exceed the injection rate. If this happens, the Bank of Portugal may supply funds through a securities repurchase agreement to stabilize interest rates. The injection rate has been one percentage point higher than the mop-up rate since mid-1993.

At times of market turmoil, the Bank frequently suspends one or both rates, intervenes on an occasional basis (see below), and may resort to open market operations, such as auctions of bank certificates and short-term credit instead.

The Bank introduced the **daily lending facility rate** for resident banks in July 1993, published daily [BPDQ]. It is usually higher than the liquidity injection rate but still does not set an absolute ceiling on money market rates. When liquidity is tight, the overnight rate may exceed the daily lending facility rate.

How does the central bank influence the money market?

■ Regular and occasional intervention

Bank of Portugal intervention consists mainly of liquidity injection/mop-up operations at short maturities (seven to 10 days) through the repurchase/sale of Treasury and central bank securities. These include Treasury bills, central bank monetary certificates (TRMs), issued with maturities of up to 14 days, and central bank intervention bills (TIMs) with maturities of 4, 9, 13, 26 and 52 weeks. The Bank prefers to use Treasury bills when it wishes to inject liquidity.

As a rule, the Bank of Portugal announces on the first working day of each maintenance period, operations with a same-day value date which mature on the first working day of the following maintenance period. This is its *regular* intervention. Interest rates on these operations are known as liquidity mop-up or injection rates.

On the remaining days of the maintenance period, the Bank of Portugal may conduct operations on a very short-term basis, maturing within the current maintenance period or the next one. Interest rates on these operations are known as *occasional* liquidity mop-up or injection rates.

■ Standing facilities

• Daily lending facility

This is a mechanism which enables the central bank to inject overnight funds into the money market through securities repurchase operations. The facility is available to resident banks subject to a quota at a pre-announced interest rate called the daily lending facility rate. Quotas are set according to each bank's share of reserve requirements. The rate may be changed at 09.00 local time each day when the Bank of Portugal announces its conditions to the money market.

• End-of-period emergency lending facility

This is an overnight emergency lending facility which allows domestic institutions short of funds to meet their reserve requirements. Operations under this mechanism mature on the following business day. Funds are granted at a penalty rate set one percentage point above the highest of either: 1) the highest interbank rate, on the same day, for maturities of up to five days; or 2) the highest liquidity injection rate in the same reserve maintenance period. These rates apply unless the Bank of Portugal specifically announces a lower rate. The end-of-period lending facility is available within 30 minutes after the close of the money market on the last working day of each seven-to-10-day maintenance period.

(Only resident financial institutions have access to domestic money market operations conducted through SISTEM, the Bank of Portugal's money market telephone system. Non-resident banks must arrange all their funding with resident financial institutions.)

■ Reserve requirements
There are four accounting periods each month of about a week, during which institutions must meet the Bank of Portugal's cash reserve requirement. They have to hold deposits with the central bank equal to a percentage of reservable liabilities, on an average basis, over the maintenance period. The Bank pays an interest rate on reserves close to that prevailing in the money market. The rate is announced at the beginning of each quarter.

■ Discount rate
The discount rate has little significance for monetary policy. It is mainly used by banks to set interest payments on loans to their employees and to set coupon payments on some private sector bonds.

Who controls the interest rate levers?

The Bank of Portugal conducts monetary policy and sets its intervention rates autonomously.

What drives interest rate policy?

Targets:

■ Operational
Short-term money market rates.

■ Intermediate
Escudo stability within the exchange rate mechanism (ERM).

■ Final
The government sets an inflation target each year designed to take the rate down to the European average by 1999.

How do official rates affect commercial ones?

Corporate

Most bank loans are floating-rate. Those for larger companies are related to the prime rate, which tracks money market rates. Small- and medium-sized companies pay a bigger premium over prime.

Mortgages

Most mortgages are floating-rate, though the proportion is falling. Borrowers can now usually opt for a fixed-rate mortgage.

Timing

The Bank of Portugal announces its intervention rates, or any proposed alternative arrangement, at about 09.00 on the first working day of each reserve maintenance period.

The Bank announces its plans to intervene in the market through the sale of short-term certificates or the offer of short-term credit at about 09.00 local time each trading day. The results of its offers to inject or drain liquidity are announced later in the day.

Interbank trading begins at 09.00 and resident banks are legally obliged to conclude their business by 15.00. Foreign banks can trade for longer.

Key Reuter pages

Monitor

Bank of Portugal pages:

BPDA-M, BPDQ-S	Full range
BPDA	Index page for the domestic money market
BPDF-G	Intervention operations
BPDH	Results of new Treasury bill placements
BPDQ-S	Money market conditions and other announcements, including the results of fixed-rate Treasury bond placements
BPDQ	Daily lending facility rate
BPEI	Credit and monetary aggregates
BOPL	Indicative exchange rates

Other pages:

LBOA	Lisbor rates at 1, 3, 6 and 12 months, updated at 11.00 local time
EPRI	Portuguese prime rates

Cont.

(cont.)

LBOC-D	Contributed one-, three-, six- and 12-month money market rates
LBOC-D	Contributed one-, three-, six- and 12-month money market rates
LBOF	Lisfra (Lisbon forward rate agreement) rates at 1, 3, 6 and 12 months, updated at 11.00 local time
MVNK-L	Treasury bond and other government security prices quoted on the stock exchange
PMMI	Contributed overnight, tomorrow/next, one-week and two-week money rates
PTEP-Q	Escudo/mark multi-contributor page

News 2000

MMT <F9> Topic code

Chapter 16

Spain

The rates to watch

- 10-day repo rate (intervention rate)
  - *signals a general change in interest rates and sets the floor for money market rates*

- Daily intervention rate (overnight cash or repo rate)
  - *sets the tone for money market rates*

- Rate on *contra poliza* (second window) loans
  - *usually sets the ceiling for money market rates*

The repurchase agreement is the Bank of Spain's key monetary policy instrument and, as such, is the main way in which the central bank affects money market liquidity.

The key rate is the 10-day repo rate for the coming reserve maintenance period, which averages 10 days. (Note, however, that actual maturities can vary from seven to 12 days.)

The allotment rate on 10-day repos is known as the **intervention rate** and this usually sets the floor for money market rates. The intervention rate is also a pointer to the central bank's medium-term policy stance.

Banks which have been unable to obtain enough funds in the interbank market to meet their reserve requirements can apply for second window loans which the Bank of Spain extends at its discretion. The interest rate on these so-called *contra poliza* loans (see below) typically sets the ceiling on overnight rates.

Changes in the 10-day repo rate normally take place at the repo tender, but if the Bank of Spain urgently wants to change the rate it can pre-empt the next scheduled tender by calling a special tender. The new rate is advised ahead of the special tender and bids are invited from the banks. This occurs when the decision to change the repo rate comes close to a scheduled tender (that is, just before or just after).

If there is a long gap before the next scheduled tender, the Bank simply announces that it is adjusting the rate. In practice, this hits the market via the **daily intervention rate**. The overnight cash rate quickly adjusts accordingly since there are no funds allocated at the repo tender.

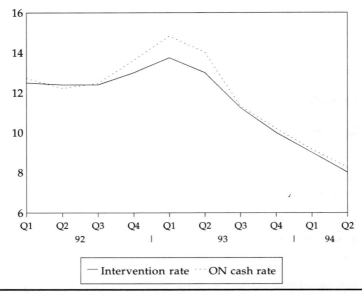

Figure 16.1   Spain: Intervention rate & overnight cash rate
Source: Datastream

The Bank of Spain may also conduct overnight (one-day) repos to meet liquidity shortages and thereby smooth short-term money market and/or exchange rate fluctuations.

An allocation of funds at the daily intervention rate set on overnight repos is usually routine, but it could be important. For example, a large change, say 25 basis points or more, may be a clear signal that the Bank plans to move official rates. More usually, however, the central bank ensures that the rate moves within a fairly narrow band around the 10-day repo rate.

The Bank of Spain allows the daily intervention rate to vary more frequently than the rates at its regular 10-day repos. The overnight rate is usually higher than the 10-day repo rate to encourage banks to meet most of their liquidity needs through 10-day repos.

How does the central bank influence the money market?

■ Repurchase agreements
Repos have become more important since the creation of a book-entry public debt market, a reduction in reserve requirements (see below) and the

parallel issue of central bank certificates of deposit (CDs) also known as CBEs or BECDs.

The system revolves around 10-day and overnight operations with funds allocated to the market through the 10-day repo tender and daily Bank of Spain intervention. Ten-day repos are always variable rate.

■ Ten-day repurchase agreements
At the beginning of each reserve requirement period the Bank auctions 10-day repos against its own outstanding central bank certificates (CBEs), Treasury bills and bonds. All institutions subject to reserve requirements can take part in the repo auctions. (Note that CBEs are tradeable *only* among institutions which are subject to reserve requirements—in practice, almost all institutions are subject to such requirements.)

CBEs have been issued only once, in March 1990, specifically to mop up the liquidity released when reserve requirements were cut (*see* 'Reserve requirements' below). They began to mature in 1993 and the last redemption will be in the year 2000.

Bids are invited the day before the tender with those above the repo rate set by the Bank of Spain allotted and those below rejected. The allotment rate is known as the intervention rate.

Tenders are almost always variable-rate although the 10-day rate often remains unchanged for long periods. The Bank only announces a fixed rate in very exceptional cases when it wants to send a direct and rapid signal on monetary policy.

■ Overnight repurchase agreements
Since the Bank of Spain does not hold ad hoc repos like the Bundesbank, the alternative is to tighten or ease its daily intervention rates through purchases or sales of CBEs and government debt.

This is done through overnight (one-day) repos with market-makers (*entidades gestoras* or *creadores de mercado*) who are registered dealers trading actively in government bonds. (Financial institutions can only take part through market-makers.) Overnight repos are also conducted at a variable rate.

Each time an auction is announced banks and savings banks inform the Bank of Spain of the amounts they require and the rates they are willing to pay (a maximum of three tenders can be accepted from each institution). The Bank allots funds to the highest bidders until the auction is complete. The daily intervention rate set at each auction is the average of the rates bid weighted by the amounts accepted.

Overnight repos mature on the next working day and are guaranteed by central bank certificates (CBEs) or government bonds. Since March 1994, the

Bank of Spain has announced the repo result as an average rate against CBEs and government debt. The Bank has often set the repo rate slightly higher against CBEs than against government debt. However, the announcement of an average rate means that it is now impossible to tell what the respective rates are.

Since the Bank does not always conduct overnight repos, and funding via the 10-day repo is normally cheaper, institutions are expected to cover their liquidity needs in the regular 10-day repos and to use overnight auctions only to satisfy their odd-lot reserve needs.

■ Second window loans (*contra poliza*)
These are loans to banks which have been unable to acquire funds in the interbank market and might therefore be unable to meet their reserve requirements. They are known locally as *contra poliza* loans. This term refers to a type of special advance against *poliza*, which is a bank's licence to operate in the money market. Such loans are granted at the central bank's discretion and secured by a loan auction contract. They are usually granted at a penalty interest rate slightly above the daily intervention rate. Forcing banks to use *contra poliza* loans is one way the Bank of Spain steers the daily intervention rate. The rate charged on these loans normally sets the ceiling for money market rates. All banks have access to second window loans.

■ Treasury debt management policy
This is significant for monetary policy, though it is becoming less important as the maturity of the Treasury's borrowing lengthens and the management of that debt therefore comes to play a reduced role in affecting short-term rates.

Nevertheless, Treasury bill results should be closely in line with short-term Bank of Spain intervention rates in order to attract funds and not interfere with monetary policy goals

Letras del Tesoro (Treasury bills) were created in 1987 as a basic government short-term financing instrument. (Treasury bill was the term previously used for *pagares del Tesoro* which are now called Treasury notes.)

■ Reserve requirements
Reserve requirements have gradually lost their role as a short-term policy instrument since they were cut to five per cent in 1990, from the 17.0 to 19.5 per cent levels seen in earlier years, and not allowed to exceed seven per cent.

They have since been reduced to 2.0 per cent alongside a widening of the eligible securities in response to a liberalization of capital flows.

Reserve requirements are usually changed to signal permanent shifts in monetary policy rather than being used merely for short-term adjustments.

As a general rule, the Bank of Spain tries to keep bank reserves close to 'normal', that is, responsive to even small changes in money market rates.

Who controls the interest rate levers?

The Bank of Spain sets interest rates. Under new statutes before Congress the Bank will be given the responsibility for controlling inflation, though its monetary policy stance should not conflict with the government's overall economic policy.

What drives interest rate policy?

Targets:

■ Operational
The Bank of Spain aims to keep bank reserves as close as possible to what it regards as 'normal' to maintain the responsiveness of the money market to changes in its interest rate levers.

■ Intermediate
The central bank has a target for ALP (equivalent to the M4 measure of broad money).

■ Final
The medium-term target is to get inflation down to the European average.

How do official rates affect commercial ones?

Spain has one of the highest rates of home ownership in the world (approximately 85 per cent). Mortgage rates have tended to be variable, but these are only reviewed once every two to three years. Thus, while mortgage rates are extremely important to the household sector, they are largely protected from short-term changes in official interest rates.

Timing

The results of the Bank of Spain's regular 10-day repos are released between 09.30 and 10.30 local time on the first working day after an auction. The Bank informs market-makers of the time the result will be announced about 10 minutes before the actual results are made available.

There is no set time for daily intervention. If there are liquidity shortages between 10-day repos, the Bank notifies market-makers that it will conduct an overnight repo.

At about 14.00 GMT, the Bank of Spain announces the average of the rates at which it intervened in the money market.

Reuters sends an alert on the intervention rate set at daily Bank interventions only in exceptional cases. This would be the case if there is a large rise/fall (say, 25 basis points or more) since, as noted above, it could be a clear signal to the market that the Bank of Spain plans to move official rates.

A significant change in the intervention rate could also be one of the Bank of Spain's front-line defences against an attack on the peseta and, in this case, its new level would also be sent out as an alert. However, a big change in the intervention rate could also reflect normal end-of-trading-period liquidity shortages, in which case Reuters does not send an alert.

Key Reuter pages

Monitor

Reuters reports:
MSP1	Money market report
PTA3	Peseta and bond market report

Bank of Spain pages
BESA-Q, DPKE-Q, FXEA-D, FXES-T	Full range
BESA	Bank of Spain announcements
BESB	Tenders of central bank certificates and daily Bank interventions
BESC	Tenders of three- and six-month and one-year T-bills
BESH	Tenders of three-, five- and 10-year T-bonds
BESQ	Reserves
FXES	Madrid official fixings

News 2000

MMT <F9> Topic code

Chapter 17

Sweden

The rates to watch

- Marginal lending/deposit rate
  - *sets the tone for money market rates*

The key rate is the **marginal lending/deposit rate** at which banks can borrow funds from, or deposit them with, the central bank (Riksbank). It sets the tone for money market rates.

The Riksbank's repurchase agreements relate to the marginal rate since this is an alternative source of funds for commercial banks. Thus, the repo rate follows the marginal rate. From the marginal rate, money market traders derive the overnight interbank rate. Money market and official rates seldom diverge by more than 10 basis points.

The marginal rate can either be a lending or a deposit rate, depending on whether banks are short of funds or have excess reserves. In August 1993, for example, it was the deposit rate, but out of force of habit money market traders and the media still called it the marginal 'lending' rate.

Until Spring 1993, the repo was the main window for policy changes. Since then, however, the main forum for marginal rate changes has been the Riksbank's board meeting (*see* 'Timing').

How does the central bank influence the money market?

There is an interest rate scale for loans from, or deposits with, the Riksbank set according to each commercial bank's capital base (see below). The more a bank borrows from the central bank, the higher the point on the scale (interest rate) it has to pay.

There are two ways in which the Riksbank can steer market rates up (or down):

i) Through a public announcement that rates will be increased (in effect, raising the whole interest rate scale).

ii) By squeezing liquidity so banks are forced onto a higher step on the interest rate scale.

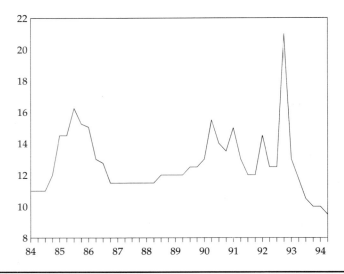

Figure 17.1   Sweden: Marginal lending/deposit rate
Source: Datastream

■ Interest rate scale

The central bank uses a graduated interest rate scale to control the overnight rate. The scale is a system of preset rates at which banks can borrow
from, or make deposits with, the central bank. The scale is symmetrical and
thus works the same way whether banks require funds or have excess liquidity to invest. The system works such that the interest rate applied increases as bank borrowing from the Riksbank rises or deposits at the central
bank fall. The interest rate scale is changed every quarter.

The Riksbank defines a different scale for each commercial bank in
which the amount it can borrow at each interest rate step is related to its
capital base. The central bank uses the aggregate of these scales to control
money market rates.

The construction of the scale gives the banks an incentive to adjust their
overnight deposit and borrowing requirements in the interbank market so
that each day ends with all banks on the same interest rate step of their individual scales. The overnight rate is equal to this marginal rate plus a
small differential.

If the Riksbank tightens market liquidity it can increase bank borrowing
(or reduce bank deposits) and thereby move the marginal rate up the interest rate scale, thus increasing the overnight interest rate.

Open market operations

■ Repurchase agreements
The Riksbank places the money market on the step of the interest rate scale it wants by using repos and reverse repos.

The Riksbank announces the marginal interest rate, then the primary dealers bid depending on their own liquidity situation. Repos usually cover periods of between three and seven days, depending on market liquidity.

A change in interest rates is usually expressed in terms of the next repo. In other words, the Riksbank says it will use a different point on the interest rate scale as its stop rate when it sets the next repo.

■ Government bills
The Riksbank sometimes intervenes in the spot market for government bills to indicate its intentions concerning money market rates. The purpose of these operations is to signal to the market that the Riksbank wants market interest rates back in line with the marginal lending rate. It is only ever needed in exceptional circumstances like those of September 1992's currency crisis.

■ Discount rate
Since May 1985, the official discount rate has not been used as a policy instrument and it therefore has no influence on bank lending and borrowing rates.

It is calculated as a weighted average of the daily market rates for six-month Treasury bills and five-year government bonds in the previous quarter, minus 2.5 percentage points, rounded to the nearest 0.25 of a point. Thus, the discount rate reflects the level of interest rates in the most recent quarter.

Nevertheless, it is still used for administrative and legal reasons, such as in private contracts and for some bank loans, and the Riksbank's Governing Board therefore makes an adjustment at its first meeting each quarter to bring it into line with market rates.

Who controls the interest rate levers?

The Riksbank sets both currency and interest rate policy. It is accountable to Parliament and not just the ruling party in government. Formally, interest rate decisions are taken by the Riksbank Council which has eight members including the central bank governor and seven others elected by Parliament for three years. Council members can be chosen from inside or outside Parliament and are elected in proportion to the representation of political parties in Parliament. The Riksbank's independence from political pressure, as opposed to just pressure from the government, depends on how many external members are elected.

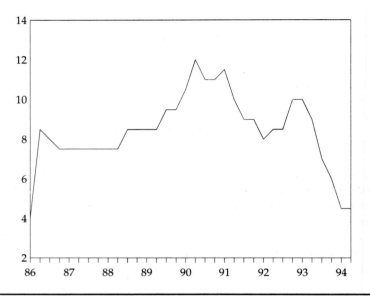

Figure 17.2   Sweden: Discount rate
Source: Datastream

What drives interest rate policy?

Targets:

■ Operational
The Riksbank controls the overnight rate by managing bank liquidity.

■ Final
Price stability. From 1995 onwards, the target is to hold inflation within a band of 1-3 per cent.

How do official rates affect commercial ones?

Corporate

According to the Riksbank, some 60-65 per cent of private sector company debt is at fixed rates. Variable-rate loans move in line with the marginal lending rate, which sets the floor for money market rates.

Mortgages

Only 8-10 per cent of mortgage lending is conducted at variable rates, leaving the housing market largely immune to short-term changes in official interest rates.

Timing

Board meetings can either be scheduled or ad hoc gatherings. [RIKG] gives the current schedule and also covers cancellations. Meetings are scheduled every Thursday at 08.30 local time and usually last about one or two hours. If an unscheduled meeting is called Reuters usually sends an alert.

At 08.30 local time, the Bank announces the terms of the next repo amount, duration, latest bid time, and implied marginal rate.

Key Reuter pages

Monitor

Reuters reports:
MSE1   Repo and T-bill report

Sveriges Riksbank pages:
RIKA-K, RIKN-Z   Full range
RIKC   Riksbank announcements of repurchase pacts. The interest rate level implied by the marginal rate on the day's repurchase pact is given on the final line
RIKG   Current schedule for Riksbank board meetings
RIKH   Riksbank announcements of a rate change
RIKO   Balance of payments
RIKS   Reverse repo results
RIKT   Discount rate
RIKU-Y   Current account breakdown
RIKV   M3 money supply
RIKX   Riksbank assets and liabilities
RIKZ   Trade in securities
TEVY   Exchange rate fixings

News 2000

MMT <F9> Topic code

Chapter 18

Switzerland

The rates to watch

- Overnight rate
  - *indicates the liquidity situation in the money market*

- Discount rate
  - *purely of symbolic importance*

- Lombard rate (floating)
  - *of limited operational significance*

The Swiss National Bank (SNB) does not set a guiding money market rate, but instead controls interest rates by regulating market liquidity. The level of banks' reserves at the central bank (sight deposits, a component of monetary base), and the overall level of money market rates, are the key indicators of the SNB's monetary policy stance.

Foreign currency operations have long been the main instrument for determining the monetary base, and hence the money supply and interest rates. Currency swaps are by far the Bank's favourite tool.

The **discount rate** is now only symbolic and there are presently no transactions under the discount facility. Nevertheless, the discount rate is still an important way for the SNB to signal or confirm a shift in its views on market rates. If the discount rate is raised or lowered, it indicates that the central bank views a change in money market rates as permanent and unlikely to be reversed immediately.

Lombard borrowings have not been significant since May 1989, when the **lombard rate** was floated. The lombard rate is set two percentage points above the average money market (call) rate over the previous two days.

The central bank has increasingly used repos to manage the banking system's short-term liquidity needs since they were introduced in September 1992.

How does the central bank influence the money market?

■ Currency swaps
The SNB estimates flows of funds into the banking system, including the forward effect of past currency swaps, and then carries out new swaps to

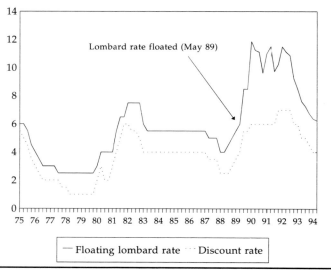

Figure 18.1   Switzerland: Floating lombard & discount rates
Source: Datastream

inject or, more rarely (*see below*), drain liquidity. The swaps are a combination of spot and forward dollar/Swiss franc transactions.

At intervention time (09.00 local, *see below*) the SNB may add liquidity through swaps by buying dollars against Swiss francs from commercial banks for a limited period. At the end of that period, the transaction is reversed at a rate agreed in advance.

Injections are generally for periods of one to three months and longer maturities often signal a more aggressive stance.

The SNB drains liquidity by buying Swiss francs against dollars. However, this rarely takes place and, if it does, is not usually carried out at the regular intervention time (09.00). Draining operations may signal a monetary tightening or concern about excess liquidity in the money market.

The interbank call money rate tends to react first to liquidity surpluses or shortages, though rate changes may also reflect technical factors.

■ Repurchase agreements (*prise en pension*)
The SNB adds liquidity by inviting banks to deposit government money market claims (*créances comptables*) into their accounts at the central bank in exchange for cash, with an agreement to repurchase the bills at a future date. The repos usually have a maturity between overnight and one week.

Note that repos are a short-term liquidity management tool used to smooth fluctuations in overnight rates and are usually discounted at prevailing money market rates.

■ Discount credits

According to the Swiss National Bank, the discount facility is "inactive at present". The SNB retains the legal right, under the National Bank Law, to conduct transactions at the discount rate at any time. The infrastructure to discount bills remains intact since the necessary trade bills are still used by banks. Thus, the discount facility could be activated to supply emergency funding to meet an exceptional money market liquidity shortage.

When activated, the SNB provides discount credits by buying trade bills outright from a select list of Swiss financial institutions before they mature. It deducts an interest charge (discount) for the remainder of the maturity period (which may not exceed six months). The interest rate applied is the discount rate [SNBS].

■ Lombard loans

To meet banks' unexpected short-term liquidity shortages, the SNB grants so-called lombard loans, at the official floating lombard rate [SNBS] against securities deposited as collateral.

Note that both the introduction of the floating lombard rate and the December 1989 increase in the surcharge over call money from one to two percentage points occurred during periods of Swiss franc weakness and caused large moves in interest rates.

The initiative both for foreign currency operations and for the open market purchase/sale of securities lies with the SNB. But in the case of lending against securities, the SNB merely fixes the terms and leaves the initiative to the commercial banks.

■ Purchases of securities

Central bank purchases of securities in the open market are limited for two reasons. Firstly, Swiss tax laws have not generally favoured issuing and dealing in securities. Second, a low level of federal short-term debt has blocked the development of a viable market for treasury bills. Purchases of securities are used by the central bank to gradually diversify its reserves.

Interest rate expectations

The price of the euro-Swiss franc contract traded on the London International Financial Futures & Options Exchange (LIFFE) provides information on market expectations for the three-month euro-Swiss franc rate. The contract is cash settled one business day before the third Wednesday of the relevant month. It is expressed as 100 minus the three-month euro-Swiss franc rate. Thus, an expected euro-Swiss franc rate of five per cent gives a contract price of 95.00. For example, if the December contract was trading at 95.00 and the euro-Swiss franc rate was currently five per cent, it would imply that the futures market expects no change in the euro-Swiss franc rate by December. Alternatively, if the December contract was trading at 93.00 that would imply that the futures market expects a two percentage point rise in the euro-Swiss franc rate, to seven per cent, by the end of the year.

Who controls the interest rate levers?

The Swiss National Bank sets monetary policy. The statutes under which it operates state that the government and the SNB must inform one another before important decisions are made. However, responsibility for both interest rate and exchange rate policy lies with the SNB.

What drives interest rate policy?

Targets:

■ Operational
The daily target is the level of banks' reserves—basically sight deposits held at the central bank.

■ Intermediate
The central bank has a target of one per cent annual growth for monetary base in the medium term.

■ Final
Price stability.

How do official rates affect commercial ones?

Corporate

Switzerland was one of the first industrialized countries to deregulate its financial markets (in the 1960s). Consequently, Swiss companies are familiar with a wide variety of financing techniques, including floating-rate finance and bond issues. There is an approximate 50:50 split between fixed- and floating-rate borrowing.

Mortgages

The Swiss mortgage market is based on floating-rate finance. There has been a move towards more fixed-rate deals at times of low interest rates but, generally speaking, the mortgage market is sensitive to changes in interest rates.

Timing

Foreign exchange swaps are conducted daily at 09.00.

The level of sight deposits, the most closely-watched indicator of money market activity, is published on the first working day after the 10th, 20th and last day of each month. (Quarter-end balances are distorted by banks' window-dressing operations.)

Information on daily operations is not available, but extraordinary operations are occasionally confirmed by the SNB's press office.

Key Reuter pages

Monitor

Reuters reports:
MSW1-3   Sight deposit levels

Swiss National Bank pages:
SNBS   SNB discount rate, floating lombard rate and average yield of government bonds
SWIS   Federal Department of Finance details of federal government bond issues

Other pages:
RTAL   Discount rate, previous rate and date of last change

News 2000

MMT <F9> Topic code

Chapter 19

United Kingdom

The rates to watch

- Money market dealing rate
    - *dictates the level of bank base rates in normal circumstances*

- Minimum lending rate
    - *dictates the level of bank base rates in special circumstances*

The Bank of England typically signals changes in commercial banks' benchmark base rates through its daily money market operations by changing the dealing rates at which it buys bills from the discount houses. But the Bank is increasingly resorting to the announcement of a new minimum lending rate to make its views on interest rates absolutely clear.

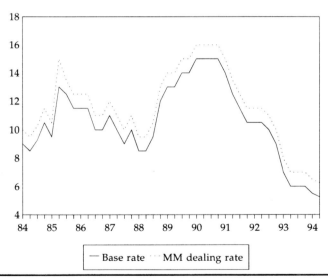

Figure 19.1   United Kingdom: Base rate & money market dealing rate

Source: Datastream

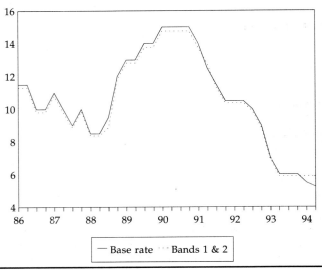

Figure 19.2 **United Kingdom: Base rate and bands 1&2 rate**
Source: Datastream

How does the central bank influence the money market?

The UK money market is unlike any other. The key players are the central bank and the commercial banks, as in other countries, but the UK also has discount houses which are unique. The discount houses are highly specialized institutions which trade and make markets in sterling money market instruments.

Commercial banks hold cash as part of their reserves. Some of this is held as 'operational balances' at the Bank of England, which are used to settle the final accounting position at the end of the day, and some is held in the form of secured funds at call or short notice with the discount houses. The clearing banks aim to keep operational balances at an appropriate 'target' level given the uncertainty of daily cashflows between themselves and the Bank.

The discount houses are the approved counterparties of the Bank of England in the money market and their role is to smooth out fluctuations in the supply of, and demand for, money. Without such a buffer, the Bank of England would have the more difficult job of negotiating with a large group of international banks.

If the balance of transactions between the commercial banks and the Bank of England (as a result of government spending, taxes etc.) is a net payment to the government, the banks may find themselves short of cash by the end of the day. Since their 'operational balances' at the Bank would otherwise fall below target, they restore their liquidity by selling bills to the discount houses, by drawing down funds deposited at the discount houses, or by borrowing from the discount houses in the interbank market.

In this way, any cash shortage (or surplus) ends up with the discount houses. The Bank of England will always provide the discount houses with the money they need.

To relieve shortages, the Bank normally invites discount houses to offer it eligible bills for outright sale. (Eligible bills are essentially post-dated cheques issued by companies, but which carry a bank guarantee.) The maturity bands of the bills being offered are defined in terms of their remaining, not the original, maturity and comprise:

Band 1:	1-14 days
Band 2:	15-33 days
Band 3:	34-63 days
Band 4:	64-91 days

The key to the Bank of England's control of the money market is the creation of shortages, which require the banking system to borrow from the Bank, and the rates at which money is made available to the discount houses through the purchase of bills or direct lending.

Open market operations

■ Money market dealing rates
The Bank can change its money market dealing rates (that is, the discount rates at which it buys bills from the market to provide liquidity). This is the most common signal.

Discount houses are invited by telephone to offer bills in what is called the 'early round' at 09.45 [RTCA]. If the Bank wants to signal a cut in interest rates it will give the discount houses, in the words of one senior money market analyst at a bank in the City of London, "a nice subtle hint" such as: "Why don't you bid (for funds) one point lower?". This can also happen at 12.00 [RTCB] or 14.00 [RTCC].

The Bank will make an announcement like:

> "The Bank has purchased bills totalling stg xxx million:
> Band 1 bank bills stg x million at x pct
> Band 2 bank bills stg x million at x pct"

If the rates are ¼, ½, or one point lower or higher than the previously established rates, it means the Bank has changed its money market dealing rates and will trigger a Reuters headline like:

"Bank of England says it raises/cuts money market dealing rates *xx* point."

Note that the Bank may deal at different rates in each band. The last time the rates in bands 1 and 2 were not the same was July 1991.

The Bank also sometimes operates in bands 3 and 4, though this is more unusual and does not always indicate a more general interest rate change.

For example, the Bank shaved its rates in bands 3 and 4 on three consecutive days in April/May 1992 before signalling a cut in banks' base rates by reducing its dealing rates in bands 1 and 2. The action was taken to prepare the market for a possible rate cut, and to test its likely reaction to it.

However, the next time the Bank shaved rates in bands 3 and 4 it was a purely technical operation to bring them more into line with the rates in bands 1 and 2 and was not an attempt to prepare the market for a wider rate cut.

■ Money market lending rate
A change in the money market lending rate (that is, the rate at which the Bank may lend to the discount houses at 14.30) can also happen at 09.45 [RTCA], 12.00 [RTCB] or 14.00 [RTCC] but is becoming increasingly rare. The Bank generally signals rate changes in the 'early round' at 09.45 local time.

After publishing or revising its forecast for the day's money market shortage, the Bank will make an announcement like:

"Those houses wishing to use their borrowing facilities at the Bank are invited to do so at 2.30 pm (14.30) when the rate will be *xx* pct."

Such an announcement may also be made when the market is pressing for a change and the Bank wishes to underline the current base rate level. On these occasions the rate specified will equal the current base rate (*see* (a) under 'Other signals' below).

Limits on the size of borrowing facilities are suspended for 14.30 lending, and the amount outstanding over the duration of the lending does not count against each discount house's borrowing facilities for late assistance on subsequent days.

■ Minimum lending rate

The Bank can re-introduce minimum lending rate (MLR) which, for a short period ahead, applies to any lending to discount houses.

Until sterling was withdrawn from the exchange rate mechanism (ERM) of the European Monetary System (EMS) on 16 September, 1992, the Bank had only reintroduced MLR twice since it was abolished in 1981 when the Bank introduced a new system for day-to-day market operations.

However, more recently, the Bank has resorted to using MLR on a more regular basis. There is no standard format but the Bank would announce something like:

"Minimum lending rate reintroduced at *xx* per cent for *xx* days effective *xxxx*"

or,

"Minimum lending rate has been set at *xx* per cent for today"

■ Other signals

These are given when the market is pushing for a change in interest rates and the Bank wants to make it clear that rates will not be changed.

In this case the Bank:

a)   Makes an announcement like,

"Those discount houses wishing to use their borrowing facilities at the Bank are invited to do so at 2.30 pm [14.30] when the rate will be *xx* pct."

The rate will equal the current base rate.

b)   Buys bills at its established rate or rates.

c)   Does not operate in the market at its usual intervention times. This is chiefly relevant when the market is pushing for a cut in interest rates which the Bank does not wish to accommodate. In that case, not operating is a relatively strong signal which may be expected to tighten money market conditions significantly.

The Bank can also tighten conditions in a more subtle way by refusing a substantial proportion of the bills offered to it at an intervention round, or by not offering a repo when the shortage is sufficiently large that a repo would usually be offered.

The Bank of England experiences particular problems with the normal working of the discount market if there is a widespread belief that a change in interest rates is imminent.

At such times, neither the banks nor the discount houses want to sell bills which will rise in price if interest rates are reduced. Under those circumstances, the banks may not offer bills to the discount houses and the latter, in turn, may prefer not to offer them to the Bank of England. This may leave the market short of funds and may drive the overnight rate up.

The Bank can penalize the discount houses for not fulfilling their function of relieving a money market shortage by selling their bills. If the market is pushing for a reduction in interest rates, and the Bank does not want to cut rates, it can engineer a money market shortage and then charge a penal interest rate for so-called 'late assistance'.

■ Late assistance

At 14.45, gilt-edged market-makers (GEMMs) and stock exchange money brokers, as well as the discount houses, may ask for late assistance. The facility for each institution is in two tranches related to its capital base; drawings on the second tranche normally bear a higher rate of interest than those on the first tranche, but the terms are at the discretion of the Bank. The loans are provided against approved collateral.

On [RTCC] (*see* 'Timing') there will be an announcement of the amount of funds supplied to the discount houses in late assistance at 14.45 in millions of pounds, but the Bank does not reveal the interest rate charged. Late assistance is also given after 14.45, until 15.30, when institutions may, by telephone, seek to borrow further funds. These transactions are at the discretion of the Bank and normally attract increasing rates of interest. The amount of funds provided to the market in this way is not announced. The message that the Bank does not want to cut rates would get through to the discount houses, but not publicly.

The Bank has discretion on the interest rate it charges for late assistance. It does not usually provide late assistance too cheaply, but the rate at which it is given depends on market conditions and is not always penal. The Bank's aim is to provide lender of last resort funds at a reasonable interest rate to put money back into the market. Whether or not a punitive rate is charged depends on why the Bank thinks the discount houses have come in for late assistance.

(Note that late assistance at 14.45 is not *only* offered when the market expects a cut in interest rates. It may be on any given day that the market is shorter of funds than expected at the time of the last round of bill operations; or that the daily shortage is unusually large; or that bills are in short supply for various reasons.)

■ Sale and repurchase agreements in gilts
In the period leading up to sterling's exit from the ERM in 1992, the heavy foreign exchange intervention needed to support the pound resulted in a large drain of liquidity from the money market. As a result, daily shortages of one billion pounds or more became a regular occurrence.

This would not have mattered but for the problems caused by the clearing banks who were 'hoarding' bills until the last minute to push up overnight rates so that they could earn a high rate of return on overnight loans. With the discount houses left short of bills, it is difficult for the Bank of England to smooth out volatile money market rates caused by liquidity shortages.

Accordingly, the central bank has introduced a system of fortnightly gilt repos through which banks, building societies and other financial institutions can borrow from the Bank of England by selling gilts which they agree to buy back at a fixed price within three to five weeks. Previously, the Bank had not dealt directly with commercial banks in its routine operations. The repos are basically an alternative way of easing money market shortages.

Note, however, that the significance of the repos for the general level of interest rates is fairly limited. *The Bank of England has stressed that the repos will not be used to signal changes in monetary policy.*

■ Treasury bill tender
Treasury bills are short-term (usually three- or six-month) IOUs issued through the Bank regularly each week. Their main purpose is not to finance government spending, but to take cash out of the money market to facilitate the operation of monetary policy. The amount of Treasury bills issued each week therefore varies to reflect the Bank's assessment of future flows to and from the government.

Weekly tenders for sterling Treasury bills are held on Fridays (or the last business day of the week). The Bank announces the amount and maturity of Treasury bills to be offered a week in advance when announcing the result of the previous week's tender. The Bank may allot less than the amount announced the previous Friday, but not more. (Even if a large cash shortage is expected the following week (as is normally the case) some Treasury bills will be offered to preserve a market, unless there are exceptional circumstances.)

During a period of large surpluses, or to relieve expected future shortages, the weekly Treasury bill tender may be increased.

■ Special deposits
Financial institutions with eligible liabilities of £10 million or more can be asked to place special deposits with the Bank.

These would normally earn an interest rate close to the equivalent of the average rate of discount at the most recent Treasury bill tender and would be called in amounts set as a percentage of eligible liabilities.

Special deposits have not been called since December 1979, but are still available as a means of withdrawing cash from the banking system.

Since a call for, or repayment of, special deposits requires a period of notice, the scheme is best suited to when there is likely to be a lengthy period of surplus cash that the Bank wants to offset.

Once called, special deposits can be released to match an expected money market shortage.

Who controls the interest rate levers?

The Treasury controls monetary policy. However, since the debacle of 'Black Wednesday' on 16 September 1992, when sterling was withdrawn from the ERM, the Bank of England has been granted a limited amount of independence: the governor of the Bank of England has said that he will speak out if he believes government monetary policy threatens its inflation target; the minutes of monthly meetings between the chancellor and the governor are now published, albeit with a six-week delay; and the Treasury has yielded the decision over the precise timing of interest rate changes to the Bank.

The Treasury still sets interest rate policy, but Bank of England comments carry more weight now than they used to.

What drives interest rate policy?

Targets:

■ Operational
The level of commercial banks' base rates.

■ Intermediate
There are no intermediate targets. However, the exchange rate (both the Bank of England's trade-weighted index and the rate against the mark), money supply (M0, M4), and asset prices give useful information to the authorities on the prospects for future inflation.

■ Final
The government has a target range for underlying inflation (retail prices excluding mortgage interest payments).

How do official rates affect commercial ones?

Changes in short-term official UK interest rates are possibly the most politi-cally-sensitive among the major industrialized countries, because banks conduct most of their lending at variable rates.

Corporate

The Bank of England estimates that 85 per cent of loans to small companies (those with a turnover of less than 10 million pounds a year) are at floating rates—normally related to banks' base rates which move in line with the Bank's dealing rates. For the corporate sector as a whole, the proportion is much lower since large companies tend to side-step the commercial banks and borrow on the capital markets often at fixed rates.

The structure of interest rates charged by commercial banks is based on a margin over base rate calculated according to the credit risk associated with the borrower. Each bank has its own criteria for deciding what that margin should be. The more creditworthy the borrower, the lower the interest rate charged. Customers may therefore switch their accounts between banks to take advantage of different interest rates.

Many borrowers also have loan facilities at interest rates linked to the London interbank offered rate (Libor).

Mortgages

Although, in recent years, there has been a move towards fixed mortgage rates, the majority of home loans are still either floating or are fixed for short periods. They are, therefore, heavily influenced by changes in short-term official interest rates.

Interest rate expectations

The price of the short sterling contract traded on the London International Financial Futures & Options Exchange (LIFFE) provides information on market expectations for interest rates. The contract is deliverable on the third Wednesday of the relevant month (usually around the 18th). It is ex-pressed as 100 minus the three-month interest rate to be delivered. Thus, an expected interest rate of six per cent gives a contract price of 94.00. For example, if the December contract was trading at 94.00, and base rates were currently six per cent, that would imply that the futures market expects no change in bank base rates by December. Alternatively, if the December con-tract was trading at 92.00 that would imply that the futures market expects a two percentage point rise in base rate, to eight per cent, by the end of the year.

Timing (local time)

09.45 [RTCA]
- The Bank's morning forecast of the daily liquidity position is announced at this time. The forecast includes the overall figure (rounded to the nearest £50 million) and a summary of the main contributory factors.

If there is a liquidity shortage, the Bank will usually invite, by telephone, an 'early round' of bill offers from the discount houses for outright sale to the Bank or, also, for subsequent resale. The Bank only offers a bill repo as well if the shortage is over about £800 million.

Note that an early round is not a prerequisite for an interest rate signal at this time.

Once the Bank has decided which offers, if any, to accept, it announces the results of its operation [RTCA], disclosing the amounts and types of bills purchased in each maturity band and the spread of discount rates at which it has dealt in each band.

Note that if the forecast shortage is very small, or there is a surplus, the Bank need not invite business at any time during the day.

12.00 [RTCB]
- If the forecast of the daily liquidity position has changed by noon, the Bank announces a revised figure, but does not publish the factors responsible for the revision.

Having taken account of the factors affecting liquidity the Bank decides, shortly after midday, whether to invite a round of eligible bill offers. Whereas the early round of offers is normally invited only when a particularly large shortage is forecast, the noon round normally takes place unless the forecast shortage is very small.

14.00 [RTCC]
- At this time, the Bank usually announces any further significant revision to its estimate of the market's position for the day. Once again, the Bank considers its forecast together with other indicators in deciding whether to invite business with the discount houses.

If a surplus is forecast then, unless it is very large, the Bank normally acts only in the afternoon session to absorb it, since an overall surplus is unlikely to show fully in the morning. To take out a surplus, at 14.00, the Bank invites discount houses and clearing banks to bid for Treasury bills of one or more specified maturities.

14.45 [RTCC]

- If a discount house finds itself short of funds after the Bank's main bill business has been concluded, it may, by telephone, ask to borrow on a secured basis under its facilities. The gilt-edged market-makers (GEMMs) and stock exchange money brokers may also borrow at this time.

The Bank announces the total amount of this 'late assistance' but not the terms. Up to now, this has never been used to announce a rate signal.

After 14.45 the discount houses may, by telephone, seek to borrow further, but such transactions are at the discretion of the Bank and normally attract increasing rates of interest.

Key Reuter pages

Monitor

Reuters reports:

MMB1	Bank of England money market operations
MMB3	Full money market report

Bank of England pages:

RTCA	Morning forecast of the daily liquidity position and the main factors affecting it (09.45)
RTCB	Revised forecast of the daily liquidity position (12.00) and assistance provided at the 09.45 and 12.00 operating rounds
RTCC	Revised forecast of the daily liquidity position (14.00) and assistance provided at the 14.00 round. Total amount of any 'late assistance' (14.45) but not the terms
RTCE-F	Treasury bill tenders
RTCG	Euro-commercial paper rates
FXEU	Spot rates for SDR calculation
MSAA-H	Monetary aggregates
GBAA-J	ECU Treasury bill tenders

Other pages:

YLDS	Key interest rates from overnight to 30 years

News 2000

MMT <F9> Topic code

132

Chapter 20

United States

The rates to watch

- Federal (Fed) funds rate
  - *sets the tone for money market rates*

- Discount rate
  - *usually sets the floor for the Fed funds rate*

The Fed funds and discount rates are the two key interest rates. Depository institutions hold non-interest-bearing reserve accounts at the Fed to meet reserve requirements and handle interbank transactions. Deposits above the minimum required are traded overnight and the **Fed funds rate** is what banks charge each other for these overnight loans.

The Fed has an objective for the funds rate which is never formally published. However, so-called 'Fed watchers' can usually tell what the target is by observing where the funds rate trades in conjunction with the Fed's money market operations.

The *first* time the Fed announced a rise in interest rates at the time it took place was on 4 February 1994, when it issued a statement saying that the Federal Open Market Committee had decided to increase slightly the degree of pressure on reserve positions. However, a series of rate rises in early 1994 were accompanied by formal Fed statements, which the markets believe were designed to make its intentions clear. What is not clear is whether this will become the standard method by which rate changes are signalled.

Traditionally, Fed watchers had to wait until the release of the minutes of the regular Federal Open Market Committee meetings, which are published six weeks afterwards, for confirmation of any perceived change in monetary policy.

All institutions with reservable deposits can borrow at the **discount rate** from the Fed's discount window for short-term adjustment purposes and limited other uses.

The Fed funds rate is usually above the discount rate. When the funds rate is at, or below, the discount rate, there is little use of the discount window by healthy banks which have access to the funds market.

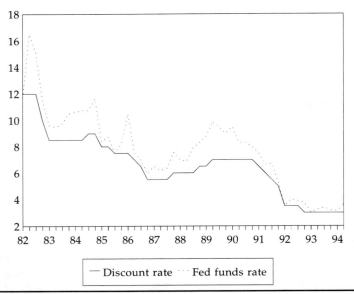

Figure 20.1   United States: Discount rate & Fed funds rate
Source: Datastream

(Note that there is no US equivalent of the lombard rate, which other central banks use to penalize institutions requiring emergency funds. However, there are circumstances when the Fed may charge a market rate above the basic discount rate. For example, borrowing under the seasonal program (*see* 'Discount rate' subsection) is at a market rate average of Fed funds and certificates of deposit (CDs). Extended credit borrowing by banks in difficulty can also be at an above market rate).

In recent years, discount window borrowing for more than seasonal needs has been limited and has not been a meaningful operating target. Still, Fed officials are reluctant to replace the reserve measure with the funds rate as their formal target (*see* 'Reserve requirements') and so are unlikely to set a funds rate target below the discount rate. Thus, the discount rate usually continues to set the floor for the Fed funds rate. However, the Fed does not consider the discount rate to be the floor for money market rates. Indeed, the funds rate often falls to very low levels late in the trading day which may take it below the discount rate.

In general, when the Fed eases money market rates, the discount rate is often cut to make it easier for the central bank to achieve its funds rate target, which may be lower than the previous discount rate.

Discount rate changes are announced by press release from the Fed's Board of Governors. The release usually gives reasons for the change and therefore a clue to the size of an adjustment to the Fed funds target. Any indications that the discount rate was changed partly to bring it into line with market rates imply that any change in the funds rate will be less than the change in the discount rate. However, between changes the discount rate is often out of line with money market rates.

The two key policy signals are:

1)   Open market operations inconsistent with the prevailing Fed funds rate or reserve requirements.

Less aggressive customer repos are sometimes used to indicate satisfaction with the prevailing Fed funds rate instead of system repos, which might be interpreted as signalling a lower desired rate.

Overnight or over-the-weekend system repos are often used by the Fed to protest the level of the funds rate at intervention time. If the Fed funds rate is at, or below, a previously acceptable rate, such an operation may signal a policy shift to a lower rate.

Both the Fed, and market participants, regard overnight customer repos as having a less aggressive message than overnight system repos. Part of the reason for the different interpretation given to the two operations results from a tradition of using them differently. Note that customer repos are also usually smaller than system repos.

On rare occasions, early intervention has been used for system repos, or matched sales, when the Fed wants to make a strong protest against the prevailing funds rate, especially if many market players perceive a policy shift where none was intended. However, it is more usual for early intervention to occur around holidays when the money market is closing early.

2)   Changes in the discount rate.

The discount rate is often underrated as an instrument of monetary policy. Because of the clearly greater importance of the Fed funds rate, many market analysts and Fed watchers view it as a merely 'cosmetic' rate of little practical importance.

However, the discount rate is still an important indicator of the Fed's policy intentions and has several key functions as a policy tool. It is the only interest rate the Fed formally admits to controlling. Thus, when it changes the rate, the Fed is making a particularly strong statement about the direction in which it wants short-term rates to move. This is particularly true of rate increases, since the Fed always has the option of raising the funds rate without increasing the discount rate.

In the past, adjustments in the discount rate were sometimes matched by adjustments in the funds rate, but under Chairman Alan Greenspan the Fed has typically moved the discount rate in 50 basis point intervals and the funds rate by 25 basis points.

Other signals include statements by the Fed chairman and press reports quoting senior Fed officials. Statements by the Fed chairman are usually monitored because of the clues they provide about the Fed's overall view of economic priorities and general policy direction. Moreover, they have sometimes been used to foreshadow imminent policy changes particularly when the chairman stresses a new concern or view of developments. Statements by FOMC members other than the chairman should be treated more cautiously as they often reflect differing personal views rather than the 'official' or consensus view.

■ Fed funds
Fed funds are balances loaned on a daily basis and available immediately, rather than on the following business day. They are borrowed or loaned by commercial banks and others to invest excess reserves or to acquire reserves to meet requirements. The demand for, and supply of, funds varies widely each day reflecting the reserve adjustments of individual banks and rates are very volatile as a result. When funds are available from other banks in the funds market, the use of the discount privilege by member banks is reduced.

The Fed signals or confirms changes in its funds rate target with open market operations (see below) which are also used to meet reserve needs. Thus, a key task for 'Fed watchers' is to distinguish policy from 'technical' actions.

The Federal Open Market Committee (FOMC) votes on a directive, which is passed to its trading desk at the New York Fed, in terms of "the degree of pressure on reserve positions" of banks. The directive does not specify the level of the funds rate, but a "greater degree of pressure" means a higher funds target and a "lesser degree of pressure" means a lower target.

Sometimes, the committee votes for a change to be implemented immediately after a meeting (the FOMC meets eight times a year, with about six weeks between meetings) but often indicates a bias (or lack of one) as to the direction of change between meetings.

Fed watchers estimate the Fed's 'technical' need to add or drain reserves in each two-week reserve period and try to determine policy-neutral activity. Deviations from those estimates may indicate a policy move. They also watch the funds rate at which operations are conducted. The Fed rarely either aggressively adds reserves when the rate is below its target, or aggressively drains reserves when it is at or above target.

In Chairman Alan Greenspan's era, the Fed has generally tried to signal policy moves clearly. An easing is usually signalled in one of two ways:

a) An overnight system repo when the funds rate is near (or slightly below) its previous target, but above the intended target.

b) A customer repo when market expectations have already driven the funds rate towards its new target level.

A tightening may be signalled by:

a) Overnight matched sales at a rate near the previous target, but below the new one.

b) No action in response to a funds rate well above the previous target.

(For an explanation of repos and sales, *see* 'Open market operations' below.)

Note that, even under Greenspan, there have been no rigid and permanent rules relating specific types of operation to policy changes, and both the markets and some Fed watchers have occasionally misread operations either by detecting a policy change when there wasn't one, or by failing to spot a change.

■ Discount rate
The discount rate is the rate at which Federal Reserve banks make collateralized advances to depository institutions. Virtually all borrowing at the discount window is through advances. Discount window loans must be secured by acceptable collateral, such as Treasury and agency securities, short-term funds and commercial paper.

Fed advances to borrowers are usually temporary, and for very short periods, since the Fed opposes operating on the basis of borrowed reserves. Borrowing institutions have therefore been pressured to restrict their lending so they can pay off such debt as soon as possible. Banks are also not supposed to borrow from the discount window and be net sellers of Fed funds on the day.

The Fed considers access to the discount window to be a privilege. Such adjustment borrowing can therefore only be undertaken occasionally (the Fed does not publicly specify the frequency). If the facility is used too often, the banks concerned receive a counselling call from the Fed.

Nevertheless, institutions requiring funds for seasonal needs or because of exceptional circumstances, and which do not have access to other sources, may borrow from the Fed for longer periods.

The many periods of banking stress since the problems at Continental Illinois in 1984 have raised the reluctance of some institutions to borrow at the discount window because of a concern about their image. However, not all banks feel that way, and even those that do still borrow at the discount window in the appropriate circumstances.

Tight administrative control of discount window borrowing has prevented it rising too far as a result of the discount rate being below money market rates. Thus, total borrowings outstanding at the discount window must be interpreted carefully as an indicator of money market conditions or Fed policy.

How does the central bank influence the money market?

Open market operations

These are conducted with a group of primary dealers in government securities (about 40) which are mainly subsidiaries of bank holding companies and securities houses. Eligible paper includes Treasury bills, notes, bonds and, for repos, government agency securities.

■ Repurchase agreements

The Fed conducts short-term repurchase agreements (repos) daily, as needed, either to offset temporary liquidity shortages or to signal a policy shift to lower interest rates. The Fed temporarily buys government securities to inject funds into the money market.

System repos are conducted for accounts within the Federal Reserve System, while customer repos are transacted in the market on behalf of customers, that is, central banks and supranationals.

Multi-day system repos are generally used to meet reserve needs that are expected to persist over much of the two-week reserve maintenance period, and do not usually have much policy significance. Collateral used in multi-day withdrawable repos may be 'pulled' back by dealers after the first day, sometimes forcing the Fed to repeat the repo operation on succeeding days. Fixed-term repos are used occasionally when the Fed wants to be sure the reserve injection sticks.

Customer repos, which, unlike system repos, are of a pre-announced size, are normally used to meet small reserve needs and are always overnight or over-the-weekend in term. Originally used primarily to avoid reserve drains when foreign central bank 'customers' left short-term money at the Fed (and thus, directly or indirectly, removed it from the commercial banks), they are now another tool used by the Fed to meet overall reserve needs.

■ Matched sales
If the Fed believes there is a temporary excess of liquidity or if it wishes to signal a policy shift towards higher interest rates, it conducts matched sale-purchase agreements (or reverses). Matched sales are a way of temporarily absorbing reserves by selling securities under an agreement to repurchase them subsequently. If the Fed believes there is a temporary excess of liquidity, or if it wants to signal a policy shift towards higher interest rates, it conducts matched sales.

The Fed does not conduct open market matched sale/purchase arrangements for official customers but, in 1992, it said that sometimes it would arrange collateralized financing for customers in small, behind-the-scenes transactions with primary dealers.

Multi-day matched sales are comparable to multi-day system repos, except the securities must be borrowed for the full term of the operation and the size is therefore fixed over the term.

Overnight or over-the-weekend matched sales are comparable to overnight system repos.

■ Outright purchases and sales of government securities
Outright purchases of government securities are made several (usually between four and eight) times a year to provide reserves on a permanent basis. These purchases are normally made in reserve settlement periods in which there is a particularly large liquidity shortage (such as around tax dates, or towards the end of the year when there is a strong demand for currency and high levels of reserve transactions deposits).

Individual purchases are restricted to bills ('bill pass') or notes and bonds ('coupon pass'). The arrangement of an outright purchase almost never sends a policy signal, though the timing and size of these purchases have occasionally been used to 'frontload' reserves, thereby putting downward pressure on the Fed funds rate in anticipation of an easing signal later in the maintenance period.

Outright sales of government securities are comparable to outright purchases, but much less common since reserve needs tend to grow over time. Although the Fed could sell bills and coupons, it has so far only sold bills outright.

'Behind-the-scenes' purchases and sales of government securities from and to foreign central bank customers are technically not open market operations, but they are often used to meet reserve needs. Although these transactions are initiated by the customer, the Fed will neutralize the effect on its own portfolio (by passing the transaction through to primary dealers) unless they are consistent with the reserve balance in a given maintenance period. Occasionally, the Fed may absorb customer transactions into its portfolio if meeting reserve needs through open market transactions might risk sending misleading signals about the funds rate.

■ Reserve requirements

Under law, all depository institutions in the US with deposit balances above a certain minimum size must hold reserves in vault cash or deposits at the Fed. They must keep an average amount of reserves over the two-week maintenance period. The reserve measure is the Fed's formal monetary target and drives the whole money market system. If the Fed cuts reserve requirements, it effectively adds money to the banking system and vice versa.

Timing

Repos and matched sales are normally arranged at 'Fed time', around 11.30 local time, for settlement that day. Early intervention (usually around 10.30) is often used on market half-days or when a particularly large technical operation is required enabling the Fed to 'lock up' collateral before it is financed elsewhere.

Outright purchases are normally arranged between 12.30 and 13.15 for settlement the next day, or two days forward. The level of the Treasury's cash balance at the Fed, which is often a major factor affecting reserves, is published daily, with a one-day lag, at about 16.00.

Reserve data needed to estimate the Fed's policy-neutral operations and to help determine their actual size are reported at 16.30 on Thursdays. Most of the data are reported weekly in Fed release H.4.1 (*Factors Affecting Reserves*). A New York Fed press conference accompanies the release of the H.4.1 data. The New York Fed highlights errors in the Fed's own projections of technical reserve factors and unusual factors not reported separately, such as warehousing of foreign currency obtained by the Treasury.

New information on several reserve factors including required reserves, vault cash used to meet reserve requirements, excess reserves and the monetary base, is available publicly only on a settlement period basis (bi-weekly), though it is updated weekly. These data are in Fed release H.3. (*Aggregate Reserves of Depository Institutions and the Monetary Base*).

Who controls the interest rate levers?

Basically, the Fed controls US monetary policy. It is often described as 'independent', and in a narrow sense this is true: the Fed is self-financed and does not require presidential approval to change interest rates.

Occasionally, it appears genuinely capable of following its own line most recently in the early 1980's when President Carter's appointee Paul Volcker raised interest rates to 20 per cent to stop an inflationary spurt in its tracks, thereby driving the economy into recession. But that episode is regarded as an exception caused by the coincidence of an extremely strong Fed chairman working within a policy vacuum created by a change of Administration.

More generally, the Fed is very obviously a creature of Congress. It can be abolished or have its terms of reference changed by Congress. The chairman is appointed by the president for a four-year term only and is conventionally a political appointee.

In practical terms, therefore, it is virtually impossible for the Fed to follow an interest rate policy significantly at odds with that desired by the US Administration.

How do official rates affect commercial ones?

Corporate

Large companies do not use bank loans to any significant extent but small and medium-sized enterprises do. The reference point for pricing commercial loans is the prime rate, the base level from which the banks calculate their lending rates. The majority of borrowers pay a margin over prime.

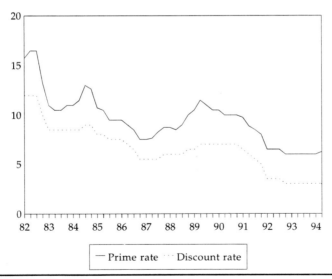

Figure 20.2   United States: Prime rate & discount rate

Source: Datastream

It is estimated that the interest rates on $150 billion in commercial loans and $100-150 billion in household loans are related to the prime rate. The interest rates charged on many bank credit cards are also set a specific number of percentage points above the prevailing prime rate.

There is no cast iron rule for relating the prime rate to official short-term interest interest rates, since it is set by commercial banks in response to market forces. Prime is always set above short-term official rates, reflecting the extra costs involved in supplying retail, rather than wholesale, funds.

Broadly, the prime rate moves in step with the discount rate. But when there is a clear trend in official interest rate policy, reflected in the way the Fed funds rate is moving, commercial banks may change their prime rates before the Fed announces a change in the discount rate.

The St. Louis-based SouthWest Bank tends to beat the pack in anticipating prime rate cuts by the so-called Moneycenter banks (Citibank, Chase Manhattan, Chemical etc.). It has, however, been known to misread the trend.

In the 10 years to 1991, the average margin between the prime and discount rates was just under two percentage points. The margin tends to widen in recessions when the perceived riskiness of lending to companies increases.

Mortgages

The cost of borrowing for house purchase can be either fixed- or adjustable-rate. Mortgage finance at fixed interest rates is typically one to two percentage points above medium- and long-term Treasury bond yields. Adjustable-rate mortgages are also common. They are usually priced off Treasury bill rates.

Interest rate expectations

The three-month eurodollar futures contract traded on the Chicago Mercantile Exchange (CME) allows speculation on where interest rates will be in future. The contract is volatile, but the best guide there is to interest rate expectations.

For example, the March contract gives a guide to what the markets think three-month eurodollar rates will be at that time. Similarly for the June, September and December contracts. The contract tends to track the Fed funds rate near expiry.

The contract is specified as 100 minus the three-month interest rate to be delivered ($100 - CP$ = expected interest rate, where CP is the contract price). The cash market offered rate for three-month eurodollar time deposits (the

London interbank offered rate, or Libor) is deducted from 100 to determine the final contract settlement price.

Thus, if the March contract is at 94.50 that implies markets expect the three-month interbank rate to be 5.50 per cent (100 - 94.50) in March. If interbank rates are currently 5.50 per cent, the implication would be that the markets expect no change in the level of rates by March.

The contract is deliverable on the second London business day before the third Wednesday of the contract month.

Key Reuter pages

Monitor

Reuters reports:
FEDS   Fed's reserve operations
NYNB   North American news/moneygraph index

Federal Reserve pages
1DIZ-JA   Fed index page
1ART   Fed statistical data
1FED-F   Federal Reserve Bank of New York
FEDM   Daily selected money market rates
NYND   Fed money market operations
NYNE   Fed weekly money supply
NYNF-J   Fed weekly banking data
NYNK   Weekly M2 components
NYNP   Fed dealer positions
NYMM   Percentage changes in M2
RTNA   Definitions of Fed operations

Other pages:
RTAL   Latest discount rate
YLDS   Key interest rates from overnight to 30 years
IZYP   Reuters weekly survey of money supply forecasts

News 2000
MMT <F9> Topic code

144

Glossary

A

ad hoc repurchase agreement (fast tender, quick tender)
Germany: A shorter maturity repurchase tender offered by the Bundesbank at times of extraordinary liquidity needs to fine-tune the money market. Such repos are offered only to banks operating in the money market for same-day settlement.

American auction (non-competitive bid)
A method of buying US Treasury bills without having to meet the high minimum purchase requirements of the regular Dutch auction. The process of bidding for Treasury bills is split into two parts: competitive (*see* **Dutch auction**) and non-competitive. Non-competitive bids are submitted by smaller investors through a Federal Reserve Bank, the Bureau of Federal Debt, or certain commercial banks. These bids are executed at the average of prices paid in all the competitive bids accepted by the Treasury.

anticipazioni a scadenza fissa
See **fixed-term advances rate**.

auction
See **competitive auction, American auction, Dutch auction, English auction**.

B

band (1, 2, 3 and 4)
UK: The maturity bands in which the Bank of England is willing to purchase eligible bills. The maturity bands of the bills being offered are defined in terms of the remaining, not the original, maturity of the bills and comprise:

Band 1: 1-14 days
Band 2: 15-33 days
Band 3: 34-63 days
Band 4: 64-91 days

bankers' acceptance
A draft or bill of exchange (basically, a short-term negotiable discount note) drawn on, and accepted by, a bank or trust company which guarantees payment of face value at maturity.

bank rate
Canada: The bank rate is the minimum rate at which the Bank of Canada lends overnight funds to the directly-clearing members of the Canadian Payments Association (CPA) including banks. The Bank rate applies to the pricing of regular purchase and resale agreements (PRAs) with dealer jobbers. The rate, which acts as a benchmark for money market rates is set 25 basis points (0.25 of a percentage point) above the average tender rate on three-month Treasury bills. *See* **PRA**.

base rate
UK: The benchmark interest rate used by commercial banks as a base from which they set their borrowing charges on loans to customers and the rates they pay for deposits from customers.

basis point
1/100th of 1 per cent, i.e. 0.01 per cent.

bausparkassen
Austria, Germany: Similar to UK building societies or US savings & loans. *See* **building society, Savings & Loan Association**.

bearer security
A negotiable security, the title of which belongs in law to the bearer (holder). The title to bearer securities is transferred by delivery. For exam-

ple, in New Zealand, the transferable certificates of deposit used in open market operations are held in bearer form. *See* **certificate of deposit**.

BECD
See **CBE**.

behind-the-scenes purchases/sales
US: Purchases/sales of government securities from/to foreign central banks customers at their request. These are technically not open market operations, but they are often used to meet reserve needs. Although these transactions are initiated by the customer, the Fed will neutralize the effect on its own portfolio (by passing the transaction through to primary dealers) unless they are consistent with the reserve balance in a given maintenance period. *See* **outright purchases/sales**.

bid
The price or yield at which a purchaser wants to buy a given security.

bill
A short-term non-interest-bearing discount security issued by the Treasury (Treasury bill or T-bill) and sold by the central bank to control the money market or to finance the national debt. *See* **Treasury bill, Reserve Bank bill**.

bill of exchange
Negotiable instrument of exchange in international trade. It is an unconditional order in writing addressed by one person to another, signed by the person giving it, requiring the person to whom it is addressed to pay on demand, or at a fixed or determined future time, a certain sum in money to, or to the order of, a specified person or the bearer. *See* *tegata*.

bill pass
US: Individual purchases of Treasury bills by the Federal Reserve to provide reserves to the banking system on a permanent basis. *See* **outright purchases/sales**.

BOT
Italy: Treasury bill.

bp
market abbreviation for basis point (1 bp = 1 basis point).

British clearer
The large cheque-clearing banks that dominate deposit-taking and short-term lending in the domestic sterling market in Great Britain.

building society
UK: Non-profit making institutions which accept savings deposits and invest the funds in mortgages. They are the main source of mortgage lending in the UK.

Bulis
See **liquidity paper**.

C

call for tender rate
See **intervention rate.**

call money rate
The interest rate financial institutions pay to borrow immediate funds. *See* **overnight lending rate, uncollateralized overnight call rate.**

call money deposit rate
Finland: The interest rate at which banks can deposit overnight funds at the Bank of Finland.

cash reserve
See **money market cash reserve.**

cash target
New Zealand: Central bank target for settlement cash used to determine how much it needs to inject into or withdraw from the money market. The central bank sets the target by forecasting daily influences on settlement cash mainly flows between the government and the private sector. The cash target is rarely hit precisely since many of the flows cannot be accurately forecast.

CBE
Spain: Certificates of deposit issued by the central bank on behalf of the Treasury against which the Bank auctions 10-day repos (the latter being the central bank's main policy instrument). These CDs have only been issued once, in March 1990, specifically to mop up the liquidity released when reserve requirements were cut. They began to mature in 1993 and the last redemption will be in the year 2000. Overnight repo rates against CBEs are set slightly higher than those against government debt since the central bank wants to encourage institutions to hold Treasury bills and bonds in their portfolios. *See* **daily intervention rate, intervention rate, repurchase agreement.**

central bank intervention bills
See **TIM.**

central bank monetary certificates
See **TRM.**

central rate
Belgium: The central bank's key interest rate at which the 15 primary dealers in government debt can get overnight funding from the central bank. It is equal to the tender rate (*see* **tender rate**) and is thus similar to the Bundesbank's repo rate, but for a shorter maturity.

certificate of deposit (CD)
A negotiable certificate with a specific maturity issued by a bank as evidence of a time deposit with that bank. If interest-bearing, it may carry a fixed- or floating-interest rate. Large-denomination CDs are typically negotiable. *See* **Treasury certificate of deposit**.

certificate of deposit (CD) rate
Denmark: The rate at which the Danmarks Nationalbank sells 14-day CDs at a weekly sale designed to help banks manage their liquidity needs. The Bank can also add liquidity by buying back CDs from the banks before they expire. This may happen on any business day. The rate at which the Bank buys back CDs includes a special buy-back fee, usually 0.10 per cent. At times of market turmoil the buy-back fee may be removed so that the Bank buys and sells CDs at the same rate. Along with the repo rate, the 14-day CD rate is the main instrument through which the central bank manages the money market. It sets the tone for money market rates.

clearing bank
Any commercial bank that settles corporate and government securities and cheques for dealers and customers. The clearing bank agrees to deliver and receive securities and cheques, taking cash against delivery.

club money
UK: Funds commercial banks had to hold on deposit with the discount houses in the 1970s in the form of secured callable deposits according to a central bank ruling. This cash averaged about five per cent of a bank's eligible liabilities (or liquid funds). It gave the discount houses an assured source of easily identifiable liquid funds at below-market interest rates which the banks could call on in an emergency. The formal 'club money' requirement was dropped in 1988, but there was an understanding that it should continue to be negotiated bilaterally with each commercial bank. However, since mid-1991, the practice has faded and commercial banks no longer have to place a minimum level of funds with the discount houses. *See* **discount house**.

collateralized financing
Securities which the issuer secures with an asset, frequently a mortgage.

commercial paper (CP)
A short-term unsecured promise to repay a fixed amount (borrowed funds plus interest) on a predetermined future date. The paper is backed by the credit rating of the borrower (issuer) or by a third party who has to repay the loan if the issuer defaults. The US has the most active commercial paper market.

competitive auction
A Dutch or English auction for securities (usually Treasury bonds). *See* **Dutch auction, English auction.**

competitive bid
A bid tendered in a Treasury auction by an institution for a specific amount of securities at a specific yield or price. *See* **Dutch auction.**

contra poliza
Spain: *See* **second window loans.**

coupon pass
US: Individual purchases of Treasury notes or bonds by the Federal Reserve to provide reserves to the banking system on a permanent basis. While the Fed can *sell* both coupons and bills outright, it has so far only sold bills outright. *See* **bill pass, outright purchases/sales.**

creadores de mercado
Spain: Market-makers who are registered dealers trading actively in government bonds. Overnight repos are conducted through *creadores de mercado*. *See* **daily intervention rate.**

créances comptables
Switzerland: Government money market claims.

credit ceiling
Central bank limits on the amount of credit banks can grant customers.

credit quota scheme
Netherlands: A limit on the amount banks can borrow through the central bank's regular credit facilities at the secured loans rate. The limit, fixed by the central bank every three months, sets a daily average for commercial bank borrowing at the central bank at the secured loans rate. *See* **secured loans rate.**

credit rate
Norway: *See* **deposit rate**.

currency swap
An agreement between two parties to exchange future payments in one currency for payments in another. Unlike interest rate swaps, currency swaps include an exchange of principal at maturity. However, neither party faces a currency risk because exchange rates are fixed in advance.

customer repos
US: Repurchase agreements transacted in the market on behalf of customers of the Federal Reserve System such as central banks and supranationals. Unlike system repos, customer repos are of a pre-announced size and are normally used to meet small reserve needs. They are always overnight or over-the-weekend. (Overnight or over-the-weekend system repos are often used by the Fed to 'protest' the level of the Fed funds rate at intervention time. If the Fed funds rate is at or below a previously acceptable rate, such an operation may signal a policy shift to a lower rate.). Customer repos were originally used mainly to avoid reserve drains when foreign central bank 'customers' left short-term money at the Fed and thus, directly or indirectly, removed it from the commercial banks. They are now another tool used by the Fed to meet overall reserve needs. The less aggressive customer repos are also sometimes used to indicate satisfaction with the prevailing Fed funds rate, in lieu of system repos which might be interpreted as signalling a lower desired rate. *See* **Federal Reserve System, Fed funds rate, system repos**.

D

D-loans (overnight loans)
Norway: A borrowing facility whereby overnight lending takes place automatically through the right of commercial and savings banks to draw up to a specified amount on their current accounts with the central bank. The central bank fixes the interest rate on D-loans and this can, in principle, be changed every day. The limits on D-loans, set on the 1st and 16th of each month, are based on a percentage of banks' equity and subordinated capital minus their subordinated loan capital. However, the central bank has announced plans to change the basis for the D-loans limit to a bank's total assets. *See* **F-loans**.

daily intervention rate (overnight repo rate)
Spain: The interest rate at which the central bank provides funds to the money market via purchases or sales of Bank of Spain certificates of deposit (CBEs) and government debt. The daily intervention rate is usually slightly higher than that set for 10-day repos and sets the tone for money market rates. *See* **CBE**, **overnight repos**, **repurchase agreement**, **ten-day repo**, **ten-day repo rate**.

daily lending facility
Portugal: A mechanism for injecting overnight funds into the money market through securities repurchase operations. The facility is available to resident banks subject to a quota at a pre-announced interest rate called the 'daily lending facility' rate. Quotas are set according to each bank's share of reserve requirements. *See* **daily lending facility rate**.

daily lending facility rate
Portugal: A pre-announced interest rate charged on overnight funds injected into the money market through securities repurchase operations. It is usually higher than the liquidity injection rate and sets the ceiling for money market rates in normal circumstances. However, it still does not set an absolute ceiling on money market rates because, when liquidity is tight, the overnight rate may exceed the daily lending facility rate. *See* **overnight rate, repurchase agreement**.

deposit rate
The interest rate banks receive for placing excess funds overnight at the central bank. The deposit rate usually sets the floor for money market rates. *See* **overnight lending rate**. (Sweden: *see* **marginal lending rate**; Denmark: *see foliorente*.)

Deutsche Terminbörse
Germany: Futures exchange based in Frankfurt.

discount
The difference between par and the price of an issue when the price is lower than par.

discount bill
A bill trading below par.

discount house
UK: Institution acting as intermediary between the Bank of England and the banking system. It enjoys lender of last resort facilities at the Bank of England and participates in underwriting the weekly UK Treasury bill auction. Discount houses use call and overnight money obtained from banks to invest in and trade money market instruments.

discount rate
The rate of interest charged by a central bank to financial institutions that borrow at the discount window. Thus, the central bank may discount, or refinance, commercial bills for depository institutions at the discount rate to ease liquidity shortages. (In some countries, such as the US, the central bank makes collateralized advances to institutions instead of actually discounting eligible bills.) The discount rate is preferential and the lowest official rate; it therefore sets the floor for money market rates. In some countries, for example Japan, it is formally known as the official discount rate (ODR).

discount securities
Non-interest-bearing money market instruments issued at a discount and redeemed at maturity for full face value.

discount window
Facility provided by central banks enabling financial institutions to borrow reserves against collateral in the form of government or other acceptable paper.

diskonto
Danish for discount rate.

DTB
See **Deutsche Terminbörse**.

Dutch auction (competitive bid)
Auction in which the lowest price (highest yield) necessary to sell the entire offering becomes the price at which all securities offered are sold. In other words, bidders buy securities at the stop price if their bid is above that price. This technique has been used in US Treasury auctions and is used in UK gilt auctions. *See* **stop rate**.
US: In the US, these so-called competitive bids are made by large government securities dealers and brokers who buy millions of dollars worth of bills. They offer the best price they can for the securities and the highest bids are accepted by the Treasury in what is called the Dutch auction. *See* **American auction**.

E

early round
UK: Bank of England invitation to discount houses to offer bills for outright sale to the Bank or, also, for subsequent resale when there is a liquidity shortage. An early round of bill offers is usually invited at the same time as the Bank's morning forecast of the daily liquidity shortage in the money market, announced at 09.45 local time. The Bank may offer a bill repo as well if the shortage is over about £800 million.

eligible
Acceptable as collateral by the central bank at the discount window. An instrument is eligible when the accepting bank can sell it without becoming subject to a reserve requirement.

eligible bankers' acceptances
In the bankers' acceptance market an acceptance may be referred to as eligible because it is acceptable by the central bank as collateral at the discount window and/or because the accepting bank can sell it without incurring a reserve requirement.

eligible bills
Essentially post-dated cheques issued by companies, but which carry a bank guarantee.

emergency lending rate
Belgium ('special overdraft rate'): Special penalty overnight rate for financial institutions in the Belgo-Luxembourg Economic Union (BLEU) charged on the part of any overdraft exceeding each institution's credit line at the central bank. There is no volume limit provided that, as for other lending facilities, there is sufficient collateral. Also known as the special overdraft rate or the rate for current account advances beyond credit lines. The emergency lending rate is always higher than the end-of-day rate, sometimes by a large margin. It is the central bank's highest rate, but is not commonly used. (*See* **end-of-day rate**).

end-of-day rate (overdraft rate)
Belgium: The overnight lending rate for financial institutions in the Belgo-Luxembourg Economic Union (BLEU) charged on borrowings up to the limit of each institution's credit facility at the central bank. Also known as the overdraft rate or the rate for current account advances within credit lines. There is a limit on the amount of funds that can be drawn at the

end-of-day rate which is equal to the central rate plus a margin. The end-of-day rate sets the ceiling for call money. (*See* **central rate**).

end-of-period emergency lending facility

Portugal: This is an overnight emergency lending facility which allows domestic institutions short of funds to meet their reserve requirements. Operations under this mechanism mature on the following business day. Funds are granted at a penalty rate. The facility is available within 30 minutes after the close of the money market on the last working day of each seven-to-10-day reserve maintenance period. *See* **end-of-period emergency lending facility rate**.

end-of-period emergency lending facility rate

Portugal: A penalty rate applied to funds granted under the end-of-day emergency lending facility. The end-of-day emergency lending facility rate is set one percentage point above the highest of either: 1) the highest interbank rate, on the same day, for maturities of up to five days; or 2) the highest liquidity injection rate in the same reserve maintenance period. These rates apply unless the Bank of Portugal specifically announces a lower rate. *See* **end-of-period emergency lending facility.**

English auction

An auction at which bidders buy securities at their bid price if they bid above the stop price. If they bid below the stop price they receive any unsold securities.

entidades gestoras

Spain: Market-makers who are registered dealers trading actively in government bonds. Overnight repos are conducted through *entidades gestoras*. *See* **daily intervention rate**.

European currency unit (Ecu)

A composite, or basket, currency made up of fixed amounts of the individual currencies of each of the members of the European Monetary System (EMS). *See* **European Monetary System**.

European Monetary System (EMS)

An exchange rate system launched in 1979 among member states of the European Union (EU). The main components are the European currency unit (Ecu) and the exchange rate mechanism (ERM). Countries are always members of the EMS but can, at times of exchange rate turmoil, leave the ERM after which they may apply to rejoin at any time. *See* **exchange rate mechanism**.

exchange rate mechanism (ERM)

A currency system designed to limit short-term movements between the exchange rates of the members of the European Union (EU). In August 1993, after a severe bout of exchange rate turmoil, member currencies were allowed to float by 15 per cent either side of their central rates.

F

F-loans (fixed-interest rate loans)
Norway: A borrowing facility introduced for private banks in 1987 to supplement the D-loan facility. The interest rate on the loans, set through periodic auctions, is fixed for up to a year though usually they have a maturity of less than four weeks. F-loans provide a more stable supply of liquidity to banks which shelters them from sharp fluctuations in short-term interest rates. The limits on F-loans are set each quarter and equal a bank's equity and subordinated capital minus its subordinated loan capital. *See* **D-loans**.

Fast tender
See **ad hoc repurchase agreement**.

Fed
See **Federal Reserve System**.

Federal funds
Non-interest-bearing reserve accounts held by depository institutions at the Federal Reserve to meet reserve requirements and handle interbank transactions. Fed funds are loaned on a daily basis and are available immediately rather than on the following business day. The demand for, and supply of, funds varies widely each day reflecting the reserve adjustments of individual banks. The Fed funds rate is therefore very volatile as a result. *See* **Fed funds rate**.

Fed funds rate
The interest rate at which Fed funds are traded; that is, the rate paid by one bank when it borrows reserves from another. The rate is influenced by the Fed through its open market operations. The Fed has a target for the funds rate which is never formally published. However, so-called 'Fed watchers' can tell what the target is by observing where the funds rate trades in conjunction with the Fed's money market operations. More recently, the Fed has made an announcement when it plans to increase pressure on reserves to boost short-term money market rates. It has thus become much easier to discern the Fed's objective for the funds rate. The Fed funds rate is usually above the discount rate. When the funds rate is at or below the discount rate, there is little use of the discount window by healthy banks which have access to the funds market. *See* **discount rate**, **Federal funds**, **open market operations**.

Federal Reserve bank
See **Federal Reserve System.**

Federal Reserve Open Market Committee (FOMC)
A committee of the Fed which establishes and executes monetary policy. It usually meets on the third Tuesday of each month to issue guidelines to the trading desk at the Federal Reserve Bank of New York. A summary report of each meeting is released the Friday after the subsequent meeting.

Federal Reserve System
The central banking system of the US. There are 12 regional Federal Reserve Banks but virtually all the policy-making powers are lodged in the Board of Governors of the Federal Reserve System in Washington. This has seven members appointed by the US president for 14-year terms. The president chooses one of these to be chairman for a four-year term.

Fibor
See **Frankfurt interbank offered rate**

five-to-10-day lending rate (*pensions de cinq à 10 jours*)
France: The interest rate charged by the Bank of France on five-to-10-day loans. Five-to-10-day loans are available through what is an emergency facility always (with one exception) available to commercial banks which can draw funds in unlimited amounts as a last resort. Such loans are granted through securities repurchase agreements. The five-to-10-day rate is typically about 75 to 100 basis points above the intervention rate. Similar to Germany's lombard rate (though the latter is only available in fixed quotas.) *See* **intervention rate.**

fixed-rate repo
See **repurchase agreement.**

fixed-rate tender
See **volume tender.**

fixed-term advances rate (*anticipazioni a scadenza fissa*)
Italy: The interest rate charged to banks who apply for extraordinary funding from the Bank of Italy to meet special short-term needs. The loans are made to individual banks and cover a prearranged maturity of between one and 32 days on collateral of tradeable securities. Banks can only apply for fixed-term advances when they have used up all the credit available to them under ordinary advances. The Bank of Italy is allowed to set the fixed-term advances rate at a premium of up to 1.75 percentage points

above the ordinary advances rate. This rises with the frequency of renewal. *See* **ordinary advances**.

fixed-term repo
US: A repo covering a fixed time period used when the Fed wants to be sure a reserve injection sticks.

floating lombard rate
Switzerland: The lombard rate was floated in Switzerland in May 1989 since when it has been set two percentage points above the average money market rate over the previous two days. *See* **lombard rate.**

foliorente
Denmark: Interest-bearing current account deposits at the central bank which attract the deposit rate. This shadows the discount rate and sets the floor for very short-term money market rates. *Foliorente* is Danish for folio (deposit) account. *See* **deposit rate**.

FOMC
See **Federal Reserve Open Market Committee.**

foreign currency swap
See **currency swap.**

foreign currency repos
Germany: A repo under which the Bundesbank transfers claims to the delivery of specific foreign assets it holds to banks for a limited period. Occasionally used by to inject liquidity into the money market.
Italy: A repo using foreign currency-denominated securities to reduce the impact of temporary shortages of lira-denominated securities and to help rebuild foreign exchange reserves. Effectively like a currency swap, the Bank of Italy began using them in October 1992 because it was having difficulty covering liquidity shortages through repos on lira-denominated government debt alone.

forward repurchase agreement
A repurchase agreement under which liquidity is supplied over subsequent days. *See* **repurchase agreement.**

Frankfurt interbank offered rate (Fibor)
The rate at which prime banks offer to make Eurocurrency deposits with other prime banks for a given maturity in Frankfurt.

G

geldmarktbuchforderungen
Switzerland: Short-term money market claims issued by the federal government.

GEMM (gilt-edged market-maker)
UK: A market-maker in British government bonds (gilts). *See* **gilt-edged security**.

gensaki
A Japanese bond repurchase contract.

gilt-edged security
British government bond. Basically, a domestic sterling-denominated security issued by the UK Treasury. The name comes from the gold edge on the original certificates, since replaced by green certificates.

Gomex rate:
Austria: The money market intervention rate. It is the effective floor for short-term money market rates.

H

Helibor
See **Helsinki interbank offered rate.**

Helsinki interbank offered rate (Helibor)
The rate at which prime banks offer to make Eurocurrency deposits with other prime banks for a given maturity in Helsinki.

I

interbank rate
The rate at which banks bid for and offer deposits to each other. *See* **Libor**.

interest rate on advances
See **secured loans rate**.

interest rate scale
A series of discrete steps on a scale used by some central banks (for example Sweden's Riksbank, the Swiss National Bank) to set interest rates.
Sweden: In Sweden, the interest rate scale is symmetrical and thus works the same way whether banks have excess liquidity to invest or require funds. On loans above 15 per cent the central bank decides the interest rate on an ad hoc basis. The Bank defines a supply function for each bank in which the size of the steps on the scale are related to a bank's capital base.

interest rate tender
See **repurchase agreement**.

intervention rate
France: The interest rate at which the central bank allocates funds on securities repurchase agreements (*opérations sur appel d'offre*). Also known as the 'call for tender rate'. It is seen as the most powerfully symbolic of the Bank of France's interest rates and usually sets a notional floor on short-term money market rates.
Spain: The interest rate at which the central bank allots funds to the money market through 10-day repos. These tenders are almost always variable-rate, although the 10-day rate often remains unchanged for long periods. The Bank only announces a fixed rate in very exceptional cases when it wants to send a direct and rapid signal on monetary policy. The intervention rate is the Bank of Spain's key interest rate and the main pointer to its monetary policy stance. It also sets the floor for money market rates. *See* **CBE, daily intervention rate, repurchase agreement, ten-day repo**.

J

JGBs
Japanese government bonds

L

late assistance:
UK: Bank of England loans to discount houses which find themselves short of funds after the Bank's main bill business has been concluded by 14.45 local time. At this time the discount houses may ask to borrow on a secured basis under its facilities. The Bank announces the total amount of 'late assistance' at 14.45, but not the terms. Late assistance is also given after 14.45, until 15.30, when institutions may seek to borrow further funds.

lender of last resort
The central bank always stands ready to lend money to a limited number of financial institutions (on its own terms) it they are unable to obtain finance from market sources. In practice, this permits the central bank to influence the level of interest rates and the money supply as well as providing a basis of confidence for the banking system.

letras del Tesoro
Spain: Treasury bills. They were created in 1987 as a basic short-term financing instrument. (Treasury bill was the term previously used for *pagares del Tesoro* which are now called Treasury notes. *See* **pagares del Tesoro**.)

liability
A financial obligation.

Libor
See **London interbank offered rate**.

linea di credito
Italy: Individual bank's maximum credit line for ordinary advances at the Bank of Italy.

linear bonds
Belgium: *Obligation linéaire obligatie* bonds (OLOs).

liquidity credit rate
Finland: The interest rate at which banks can borrow overnight funds from the Bank of Finland. It is tied to the Bank of Finland's tender rate. *See* **tender rate**.

liquidity injection rate
Portugal: The intervention rate at which the central bank buys Treasury and central bank bills and certificates to inject liquidity into the money market. The injection rate is set at the start of each accounting period for commercial bank reserves. It sets an indicative ceiling for money market rates. Traditionally, the Bank has set a fixed rate. However, since the ERM crisis in July 1993, it has set the rate through auctions of Treasury bills, central bank monetary certificates (TRMs) and central bank intervention bills (TIMs). *See* **TIM, Treasury bill, TRM.**

liquidity mop-up rate
Portugal: The intervention rate at which the central bank sells Treasury and central bank bills and certificates to drain liquidity from the money market. The mop-up rate is set at the start of each accounting period for commercial bank reserves. It usually sets the floor for money market rates. Traditionally, the Bank of Portugal has announced a fixed rate. However, since the ERM crisis in July 1993, it has set the rate through auctions of Treasury bills, central bank monetary certificates (TRMs) and central bank intervention bills (TIMs) which have the same maturity as the period just starting. *See* **TIM, Treasury bill, TRM.**

liquidity paper (*Bulis***)**
Germany: Paper sold by the Bundesbank to absorb money market liquidity.

Lisbon interbank offered rate (Lisbor)
Portugal: The benchmark interest rate for medium-term loans. It is set by a cartel of eight leading banks which quote one, three, six and 12-month interbank rates. Reuters automatically calculates an average at 11.00 local time each trading day (LBOA). This is used by the market as the benchmark Lisbor rate for the day.

Lisbor
See **Lisbon interbank offered rate.**

Lisfra
Lisbon forward rate agreement.

local authority bill
A bill issued by UK municipalities. These bills do not carry a government guarantee.

local authority bond
A bond issued weekly by UK municipalities, usually with maturities of one year, sometimes up to five years. These bonds are not guaranteed by the government.

lombard rate
The rate of interest charged by the central bank for a secured overnight loan. For example, Section 19 of the Bundesbank Act allows the central bank to grant overnight loans to the banking system at the lombard rate against collateral including specific securities and Debt register claims, such as federal government bonds. The lombard rate usually sets the ceiling for short-term money market rates because lombard loans are intended to be used temporarily in special circumstances, such as when liquidity is tight, and not to subsidize banks.
Austria: The interest rate charged on short-term loans of up to three months' maturity granted against collateral. The lombard rate in Austria has historically been about two percentage points above the discount rate. It is the least important of the Austrian National Bank's three leading rates and loans at this rate do not account for any routine bank refinancing.

London interbank offered rate (Libor)
The rate at which prime banks offer to make eurocurrency deposits with other prime banks for a given maturity which can range from overnight to five years in London.

long-term prime rate
Japan: The rate which banks charge their best corporate customers on loans with maturities of over one year. It is traditionally set 90 basis points over interest rates on five-year bank debentures which long-term credit banks issue monthly.

M

Marché à Terme International de France
France: Futures exchange based in Paris.

margine disposible
Italy: The undrawn margin of an individual bank's credit line at the Bank of Italy.

marginal lending rate (deposit rate)
Sweden: The lowest step on the Riksbank's (central bank's) interest rate scale at which banks can deposit or lend funds at the central bank. It sets the tone for money market rates. The Bank holds repos and then always announces the interest rate implied by the marginal rate on the day's pact. (Until spring 1993, repos were the main window for policy changes but since then the main forum for marginal rate changes has been the central bank's weekly board meeting.) From the marginal rate, money market players derive the overnight lending rate. The marginal rate can either be a lending or a deposit rate, depending on whether banks have excess reserves or are short of funds. However, the market and media always refer to it as the marginal 'lending' rate.

matched sale-purchase agreements (reverses)
US: The opposite of a repurchase agreement. Matched sales are a way of temporarily absorbing reserves by selling securities under an agreement to repurchase them subsequently. If the Fed believes there is a temporary excess of liquidity, or if it wants to signal a policy shift towards higher interest rates, it conducts matched sales. The Fed does not conduct open market matched sales for official customers, but in 1992 it said that sometimes it would arrange collateralized financing for customers in small, behind-the-scenes transactions with primary dealers. Multi-day matched sales are comparable to multi-day system repos except the securities must be borrowed for the full term of the operation and the size is therefore fixed over the term. Overnight or over-the-weekend matched sales are comparable to overnight system repos. *See* **collateralized financing, customer repos, primary dealer, repurchase agreement, reverse repurchase agreement, system repos.**

Matif
See **Marché à Terme International de France.**

MID
The computer system on which interbank funds are traded called the *Mercato Interbancario Depositi* (MID).

minimum lending rate (MLR)
UK: An administered interest rate which the central bank periodically re-introduces so that, for a short period ahead, it applies to any lending to discount houses. MLR is used when the Bank wants to enforce a particular interest rate on the market. Until sterling was withdrawn from the exchange rate mechanism (ERM) of the European Monetary System (EMS) in September 1992, the Bank had only re-introduced MLR twice since it was abolished in 1981 when the Bank introduced a new system for day-to-day market operations. The Bank has since resorted to using MLR more regularly. See **discount house, European monetary system, exchange rate mechanism**.

monetary base
Currency in circulation plus banks' reserve (sight) deposits at the central bank.

monetary intervention securities
See **TIM**.

monetary regulation bills
See **TRM**.

money market
The market in which short-term debt instruments (bills, deposits, commercial paper, bankers' acceptances, certificates of deposit etc.) are issued and traded.

money market cash reserve
Netherlands: A cash reserve set by the Nederlandsche Bank to create a liquidity shortage thereby enabling the bank to steer money market rates with special advances. *See* **special advances, special advances rate**.

money market dealing rate
UK: The interest rate at which the Bank of England buys eligible bills from discount houses to provide liquidity. *See* **discount house**.

money market lending rate
UK: The interest rate on Bank of England loans to discount houses using their borrowing facilities at the Bank. *See* **discount house**.

mop-up rate
See **liquidity mop-up rate.**

multi-day matched sales
See **matched sale-purchase agreements.**

multi-day system repos
See **system repos.**

N

Nederlandsche Bank Certificates (NBCs)
Netherlands: NBCs are interest-bearing negotiable certificates issued to drain structural money market surpluses caused by intervention sales of guilders to support other member currencies in the exchange rate mechanism. *See* **money market cash reserves**.

non-competitive auction
Auction at which all bidders receive securities at the average price.

O

obligation linéaire obligatie (OLOs)
Belgium: Linear bonds

occasional intervention
Portugal: Money market operations announced by the Bank of Portugal for the days of the seven-to-10-day accounting period remaining after the first business day of each maintenance period. Occasional intervention takes into account changes in money market liquidity and/or the trend in overnight rates. It involves operations that usually mature in the current or following accounting period, but it may include operations with a maturity of up to one year. Interest rates on these operations are called *occasional* liquidity injection/mop-up rates. *See* **liquidity injection rate, liquidity mop-up rate, regular intervention.**

offer
The price or yield at which a seller wishes to sell a given security.

official dealer
Australia: Dealers at banks authorized by the Reserve Bank of Australia to deal in Australian government securities of up to one year maturity. *See* **official overnight cash rate.**

official discount rate
See **discount rate.**

official overnight cash rate
Australia: The key money market rate set on the 'official' market and which influences banks in setting prime lending rates. Nine banks have been authorized as official dealers in Australian government securities of up to one year maturity.

official repurchase facility rate
See **five-to-10-day lending rate.**

OLO (*obligation linéaire obligatie*)
Belgium: Linear bonds

open market operations
Central bank activities in the secondary (open) market in order to affect interest rates. When the central bank buys securities the quantity of bank

reserves is increased. When the central bank sells securities banks lose reserves. The aim of most open market operations is to offset changes in the quantity of bank reserves arising from other factors. However, they are also used to affect the money supply.

operational balances
Commercial bank funds held on deposit at the central bank to settle the final position at the end of the day between the banking system and the Bank.

ordinary advances (*anticipazioni ordinaire*)
Italy: Credit lines agreed with individual lending institutions, such as banks, and guaranteed with collateral which can include state and other eligible traded bonds. Ordinary advances are the customary way banks borrow from the central bank for their ordinary everyday needs. The interest rate on ordinary advances equals the discount rate. Banks also have to pay a fixed fee equal to 0.3 per cent of their credit line every four months.

outright purchases/sales
Government securities purchased or sold outright, that is, without an agreement to subsequently sell or repurchase them through a repurchase agreement or reverse repo. Purchases are normally made in reserve settlement periods in which there is a particularly large liquidity shortage (such as around tax dates or towards the end of the year, when there is a strong demand for currency and high levels of reserve transactions deposits. Outright sales are much less common than outright purchases since reserve needs tend to grow over time. *See* **bill pass**, **coupon pass**.

overdraft rate
See **end of day rate** and **emergency lending rate**.

overnight lending rate
The rate charged by banks and other financial institutions for overnight (one-day) funds.

overnight repos
Spain: One-day variable-rate repos conducted with market-makers (*entidades gestoras*). Each time an auction is announced banks and savings banks inform the Bank of Spain of the amounts they require and the rates they are willing to pay (a maximum of three tenders can be accepted from each institution). The Bank allots funds to the highest bidders until the auction is complete. The daily intervention rate set at each auction is the average of

the rates bid weighted by the amounts accepted. Overnight repos mature on the next working day and are guaranteed by central bank certificates (CBEs) or government bonds. The Bank of Spain sets repo rates against CBEs slightly higher than those against government debt to encourage institutions to hold Treasury bills and bonds in their portfolios. Since the Bank does not always conduct overnight repos, and funding via the 10-day repo is normally cheaper, institutions are expected to cover their liquidity needs in the regular 10-day repos and to use overnight auctions only to satisfy their odd-lot reserve needs. *See* **CBE, daily intervention rate, intervention rate, repurchase agreement, ten-day repo, ten-day repo rate.**
United States: *See* **customer repos.**

over-the-weekend repos
See **customer repos.**

P

pagares del Tesoro
Spain: Treasury notes. The term was previously used for Treasury bills which are now called *letras del Tesoro*. *See **letras del Tesoro**.*

Paris interbank offered rate (Pibor)
The rate at which prime banks offer to make eurocurrency deposits with other prime banks for a given maturity in Paris.

Pibor
See **Paris interbank offered rate**.

point
100 basis points = 1 percentage point.

PRA (purchase and resale agreement)
Canada: These are regular repos which involve Bank of Canada purchases of short-term government debt that designated investment dealers, called jobbers, can buy back at any time from the next business day up to two weeks ahead. Dealers that have technical lines of credit with the Bank of Canada are allowed to obtain funds from the Bank through PRAs if call money is above the Bank rate.

PRA rate
Canada: *See* **Bank rate**.

primary dealer
A dealer in government securities recognized by, and with direct access to, the central bank.

primary liquidity
New Zealand: The amount of discountable bills in the banking system.

primary liquidity ratio
Ireland: A central bank reserve requirement fixed as a percentage of commercial bank assets.

prime bank
A bank of the highest standing.

prime rate
The rate at which banks lend to their best (prime) or most creditworthy customers. The all-in cost of a bank loan to a prime credit equals the prime rate plus the cost of holding compensating balances. Prime rate also refers to the approximate average of prime rates quoted by the major US banks on a given day.
Japan: *See* **long-term prime rate**.

prise en pension
Switzerland: Swiss name for a repurchase agreement. The Swiss National Bank adds liquidity by inviting banks to deposit government bills (créances comptable) into their accounts at the central bank in exchange for cash, with an agreement to repurchase the bills at a future date. These repos usually have a maturity between overnight and one-week.

promissory note rate
Netherlands: The promissory note rate equals the secured loans rate plus 0.5 of a percentage point. The central bank no longer conducts transactions at this rate and it is now used just as a benchmark for the rates charged by commercial banks. *See* **secured loans rate**.

purchase and resale agreement (PRA)
See **repurchase agreement**.

Q

quick tenders
See **ad hoc repurchase agreement.**

R

RBA
Reserve Bank of Australia

rediscount quota
Germany: A quota used by the Bundesbank to vary the total amount of rediscount credit available to banks at the discount rate. Individual banks' access to the overall quota is based on their capital liabilities and business structure.

rediscount rate
See **discount rate**.

refunding
Redemption of securities by funds raised through the sale of a new issue.

regular intervention
Portugal: Money market operations announced by the Bank of Portugal on the first day of each seven-to-10-day accounting period which have a same-day value date and mature on the first working day of the following main-tenance period. Interest rates on these operations are called *regular* liquidity injection/mop-up rates. *See* **liquidity injection rate**, **liquidity mop-up rate**, **occasional intervention**.

repurchase agreement (repo or RP)
Central bank purchase of securities (the collateral) from financial institu-tions (usually banks) with an agreement to sell them back at a fixed price on a predetermined future date. The central bank effectively lends the hold-ers of the securities money for the period of the agreement on terms struc-tured to compensate. The price at which the reverse transaction takes place (*See* **reverse repurchase agreement**) sets the interest rate over the period (the 'repo rate'). Dealers often use repos to finance their positions. Repur-chase agreements can be either variable or fixed. At variable-rate tenders, financial institutions bid in terms of both the amount of funds they require and the rates they are prepared to pay. The central bank decides what vol-ume of bids to accept, and which of the bids it will accept in full. Under fixed-rate tenders, the central bank sets the repo rate and banks submit bids for the amounts they want at the fixed rate. The central bank then accepts a total amount consistent with its liquidity objectives. Variable-rate repos are also known as 'interest rate tenders', while fixed-rate repos are also known as 'volume tenders'. If the central bank wants to keep a firm grip on repo

rates and give the market clear guidance, it offers repo funds at *fixed-rate* tenders. In Germany, for example, the Bundesbank has regularly offered banks repurchase funds at fixed-rate tenders in recent years to guide money market rates after a change in its key lombard and/or discount rates. The most active repo market is in the US where the Fed sets short-term interest rates by lending securities. *See* **foreign currency repos**.

repurchase rate (repo rate or RP rate)
The rate at which the central bank buys securities from financial institutions (usually banks) with an agreement to resell them at a fixed price on a fixed date.

reserve bank bill
A non-interest-bearing discount security issued and sold by the central bank to control the money market or to finance the national debt. *See* **bill, Treasury bill**.

reserve requirements
The percentages of different types of liabilities that institutions are required to hold on deposit at the central bank.

reserves
Assets held as cash or in highly liquid form on deposit at the central bank.

reverse repurchase agreements (sale and repurchase agreements, SRAs, matched sale-purchase agreements (US), reverses)
Central bank sales of securities to financial institutions (usually banks) with an agreement to buy them back at a fixed price on a predetermined future date. Also known as 'matched sales' in the US.

S

S-loans
Norway: Loans provided to banks on special terms. They are not used to manage liquidity but provide banks with funds on special application. They are provided to individual banks having difficulty raising funds in the money market or through deposits from the public. S-loans are the central bank's 'lender of last resort' facility.

sale and repurchase agreement (reverse repo, SRA, reverse)
See **reverse repurchase agreement**.

Savings & Loan Association
US: Federal or state chartered institution that accepts savings deposits and invests the bulk of the funds received in mortgages.

second window loans (*contra poliza*)
Spain: Loans to banks unable to acquire funds in the interbank market and which may therefore not meet their reserve requirements. They are known locally as *contra poliza* loans. This term refers to a type of special advance against *poliza*, which is a bank's licence to operate in the money market. Such loans are granted at the central bank's discretion and secured by a loan auction contract. They are usually granted at a penalty interest rate which is slightly above the daily intervention rate. Forcing banks to use *contra poliza* loans is one way the Bank of Spain steers the daily intervention rate. The interest rate charged on these loans normally sets the ceiling for money market rates. All banks have access to second window loans. *See* **daily intervention rate**.

secured callable deposits
UK: Deposits which can be called in at any time by the depositor and for which the borrower (for example, discount house) provides backing in the form of specific assets or revenues. *See* **club money, discount house**.

secured loans rate
Netherlands: The interest rate applied to commercial banks' daily borrowing at the central bank under the credit quota scheme. The secured loans rate is the middle one of the three key official rates and stands between the promissory note and discount rates. It sets the floor for money market rates. *See* **credit quota scheme, discount rate, promissory note rate**.

secured overnight advances
Ireland: Supplementary overnight funds provided by the central bank at a penalty rate to to credit institutions which have used up their quotas under the short-term facility. *See* **short-term facility**.

securities repurchase agreement
See **repurchase agreement**.

settlement cash
Funds used to settle outstanding flows between the government and private sector. *See* **cash target**.

short-term facility (STF)
Ireland: A facility under which credit institutions may borrow funds from the central bank against approved security at an interest rate set slightly above prevailing money market rates. *See* **secured overnight advances**.

sinking fund
Money, either cash or eligible securities, periodically set aside by a borrower (in this case, the central bank) to redeem all or part of its long-term debt issues. For example, irregular Bank of Japan open market operations include Ministry of Finance sinking fund bond purchases through the central bank which acts as agent.

SISTEM
Portugal: Money market telephone system of the Bank of Portugal.

Somali
Austria: Special open market line through which the central bank can lend extra money to banks. The Somali is used to provide funds when banks have reached their refinancing ceilings at the Gomex, discount and lombard rates. It is used only once or twice a year. *See* **discount rate**, **Gomex rate**, **lombard rate**.

special advances
Short-term liquidity pacts offered to commercial banks against collateral, mainly Treasury paper.
Netherlands: Special fixed-term central bank loans. *See* **special advances rate**.

special advances rate
Netherlands: The interest rate charged on special fixed-term central bank loans. In practice, banks are usually invited to tender for an open amount

of a special loan with a fixed rate. The rate applies to most of the central bank's last resort lending. It is thus used to steer money market rates and the guilder's value against other currencies, especially the mark.

special deposits
UK: Deposits which financial institutions with eligible liabilities of £10 million or more can be asked to place with the central bank. Special deposits would normally earn an interest rate close to the equivalent of the average rate of discount at the most recent Treasury bill tender. They have not been called since December 1979, but are still available for withdrawing cash from the banking system.

special deposit rate
Belgium: The interest rate banks receive for placing excess funds overnight at the Rediscount and Guarantee Institute (RGI). The special deposit rate is the lowest rate paid on such deposits and is below the deposit rate which also applies to such deposits. The special deposit rate is currently the central rate minus 2.0 percentage points.

special lending facility
A facility under which the central bank may grant temporary loans to institutions in exceptional circumstances to fine-tune the money market. For example, the Bank of England re-introduced a special lending facility to provide commercial banks with funds in the run-up to sterling's exit from the exchange rate mechanism (ERM) in September 1992. (The special facility was subsequently made permanent as part of the Bank's move to regular repos in early 1994.) Japan also has a special lending facility, but this has so far never been used.

special official lending rate
Japan: A special rate set independently of the official discount rate. It can apply to temporary and exceptional loans to private financial institutions under a special Bank of Japan lending facility. So far, however, it has never been used.

special overdraft rate
See emergency lending rate.

special repos (specials, special purchase and resale agreements (SPRAs) or PRAs)
A repurchase agreement at the amount and rate chosen by the central bank; for example, central bank purchases of Treasury bills with an agreement to

sell them back at a later date. Specials provide liquidity and are normally used to offset upward pressure on the overnight rate.

special term loans (S-loans)
See **S-loans**.

SPRA (special purchase and resale agreement)
Canada: SPRAs are used by the Bank of Canada to relieve temporarily undesired upward pressure on overnight rates. *See* **SPRA rate**.

SPRA rate
Canada: The interest rate at which the Bank of Canada chooses to purchase securities under special purchase and resale agreements. This sets the ceiling for money market rates in special circumstances.

SRA (sale and repurchase agreement)
Canada: SRAs are used to offset undesired downward pressure on overnight rates. *See* **SRA rate**.

SRA rate
Canada: The rate at which the Bank of Canada chooses to sell securities under sale and repurchase agreements. This usually sets the floor for money market rates in special circumstances..

standing facilities
Portugal: *See* **daily lending facility, daily lending facility rate, end-of-period emergency lending facility, end-of-period emergency lending facility rate**.

stop price
See **stop rate**.

stop rate
The lowest rate (highest price) at which a central bank will purchase bills, bonds etc. Alternatively, the highest rate (lowest price) at which a central bank will sell bills, bonds.

swap
See **currency swap**.

system repos
US: Short-term repurchase agreements conducted for accounts within the Federal Reserve System, unlike customer repos which are transacted in the

market on behalf of customers of the Federal Reserve System (that is, other central banks and supranationals). Multi-day system repos are generally used to meet reserve needs that are expected to persist over much of the reserve maintenance period and do not usually have much policy significance. Overnight or over-the-weekend system repos are often used when the Fed wants to make a strong 'protest' against the prevailing Fed funds rate at intervention time—especially if many market players perceive a policy shift where none was intended. If the Fed funds rate is at or below a previously acceptable rate, such an operation may signal a policy shift to a lower rate. *See* **customer repos, Federal Reserve System, Fed funds rate**.

T

tegata
Japan: Bill of exchange.

ten-day repo
Spain: A variable-rate tender held at the beginning of each 10-day reserve requirement period. The Bank of Spain auctions 10-day repos against its own outstanding central bank certificates (CBEs), Treasury bills and bonds. Bids are invited the day before the tender with those above the repo rate set by the bank allotted and those below rejected. The allotment rate is known as the intervention rate. Although tenders are almost always at a variable rate, the 10-day rate often remains unchanged for long periods. *See* **CBE, intervention rate, repurchase agreement**.

ten-day repo rate
See **intervention rate**.

tender
Competitive bids from financial institutions quoting prices (yields) at which they will sell/buy government securities such as Treasury bills, Reserve Bank bills, bonds etc. *See* **volume tender**.

tender rate
Belgium: The rate at which the central bank supplies structural liquidity to financial institutions in the Belgo-Luxembourg Economic Union (BLEU) through seven-day advances or repos, by way of an auction. It is usually in line with the central rate. A change in the central rate is thus normally followed by a change in the tender rate. *See* **central rate**.
Finland: The tender rate is set through central bank auctions of one-month paper, that is, the weighted average of all the latest accepted bids for central bank funds or certificates (its own certificates of deposit (CDs), commercial bank CDs or Treasury bills) offered for sale in the money market.

TIM (central bank intervention bills or monetary intervention certificates)
Portugal: Central bank securities issued for maturities of 4, 9, 13, 26 and 52 weeks and bought/sold at auction to inject/drain liquidity. The interest rate set at auctions of TIMs is called either the 'liquidity injection' or 'liquidity mop-up' rate. *See* **liquidity injection rate, liquidity mop-up rate**.

Treasury bill
A non-interest-bearing discount security issued by the Treasury and sold by the central bank to control the money market or to finance the national debt. *See* **bill, Reserve Bank bill**.

Treasury overdraft
Italy: Facility requiring the Bank of Italy to make loans to the Treasury up to the legal limit set on the overdraft.

Treasury certificate of deposit (CDs)
Norway: short-term (one year or less) interest-bearing negotiable securities first issued by the Treasury in January 1985. The central bank is a market-maker for the securities in the secondary market. They are quoted on the Oslo Stock Exchange.

TRM (central bank monetary certificates or monetary regulation bills)
Portugal: Central bank certificates issued for maturities of up to 14 days sold at auction to drain liquidity. The interest rate set at auctions of TIMs is called the either the 'liquidity injection' or 'liquidity mop-up' rate. *See* **liquidity injection rate, liquidity mop-up rate**.

U

uncollateralized overnight call rate
Japan: The interest rate financial institutions pay to borrow overnight funds secured without the backing of any collateral. It is the most important short-term Japanese interbank money market rate. The Bank of Japan appears to have an unpublished target zone for what is called the overnight *mutan* call rate. (*Mutan* is Japanese for uncollateralized, while *yutan* means collateralized). *See* **call money rate.**

unofficial cash rate
Australia: Money market rate set in the unofficial market covering banks not authorized as official dealers in Australian government securities of up to one year maturity.

V

volume repos
See **repurchase agreement.**

variable-rate repurchase agreement
See **repurchase agreement.**

W

when issued (W/I)
Short for 'when, as and if issued'. It refers to a transaction made conditionally because a security, although authorized, has not yet been formally issued. US: The period from the announcement of a Treasury issue until the time after the sale when payment has been actually received by the Treasury.

Appendix 1

The rates to watch

Australia

- 'Unofficial' overnight cash rate

Austria

- Gomex rate
- Discount rate
- Lombard rate

Belgium

- Central rate
- End-of-day (overdraft) rate
- Emergency lending (special overdraft) rate
- Discount rate
- Tender rate
- Special deposit rate

Canada

- Overnight rate
- Three-month Treasury bill rate
- Bank rate
- SPRA rate
- SRA rate

Denmark

- Certificate of deposit (CD) rate
- Repo rate
- Deposit rate
- Discount rate

Finland

- One-month tender rate
- Call money deposit rate
- Liquidity credit rate
- Bank rate
- Three-month certificate of deposit (CD) rate

France

- Intervention rate
- Five-to-10-day lending rate

Germany

- Repo rate
- Discount rate
- Lombard rate

Ireland

- Repo rate
- Short-term facility rate
- Overnight deposit rate

Italy

- Fixed-term advances rate
- Repo rates
- Discount rate

Japan

- Uncollateralized (unsecured) overnight call rate
- Official discount rate

Netherlands

- Special advances rate
- Secured loans rate (interest rate on advances)

New Zealand

- Discount rate
- Overnight rate
- Float tender rate

Norway

- Deposit rate
- Overnight lending rate

Portugal

- Liquidity injection rate
- Liquidity mop-up rate
- Emergency lending rate

Spain

- 10-day repo rate (intervention rate)
- Daily intervention rate (overnight cash rate)
- Rate on *contra poliza* (second window) loans

Sweden

- Marginal lending/deposit rate

Switzerland

- Overnight rate
- Discount rate
- Lombard rate (floating)

United Kingdom

- Money market dealing rate
- Minimum lending rate

United States

- Federal (Fed) funds rate
- Discount rate

192

Appendix 2

Index of central banks

Australia

Reserve Bank of Australia
65 Martin Place
Sydney
New South Wales 2000

Tel: +61 2 551 8111
Fax: +61 2 551 8000
Telex: 071 121636 or 071 20106
Answerback: RESBANK AA 121636 or RESBANK AA 20106

Austria

Austrian National Bank (Nationalbank Oesterreichische)
PO Box 61
A-1011
Vienna

Tel: +43 1 40420
Fax: +43 1 40420 6609 or 6699
Telex: 114778

Belgium

National Bank of Belgium (Banque Nationale de Belgique)
Boulevard de Berlaimont 5
B-1000
Brussels

Tel: +32 2 2212111
Fax: +32 2 2213100
Telex: 046 21105
Answerback: BNBSG B

Canada

Bank of Canada
245 Sparks Street
Ottawa
Ontario K1A OG9

Tel: +1 613 782 8111
Fax: +1 613 782 8655
Telex: 0534241
Answerback: BANKCDA OTT

Denmark

Danish National Bank (Danmarks Nationalbank)
Havnegade 5
DK-1093 Copenhagen K

Tel: +45 33 141411
Fax: +45 33 148539 or 159634

Finland

Bank of Finland (Suomen Pankki Finlands Bank)
PO Box 160
FIN-00101
Helsinki

Tel: +358 0 1831
Fax: +358 0 174872
Telex: 121224
Answerback: SPFB SF

France

Bank of France (Banque de France)
39 Rue Croix des Petits Champs
Paris 1

Tel: +33 1 42 92 39 00
Fax: +33 1 42 92 39 11

Germany

Deutsche Bundesbank
Wilhelm-Epstein-Strasses 14
60431 Frankfurt-am-Main

Tel: +49 69 95 66 21 57
Fax: +49 69 56 87 56
Telex: 069 41 227

Ireland

Central Bank of Ireland (Banc Ceannais na Héireann)
PO Box No. 559
Dame Street
Dublin 2

Tel: +353 1 671 6666
Fax: +353 1 671 6561
Telex: 31041

Italy

Bank of Italy (Banca d'Italia)
Via Nazionale 91
00184 Rome

Tel: +39
Fax: +39
Telex:

Japan

Bank of Japan
CPO Box 203
Tokyo 100-91

Tel: +81 3 3279 1111
Fax: +81 3 3279 5801
Telex: 07222763
Answerback: NITIGIN

Netherlands

The Netherlands Bank (De Nederlandsche Bank)
Westeinde 1
1017 Amsterdam

Tel: +31 20 524 9111
Fax: +31 20 524 2500
Telex: 10701

New Zealand

Reserve Bank of New Zealand
2 The Terrace
PO Box 2498
Wellington

Tel: +64 4 472 2029
Fax: +64 4 473 2250
Telex: 3368
Answerback: NZX

Norway

Bank of Norway (Norges Bank)
PB 1179 Sentrum
N-0107
Oslo

Tel: +47 22 31 60 00
Fax/Telex: + 47 22 41 31 05

Portugal

Bank of Portugal (Banco de Portugal)
Rua do Comercio 148
Piso 2
1100 Lisbon

Tel: +351 1 3462931
Fax: +351 1 523938
Telex: 18565/6 or 63447
Answerback: BIGILP

Spain

Bank of Spain (Banco de España)
Alcala 50
Madrid 14

Tel: +34 1 3385000
Fax: +34 1 4203641

Sweden

Sveriges Riksbank
103 37 Stockholm

Tel: +46 8 7870000
Fax: +46 8 210531
Telex: 19150
Answerback: RIKSBK S

Switzerland

Swiss National Bank (Banque Nationale Suisse)
PO Box 8022
Zurich

Tel: +41 1 631 31 11
Fax: +41 1 631 39 11
Telex: 045812581
Answerback: BVZCH

United Kingdom

Bank of England
Threadneedle Street
London
EC2R 8AH

Tel: +44 71 601 4444
Fax: +44 71 601 4771
Telex: 885001
Answerback: BKENA G

United States

Federal Reserve Bank of New York
33 Liberty Street
New York
NY 10045

Tel: +1 212 720 5000
Fax: +1 212 720 6628

The Publisher....

Probus is a major force on the international business and finance publishing scene. We are committed to publishing the very finest books and information products. Our range of quality books in core business subjects such as investments, banking, the capital markets, accountancy, taxation, property, insurance, sales management, marketing and healthcare, is second to none. We believe that you will find many other titles in our range to be of interest. Are you a writer? If so, please feel free to refer potential publications to us.

You may wish to contact Probus direct at:

Probus Publishing Company	*OR*	Probus Europe
1925 North Clybourn Avenue		11 Millers Yard
Chicago		Mill Lane
Illinois 60614		Cambridge CB2 1RQ
USA		England
Tel: (312) 868-1100		Tel: (0223) 322018
Tel [Sales]: 1-800-PROBUS-1		Fax: (0223) 61149
Fax: (312) 868-6250		

The World's Futures & Options Markets, Nick Battley (Ed.)
1029pp, Probus Europe, 1994. ISBN 1 55738 513 0

Where in the world can you trade euroyen futures? Is there a Finnish interest rate contract available? Which is the most heavily-traded of the world's five eurodollar futures contracts? The answers to all these questions—and more—can be found in this fully-classified directory, making it **the** essential reference work for everyone with a professional or personal interest in futures and options. This major publication features detailed information on over 550 contracts, categorized by type and listed alphabetically for ease of reference. Of course, in addition to the contracts, the 51 exchanges on which they are traded are covered in full detail.

For those with an appetite for statistics, the appendices contain 7-year historical volume figures, not only for almost every contract, but also for each exchange.

To bring the world of international futures and options directly to your your desk, place an order with your bookseller, or call (0223) 322018 in the UK or (312) 868 1100 in the United States.

COPING SUCCESSFULLY WITH HAY FEVER

Coping Successfully With Hay Fever

Dr Robert Youngson

ISIS
LARGE PRINT
Oxford, England

First published in Great Britain 1995
by Sheldon Press

Published in Large Print 1996 by Isis Publishing Ltd,
7 Centremead, Osney Mead, Oxford OX2 0ES,
by arrangement with Sheldon Press

British Library Cataloguing in Publication Data
Youngson, R. M. (Robert Murdoch), 1926–
  Coping successfully with hay fever. – Large Print ed. –
(Overcoming common problems)
1. Hay fever – Popular works 2. Hay fever – Treatment –
Popular works
I. Title
616.2'02

ISBN 1-85695-074-3 (hb)
ISBN 0-7531-5122-7 (pb)

Printed and bound by Hartnolls Ltd, Bodmin, Cornwall

CONTENTS

To Elaine

INTRODUCTION

Every year, millions of people — an estimated 20 per cent of the population — suffer distress, discomfort and embarrassment whenever the pollen count rises. Seasonal misery from hay fever, with itching and watering of eyes and noses, constant sneezing, nasal congestion and redness of the eyes, popping of the ears, constant clearing of the throat and coughing, takes much of the pleasure out of the best times of the year, and can prevent people from going to areas of natural beauty. It can also cause problems for young people taking important exams during the summer. Non-seasonal forms of the disorder affect people all the year round and these sometimes develop into more serious allergies. Some ten per cent of hay fever sufferers are also asthmatics or develop asthma.

Hay fever has been becoming increasingly common and is now ranked as the sixth most prevalent persistent condition in the major developed countries. In this respect it now outranks heart disease. Hay fever is not only unpleasant in its own right, but it also features a number of complications some of which can be even more troublesome — middle ear problems, hearing upsets, sinusitis, alteration of the sense of smell, sleep disturbances and mouth-breathing. Many conditions previously unsuspected of being allergic in nature are now known to be features of hay fever.

Recent years have seen great advances in the understanding of the immune system disturbances that underlie hay fever, and with these advances have come new and better forms of treatment. If you are a sufferer, the key to your personal management of hay fever is knowledge of these new facts. This book contains a straightforward account in clear, simple language of all the essential scientific facts underlying this annoying condition. It is not a medical textbook, but if you read it carefully the chances are that you will end up knowing more about hay fever than the average health professional. More importantly, you will know much that will help you to minimize the effect of this distressing condition on your life.

This book contains a number of "case histories" illustrating important points in the story. It would not do to publish actual excerpts from clinical notes so these cases are presented in fictional form. All the events described in these cases, however, actually happened.

CHAPTER
ONE

What is Hay Fever?

Although doctors commonly use the term *hay fever* when talking to patients, they don't use it so much among themselves. This is because doctors know that the condition has nothing to do with hay and doesn't cause fever. So the more formal members of the medical profession tend to stick to the medically correct term, seasonal allergic rhinitis (see p. 6). In this book, however, I can be as informal as I like, so I'm going to carry on using the well-known colourful term, however unscientific. First, a quick look at the background to the condition.

A short history of hay fever

The term "hay fever" appears to have been used first in 1829 by a Dr Gordon writing in the now long-forgotten *Medical Gazette*. In his article on the condition he sometimes called it hay-asthma and sometimes hay-fever. There is another early reference in *Tweedie's System of Practical Medicine*, published in 1840. This early doctors' book talks of "The summer catarrh, hay-fever or hay-asthma as it is termed from its supposed connexion with the effluvium of new hay." In

1

a letter written in 1840, the popular cleric and humorist Sydney Smith wrote: "I am suffering from my old complaint hay-fever." And in Martineau's *History of the Peace*, we find a reference, dated 1951, to another noted sufferer: "The King enjoyed an exemption from his annual attack of hay-fever."

Although these were the earliest uses of the term, the condition must have been well known to sufferers long before this. So far as we know, people have suffered from hay fever from the dawn of humankind. Certainly, as soon as people started taking an interest in the things that can go wrong with the body and writing down their observations and ideas, there have been accounts of the condition. Mostly it was referred to as "catarrh" — a term applied to what we now know are several different conditions. One reference, of 1586, probably describing hay fever, goes: "Sodainely choked with catarrhes which like to floods of waters, runne downewards." In those days, the discharge from the nose and eyes was believed to come from the brain.

It was not until the 19th century that doctors began to get an idea of the real nature of hay fever. In 1819, a London physician, Dr John Bostock, wrote an account of a seasonal catarrhal condition affecting the nose. The description makes it clear that he was referring to hay fever. For a time, this condition was known as "Bostock's summer catarrh". The matter was taken a step further in 1831 when a detailed account of the condition was written by Dr John Elliotson. Elliotson's paper includes the perceptive remark by a patient that the disorder was brought on by pollen.

In 1872 and 1873 an English non-medical scientist, Charles Blackley, and an American scientist, Morril Wymann, who had been working independently on the problem for 20 years, published their results. Wymann noticed that hay fever symptoms were at their worst when ragweed flowered. He then sent parcels of ragweed to various people and produced the symptoms in those who were prone to hay fever. Blackley was a Manchester man and apprenticed to the printer and Quaker George Bradshaw of railway timetable fame. He was a hay fever sufferer and performed many experiments on himself and others to try to find the cause of the disorder. He applied pollens to many parts of his own body and even scratched some of it through the skin, causing a severe reaction. He also carried out experiments with sticky plates, some of them flown up in kites, to check for the presence of pollen in the atmosphere. Both his and Wymann's reports showed conclusively that hay fever was caused by grass and weed pollens. Another scientist was able to show that asthma could be caused in exactly the same way. These discoveries were of great interest to doctors who were, at the time, deeply concerned with the new ideas that many diseases were caused by invisible germs or microbes. This was a new idea — a disorder caused by a substance that was not a germ and did not produce an infection that could be spread to others.

By the turn of the century those who knew most about the subject were aware that some people could be affected by certain substances in such a way that, although nothing happened at the first contact, they were somehow changed so that they became unusually

3

sensitive to the substance. A second contact could then produce a severe reaction. In 1906 Dr Clemens Pirquet, working in Vienna, suggested that the new word "allergy" should be applied to this mysterious hypersensitivity. This word quickly caught on.

At the same time, what at first seemed to be a completely different line of investigation was going on. This field of study had been started over a hundred years before by the English country doctor Edward Jenner who had found an effective preventive for the dreadful disease of smallpox. Jenner had heard a milkmaid say that she could never get smallpox because she had had the trivial condition of cowpox. She was simply repeating what was, to her, a well-known country belief. People who had contracted cowpox while milking never developed smallpox, even if they were in close contact with a case. So Jenner experimented on a boy, infecting him with material from a cowpox blister and then, rather rashly, infecting him with material from a severe case of smallpox. Both Jenner and the boy were lucky. The boy remained healthy, Jenner published his work, and the quiet country doctor became world famous. It was not long before thousands of people, including the Royal Family, had been vaccinated, and in recognition of his achievement, Parliament voted Jenner £30,000.

This was the beginning of the science of immunology. During the 19th century, many other protective inoculations were developed, especially by the French scientist Louis Pasteur and the German bacteriologist Robert Koch. At first, no one had the least idea how an attack of a disease could protect against another attack, but at the beginning of the 20th century the German bacteriologist Paul Ehrlich was able to prove that when the body was infected, it produced substances that combatted the infection. These substances remained in the body and, if a further infection occurred, were again produced, but in greater quantity so that there was complete protection.

Ehrlich won the Nobel Prize in medicine in 1908. By 1937, the nature of the protective substances were known. They were soluble proteins called *globulins*. From then on, progress was rapid. Hundreds of scientists devoted their lives to working out the processes of immunology and by 1962 everything important was known about antibodies.

You may be wondering what all this has to do with hay fever. The connection is quite simple. Hay fever is an allergy and allergy is the result of the immune system going slightly off the rails. So before you can understand hay fever you have to know a bit about the immune system and how it can go wrong. This is not really as complicated and difficult as you may think and it is well worth taking the trouble. These days, the immune system is very much in the news, and all well-informed people should know at least the basics of the subject. So, as well as helping you to cope with your hay fever, this book will enable you to understand other immune system disorders, such as AIDS. The real study of the scientific basis of hay fever starts in the next chapter, but first there are a few basic but important things to be said about the condition.

What is hay fever?

Strictly speaking, hay fever should be called *seasonal allergic rhinitis*. Another official term is *pollenosis*. Both of these are a bit of a mouthful and neither seems likely to catch on with the general public, but they are worth explaining as they actually tell us a lot more than the term hay fever.

Rhinitis just means inflammation of the nose — in this case the inner lining of the nose. This word comes from the Greek root *rhino*, which means "nose" and the ending *-itis*, which means "inflammation". Every medical word ending in *-itis* is referring to inflammation of something. Appendicitis is inflammation of the appendix; gastritis is inflammation of the stomach; otitis, inflammation of the ear; dermatitis, inflammation of the skin; and so on. Rhinitis is not necessarily seasonal or allergic. Allergic rhinitis is nose lining inflammation caused by an allergy. You will learn all about allergy in the next chapter, and you may be surprised to find how interesting it is. If you are a hay fever sufferer, this is certainly something you should clearly understand.

A seasonal allergy, of course, is one occurring at a particular season of the year. This book is largely concerned with spring and summer allergic rhinitis — which are slightly different from each other — but it also deals with non-seasonal, or *perennial*, allergic rhinitis. Perennial just means "occurring throughout the year". This is due to many causes such as house dusts, house dust mites, or animal fur or skin flakes, and can affect sufferers at any time. This important form of the disorder is dealt with in Chapter 5. Here, we will concentrate on seasonal allergic rhinitis.

The word *pollenosis* sounds impressive, but it just means "a condition related to pollen". Doctors find the rather vague ending *-osis* is quite useful, as it can be used to indicate any process, state, disease condition, cause or formation. If *-itis* doesn't fit, the chances are that *-osis* will. Pollenitis would hardly do, as that would mean inflammation of pollen — which is nonsense — so it has to be pollenosis. There are plenty of medical words ending in *-osis* — words like *fibrosis* (the development of fibrous tissue); *silicosis* (a lung disease caused by silicon dusts); *acidosis* (excess acid); *psychosis* (a disease of the mind); *agranulocytosis* (a shortage of white cells in the blood); and so on. The word pollenosis really doesn't tell us very much about the nature of the condition, however, so, having understood what it means, we can ignore it.

People with hay fever have developed an allergy to one or other of these pollens, spores, dusts, mite products or other animal products. Any object that causes an allergic response in a person is called an *allergen*. Contact between the allergen and the membranes lining the nose or eyes of the sensitized person results in an attack of hay fever.

You can read all about the symptoms of hay fever in Chapter 3. It is hardly necessary to remind you of all the ways in which hay fever can interfere with your social, educational, business, professional or sexual life; if you were not concerned about this you would probably not be reading this book. But it is worth mentioning that, in Britain, up to 20 per cent of the population are affected to some degree by hay fever and some five per cent suffer significant interference with normal life and work.

Hay fever has been getting steadily more common over the whole course of the 20th century and there has been a striking increase in the incidence over the past 30 years. In Britain and America, hay fever accounts for about three per cent of all medical consultations, and a large number of sufferers never bother to consult their doctors. When allergic asthma, sinusitis and allergic skin reactions — the other diseases caused in the same way — are included, the figures are even more striking. In some countries, such as the United States, about a quarter of the population are affected. It is estimated that ten million Britons and 40 million Americans suffer from hay fever, asthma and other allergic diseases.

Pollens and other hay fever triggers

The spring type of seasonal allergy is triggered by airborne tree pollens, especially elm, birch, elder, plane, ash, pine, oak and maple. Most hay fever victims are allergic to grass pollens alone and suffer most severely a little later in the year. But some unfortunates are also allergic to tree and weed pollens, and have a bad time for months.

There are about 150 different species of grass in Britain but fortunately only about a dozen or so cause much trouble. If you are good at identifying grasses, you might be interested to know that among the common British grasses whose pollens cause hay fever are:

- Rye grass (*Lolium perenne*);
- Cocksfoot (*Dactylis glomerata*);
- Crested dog's tail (*Cynosurus cristatus*);
- Yorkshire fog grass (*Holcus lanatus*);
- Timothy grass (*Phleum pratense*).

Sometimes the problem is caused by airborne fungus spores, mainly of the genera *Aspergillus*, *Cladosporium* and *Alternaria*. You might be able to discover that you have an exclusive allergy to these if your attacks occur only at the times when they produce their spores. In Britain fungus spore production peaks in August and September. In other countries, check the situation in the late summer and early autumn (see also Chapter 11). These spores are usually released in a more localized geographic area than are tree or grass pollens. Weed pollens, such as those from the nettle dock or the water dock, can also cause hay fever. In North America, the big culprits are the green tassel-like flowers of the ragweed *Ambrosia artemisifolia*.

The heavy, sticky pollen produced by brightly-coloured flowers is not a major source of trouble. This is not because such pollen cannot cause allergies — it can — but because this kind of pollen is not, to any great extent, carried by the wind. Flower pollen of this kind is transported by insects, especially bees, when it sticks to their legs and bodies.

The timing of hay fever

Different allergens cause their problems at different times of the year. The chances are that you will be

9

affected by only one. Spring hay fever is triggered by tree pollens. Usually, oak tree pollen is the first to be released, followed by birch and plane tree pollen, then ash and pine. The summer type of allergy is due to grass and weed pollens. In the south of England, the worst time for grass pollen allergy is from mid-May until the end of July. North of Scotland sufferers have their worst time about five weeks later.

Pollen is released in the morning and rises throughout the afternoon. The grains are very small and light — only about 10–20 thousandths of a millimetre (10–20 microns) in diameter. This gives them a remarkable performance in air and they often rise to an altitude of about 3,000 metres (10,000 feet). In the country, pollen counts are usually highest between 3.30 and 6.00 pm. In town, the count rises to a peak at about 7.30 pm. The reason for the later timing in town is that, during the afternoons, rising thermal currents carry the pollen high out of harm's way. Unfortunately, during the evening, cooling of the air occurs and the pollen is brought down again.

A similar effect occurs at the seaside. Because of prevailing winds, much of the pollen is blown out to sea during the day. In the evening, however, winds tend to change and become onshore, bringing the pollen back in again. This is why sufferers at the seaside commonly have attacks during the evening.

The pollen count

Since pollen grains carried in the air are the trigger for attacks of hay fever, it is obviously of great interest to know how much pollen is in the lower atmosphere at any particular time. Pollen counting is of interest also to the meteorologists and is regularly done by them, as part of a more general measurement of atmospheric pollution.

Pollen counting is done by directing a continuous jet of the air being studied onto a stationary or moving surface specially prepared so that any pollen grains in the air will stick to it. The rate of flow of the air is known and the length of time the jet continues is accurately measured. In this way, the total volume of air involved is known. Sample areas of the surface are then counted by microscopy for adherent grains. This gives a measure of the concentration of pollen in the air.

Of course, the measurement really applies only to the area in which the measurement is done. Pollen levels can vary widely from place to place and official figures give only a general indication. They do, however, indicate that a risk is present. If the pollen count is high at the weather station where it is made, the chances are that it will be high elsewhere in the region.

Hay fever and the weather

The pollen count alone cannot fully predict whether you are in for trouble. If, however, pollen counts are taken in conjunction with the local weather situation, they can provide a much better forecast of the severity of the hay fever suffered by the population concerned. Given reliable weather forecasting, it is possible to predict the severity of hay fever to an accuracy as high as 80 per cent.

The worst kind of weather for hay fever is, unfortunately, the kind of weather most people enjoy best — no rain, plenty of sunshine and a rising temperature. In Holland, Dr F. T. M. Spieksma of Leiden University worked out a weather points system for hay fever sufferers. This gave a score of from 1 to 10. The lower the score the worse the weather and the better for hay fever victims. This score has been broadcast daily during the hay fever season on Dutch radio, giving sufferers the opportunity to adjust their treatment or modify their holiday plans.

In the lower atmosphere, the temperature is normally highest near the ground and becomes progressively cooler further up. Temperature inversion is the term given to a local situation in which the temperature is lower near the ground than at higher altitudes. The normal situation allows steady up-currents (*convection currents*) that carry up pollen and other pollutants, partly dispersing and diluting them. In a temperature inversion situation, however, convection current air flow cannot occur and the pollutants are kept down near the ground. Temperature inversion is very bad news for everyone, as it increases the concentration of all the undesirable material. It is the cause of the nasty smogs that can make so many cities uncomfortable and some, like Los Angeles, practically uninhabitable. It is particularly bad news for hay fever sufferers. Not only does it increase the pollen concentration, it also increases the other elements in the atmosphere that can make hay fever much worse.

The effect of other atmospheric pollutants

It has been known for a long time that hay fever is made worse by other pollutants in the atmosphere. The reason for this is gradually becoming clear. Many atmospheric pollutants, especially the nitrogen oxides from car exhausts and the ozone that is produced by the action of sunlight on these oxides, are damaging to the lining of the nose. Nature has provided us with a remarkable layer of lining cells to the respiratory system. These cells carry millions of fine, microscopic hair-like processes, called *cilia*, that beat backwards and forwards in a purposeful manner rather like wind blowing a field of ripe corn. This movement carries fine particles and mucus out of the sensitive parts of the nose towards the nostrils.

Nitrogen oxides, even in quite low concentrations can damage the cilia-bearing cells. For instance, 0.4 parts per million of nitrogen dioxide will interfere with the action of the cilia. Two parts per million will kill the cilia cells. If this happens, pollen grains are obviously going to be kept longer in contact with the nose lining so that they are more likely to trigger an allergic response. The levels of these dangerous oxides from traffic fumes have been rising steadily for years and have been accompanied by a similar rise in the number and severity of cases of hay fever. This association also helps to explain the surprising fact that hay fever is commoner in towns than in the country in spite of the fact that pollens are more plentiful in the rural setting.

The outlook in hay fever

You may be encouraged to learn that hay fever disappears spontaneously in some five to ten per cent of sufferers. Why this should be remains a mystery. Those who are fortunate enough to enjoy this unexpected relief are people with comparatively mild seasonal allergy which has persisted for no more than about five years. Regrettably, if that period has passed and you are still prone to attacks, you are likely to be permanently affected. The only hope for a complete cure, in such a case, lies in the rather controversial desensitization treatment (see Chapter 7).

People with established hay fever or perennial allergic rhinitis (PAR) have about one chance in ten of developing the closely associated condition of allergic asthma. There is also a small chance of developing one or other of the various complications of hay fever (see Chapter 10). Don't be too discouraged by these gloomy prognostications. The chances are that you will have no such troubles. And there is a great deal you can do to control and alleviate the symptoms you do have.

Now that we have got the preliminaries out of the way, we can get down to the real business of understanding allergy. You may find the next chapter a little difficult, but it is really the most important chapter of the book and contains facts that should be known to every well-informed person. It is of particular importance to you if you are a hay fever sufferer, as it is only by understanding the scientific basis of the problem that you can tackle your problem logically and effectively.

CHAPTER
TWO

Understanding Allergy

The term *allergy* is often used wrongly. Many substances can adversely affect the body and can do so in various ways, but these effects are not necessarily allergic. Unfortunately, the idea of allergy has caught the public imagination and some misunderstanding has resulted. Food allergy, for instance, is really quite rare, certainly far less common than is generally supposed. As for the "total allergy syndrome", this is excessively rare — almost unknown — and much more likely to be a psychological problem than an allergy.

Allergy is an abnormal bodily response due to a minor defect in the action of the immune system of the body. This is not to say that the effects of this fault are necessarily minor — you would not be reading this book if they were. Sometimes these effects are very serious. But, as we shall see, much worse things can happen to the immune system than the defect that causes allergy. You will not be able to understand allergy without a basic knowledge of the immune system and how it works. So let's take a look at what is one of the most remarkable and interesting systems of the body.

Where is the immune system?

Don't be put off by the fact that this system — unlike the other systems of the body, such as the nervous system, the digestive system or the respiratory system — is largely invisible. This is because these other systems are based on large organs like the brain, the intestine and the lungs, while the immune system is based primarily on tiny, microscopic, individual and often free-roaming, cells. The whole body is, of course, made of cells but most of these are stuck together to form tissues and organs. The cells of the immune system are everywhere — in the blood, in the tissue fluids which bathe the body cells, and even between the cells that make up every organ of the body.

The only part of the immune system that you can actually see without a microscope are the collection of *lymph nodes* (usually called "glands") and various masses of lymphoid tissue such as the tonsils, adenoids and spleen. The lymph nodes are small, soft, bean-shaped bodies found all over the body, but mainly in the neck, armpits, groins and around the main arteries of the chest and abdomen. These nodes are packed with immune system white cells, and are connected together by a fine network of clear tubes known as *lymphatics* which eventually drain into veins in the chest. The spleen is a larger, spongy organ lying in the upper left side of the abdomen, just to the left of the stomach. It has a very good blood supply and it, too, is packed with immune system cells.

How the immune system works

The object of the immune system is to keep the inside of our bodies free from living things like germs of all kinds, cancer cells and any abnormal and unwanted material that can cause damage. Without an effective immune system we are in real trouble, as people affected in some way by the AIDS epidemic know very well. Many of these invaders — viruses, bacteria, fungi and other single-celled parasites — damage local tissue and cause a reaction known as *inflammation*. The main feature of inflammation is a widening of the local blood vessels so that more blood than usual passes through the affected area. This is why an inflamed part looks red and feels hot. But this increase in blood supply serves a very useful purpose — it brings to the site of infection large numbers of the white blood cells that make up part of the immune system.

To do its job properly, the immune system has to be able to tell the difference between things that can be allowed to remain safely within the body and those that are dangerous or foreign and must be attacked. Any such foreign objects entering the body are called *antigens*. The immune system can immediately spot foreign antigens and attack them. In addition to dealing with foreign invaders, the immune system must also keep a constant watch over the body's own cells. If these are healthy, well and good. But if they have been attacked by viruses or have become cancerous, they must be destroyed. Without this constant surveillance for cells with cancerous changes, we would all have been dead long ago. Unfortunately, there is a limit to the efficiency of the immune system and, sometimes, too many cells with these changes occur for the system to deal with. In that event an established cancer develops.

The antibodies

The job of identifying foreign material is performed by certain phagocytes, known as *macrophages*. When a macrophage engulfs a foreign organism or cell it immediately alerts other cells of the immune system. These cells are called *lymphocytes* and there are two main kinds — the T lymphocytes and the B lymphocytes. These cells are so important, and have to be mentioned so often by people concerned with the immune system, that they are usually referred to simply as "T cells" and "B cells". But you should remember that they are all lymphocytes.

T cells pick up information from macrophages. The B cells have a different job. Their function is to produce certain protein substances called *antibodies*. Each B cell can produce only one kind of antibody. But there are literally thousands of different kinds of B cells, each capable of making a different antibody best suited to deal with a particular kind of foreign invader.

After the macrophages and their attendant T cells have completed the recognition process, an extraordinary thing happens. The T cells look over the range of the B lymphocytes to find the one capable of producing the most effective antibody against the invader. When they find it, they instruct this cell to multiply and produce numerous daughter lymphocytes, all identical to the one that started. A population of identical cells is called a *clone*. This clone of B cells now starts to produce large quantities of antibodies. Each one may synthesize 2,000 antibodies per minute, and the clone may contain millions of B cells. The antibodies are Y-shaped proteins that quickly bind on to and inactivate the antigens. Once this has occurred, these foreign objects and infected or diseased body cells fall easy prey to other phagocytes and are soon eaten up and destroyed.

B lymphocytes that have been activated in this way can survive for many years, preventing us from suffering a second attack of many infectious diseases. When a second infection occurs, they are ready and waiting, and will, if necessary, clone more copies of themselves to produce more of the same antibody. This is also how immunization works. It is a fairly easy matter to identify antibodies precisely from a small sample of blood. Different people who have had the same infection carry the same antibodies and these can be pinpointed in the laboratory. So it is easy to tell whether a person has had any particular infection, even if they have been cured of it years before.

More about antibodies

Antibodies are proteins. Some proteins, such as those of meat (muscle), are fairly obvious; others are not because they are dissolved in the blood. The soluble proteins include a group called the globulins and these include all the antibodies. Because these globulins are concerned with the immune system, they are called *immunoglobulins*. Although the body can produce many thousands of different antibodies, these fall into five well-defined groups. The name immunoglobulin is already rather a mouthful and, since it is often necessary to say which group you are concerned with, it is a good idea to shorten the name. Doctors therefore talk of *Ig* for immunoglobulin and then add the letter that indicates the group.

The most plentiful group of antibodies is immunoglobulin class G, usually abbreviated to *IgG* or often called *gamma globulin*. Three quarters of the immunoglobulins in the blood of healthy people are IgG. IgG antibodies are concerned with protection against a wide range of germs. Only one of the other four antibody groups need concern us here — the immunoglobulin class E. IgE is the antibody type that is involved in hay fever. It is also the antibody group concerned in causing asthma and other allergic reactions. Needless to say, you will find quite a lot about IgE in this book. Like all the other immunoglobulins, IgE is produced by B cells. These are present in large numbers in the nose lining, the tonsils and in the wall of the intestine.

People who do not have allergy problems produce hardly any IgE; people with hay fever, allergic asthma, severe allergies and eczema have lots of it. You can even cause an entirely healthy person to develop hay fever simply by giving him or her an injection of the serum from a hay fever sufferer. This serum contains IgE and by giving this immunoglobulin you can convert a non-allergic person into an allergic person.

Recent research has shown that the body can manufacture IgE only if certain types of T cells of the immune system are present. These cells, the "helper" T cells are, incidentally, the ones that get knocked out by the human immunodeficiency virus (HIV), thus causing AIDS. It seems likely that people who do not suffer from hay fever have very few of this particular group of helper T cells, whereas those who do have plenty of them.

In spite of a great deal of research, we still don't know for certain what IgE is for. The function of all the other immunoglobulin groups is clear and they are all obviously beneficial, but IgE seems to be good for nothing and when it does have an effect, that effect is harmful. There was thus great excitement among the immunologists a few years ago when it was found that people in the tropics with worm parasites had high levels of IgE in their bodies. This suggested that the original function of IgE might have been to protect against such parasites. Presumably, worms and other similar parasites are no more enthusiastic about the effects of IgE than people are. Be that as it may, the idea provides cold comfort to people who are never likely to have a problem with worms but who greet the spring of each year with sinking hearts.

How can the immune system go wrong?

This can happen in various ways. Because of AIDS, the best known, these days, is immune deficiency. This group of diseases had, however, been familiar to doctors for many years before AIDS appeared. Immune deficiency can be present at birth as a genetic disorder of various degrees of severity. In rare cases this is so complete that the baby has to be kept in a sealed chamber if there is to be any chance of surviving. Immune deficiency can also be acquired later in life in various ways. These include:

- insufficient protein intake from malnutrition to make antibodies;
- loss of antibodies in the urine as a result of kidney disease;
- radiation damage affecting the production of immune system cells;
- long-term use of antibiotics and other drugs that damage the immune system;
- the effect of old age;
- the acquired immune deficiency syndrome (AIDS).

AIDS is caused by HIV, which attacks T cells, preventing them from carrying out their normal task of identifying foreign invaders. As a result, the body becomes prone to develop infections of all kinds and is much more liable to develop cancer.

So what has all this to do with allergy?

You may be wondering why it is that, although all of us breathe in pollen grains from the atmosphere, only some of us get hay fever. The reason is that there is a genetic condition called *atopy* that causes people to react to certain substances in a certain way. Atopy is hereditary and may show itself either as hay fever or as asthma or as the skin problem *eczema*. Some unfortunates have all three but usually one or other predominates.

People who get hay fever have an inherited tendency to become over-sensitive to substances, specifically certain proteins present in pollen grains, that are completely harmless to 80 per cent of the population. These substances are commonly called *allergens*. You already know quite a number of other important things about them, but to recapitulate briefly, these are that:

- they are *antigens*;
- the body recognizes them as foreign;
- the body reacts to them by producing antibodies;
- these antibodies are proteins, known as immuno-globulins;
- they are produced by B lymphocytes;
- the antibodies produced are in a special immuno-globulins class known as class E;
- they are therefore known as IgE.

In hay fever the antigens are in the seasonal pollens in the inhaled air. These pollen grains enter the nose and are trapped by a layer of sticky mucus. The fine moving hairs (cilia) on the lining cells immediately start to try to move them out. But before they can get rid of them, a chemical activator (*enzyme*) called *lysozyme*, that is present in the tissues, digests off the outer coats of the grains and releases the protein antigens.

Now we come to the villains of the piece.

The mast cells

Back in 1877 the brilliant German scientist Paul Ehrlich — the first man to produce an effective antibacterial drug that could be taken internally — noticed some rather peculiar cells under his microscope and took the trouble to record his observations. These cells, when stained, were seen to be packed with round bodies like granules. Ehrlich assumed that these cells were phagocytes and that the granules were "food" particles that the cells had taken up. For this reason he decided to call them mast cells. (In German, the word *mast* means "a feed for fattening".) Neither Ehrlich nor anyone else had any idea what the mast cells did, so after that they were largely forgotten. Today, the mast cells are at the centre of interest of anyone concerned with allergies and especially hay fever.

Situated within and just under the lining of the nose in people who suffer from hay fever, allergic asthma and severe allergies, are millions of mast cells. These are formed in the bone marrow and are carried in the blood to all parts of the body where they lodge in most kinds of tissue. Interestingly, people who do not suffer from hay fever have comparatively few mast cells in their nose linings.

Mast cells can easily be seen with a modern microscope. If a swab or a scraping containing mast cells is stained in the usual manner for microscopy, these cells are seen to be full of tiny, deep-staining spots known as granules. These granule-filled mast cells are of basic importance in allergy. In people with hay fever the number of mast cells in the nose and throat lining increases steadily as the hay fever season advances.

The granules in the mast cells are actually tiny droplets containing a very nasty mixture of highly active substances. These substances have various effects, all of them unpleasant. The most important and best known of them is called *histamine* and this is the one you should know about. Histamine does no harm so long as it remains safely locked up in the granules of the mast cells. But if these granules are released it is free to act.

This is what histamine does:

- it causes the secreting cells in the nose lining to produce mucus and watery secretions;
- it increases the leakage of fluid from small veins so that membranes swell;
- it attacks local nerve endings causing itching and burning;
- it contracts smooth muscles, including those in the walls of the air tubes (bronchioles) of the lungs.

In addition to histamine, freed granules release protein-splitting enzymes, called *proteases*, which can damage small blood vessels. They also release substances called prostaglandins that are powerful nerve stimulators and a range of substances called *leukotrienes*, which are even more potent narrowers of the air tubes than histamine. All this, of course, leads to the general misery of the hay fever victim. This, too, is the mechanism that leads to allergic asthma.

There is another important point to be made about mast cells. If the amount of natural body steroid — the secretion of the adrenal glands situated on top of the kidneys — is increased, mast cells are seriously discouraged from appearing. As we shall see, this fact can be exploited as a way of preventing, or minimizing the severity of, hay fever.

Degranulation

The central fact to appreciate about mast cells is that they love IgE. Mast cells have thousands of special sites on their surfaces that IgE antibodies fit into perfectly. These are called IgE receptor sites. So anyone who produces a lot of the particular type of IgE produced by hay fever victims is going to have mast cells already covered with IgE. This is when another remarkable thing happens.

You already know that antibodies work by latching onto antigens. This is their whole function in life. They are, chemically, of just the right shape to fit the antigens like a key fits a lock. When IgE is in place on the mast cells and new pollen antigens come along, the latter, of course, immediately get linked to the IgE. But this happens in a rather peculiar way. Instead of one antigen attaching to one antibody, each pollen antigen bridges across two or more adjacent IgE antibodies. This causes the outer membrane of the mast cell to distort so severely that it ruptures. And, of course, when that happens, the granules pour out. This is called *degranulation*.

Degranulation occurs within 20 minutes of exposure

to the pollen antigen and it occurs even in mast cells one millimetre below the surface. Degranulation, of course, releases histamine and all the other unpleasant substances that act on the local tissues to cause the symptoms of hay fever.

Late effects

Unfortunately, this is not necessarily all that happens. For many people, hay fever is not much more than a considerable nuisance. But for others various complications may arise, and some are quite serious. You can read about them in Chapter 10. The longer you have hay fever, the more severe it tends to become. The levels of IgE rise progressively and the number of mast cells in your upper respiratory tract increases. The sensitivity to the allergen also increases so that repeated contact produces an increased release of histamine. Perhaps worst of all is the possibility that this process may lead, eventually, to permanent changes in the nose and surrounding areas, in the ears or even in the lungs. Doctors are still arguing about whether or not this latter misfortune actually occurs.

Is hay fever hereditary?

Many cases certainly are hereditary. These are hay fever sufferers with a family history of other allergic problems such as asthma, eczema, nettle-rash, severe reactions to bee and other stings (*anaphylaxis*) and sometimes food allergy. As we have seen, this tendency is called *atopy*, and such people produce far larger quantities of IgE antibodies than do non-allergic people.

Families with atopy have been studied to see whether the genetic basis of allergy can be clarified. Recent research at the Churchill Hospital, Oxford, has shown that it can. The scientists there located the gene responsible for producing the receptor sites on the mast cells to which the IgE molecules attach themselves. In June 1994 they revealed that many families with atopy have a particular variant (*mutation*) of the IgE receptor gene. Surprisingly, this abnormal gene has, in every case, been found to be inherited from the mother. The IgE receptor sites produced by this gene are only very slightly different from those on the mast cells of people without atopy. But this slight difference is enough to affect the way mast cells with IgE respond to pollen grains. It seems that the abnormal IgE receptor sites simply make the mast cells much more sensitive to the triggering effect of the pollen grains.

You will be relieved to know that we are now through the hard part and that from now on it's all pretty plain sailing. There is just one last bit of preliminary study before we go on to deal with the symptoms of hay fever.

More about the nose

Although hay fever involves parts other than the nose, this is the region that suffers the most sustained attack. So, as a hay fever sufferer, the more you know about your nose the better. You have already learned about the remarkable cilia that waft out foreign material caught by the mucus (see Chapter 1). But there is good deal more to the nose than that.

The shape of the nose is determined by a short bone that protrudes from the lower part of the forehead — the nasal bone — and a number of cartilages that are connected together by fibrous tissue. The two halves of the nose are separated by a thin partition made of cartilage in front and bone behind. This is called the *nasal septum*. It is quite easy to change the shape of a nose by sculpting away at the cartilages and to change the degree of protrusion of the nose by filing away part of the bone. The bone and cartilage is covered externally with skin and internally with a layer of mucous membrane. The inner parts of three of the cartilages on each side are curled up so as to increase the surface area over which the inhaled air must pass. These curly, mucous membrane-covered plates are called *turbinates*.

The nose has a remarkably good blood supply — a fact reflected in the ease with which it can be made to bleed. The lining of the nose and the zone between the lining and the cartilages and bone contain many blood vessels — both arteries and veins. The curled turbinates and the septum carry quite large vein channels that can swell easily when filled with blood. For this reason these are called *pseudo-erectile tissue*. The condition popularly known as "stuffy nose" is due to the swelling of these veins and the general congestion of the mucous membrane. Vein channel erection is under the control of part of the nervous system (the *autonomic* system) and, even in perfect health, this usually causes alternate swelling of one side and then the other. This alternation occurs at intervals of between two and seven hours. It is, of course, much more obvious when you have a cold or are suffering from hay fever.

This rich blood supply is capable of raising the temperature of the inspired air by as much as 25°C as it passes from the atmosphere to the back of the nose. The inner openings of the nasal passages are the narrowest part of the entire respiratory system and as a result it is quite hard to get enough air through the nose when the body's oxygen requirements are raised by strong exertion. When the requirement rises above about 30 litres per minute we are forced to open our mouths.

The lining mucous membrane is exceptional in its ability to produce watery secretion and mucus. The water production can be turned on like a tap. This is because of the profusion of glands in the mucous membrane. In the nose there are eight times as many secreting glands in each square millimetre than in the rest of the respiratory system. People who suffer from hay fever know all about the remarkable power of the nose to produce these secretions.

CHAPTER
THREE

The Symptoms of
Hay Fever

Hay fever is not so much a disease as a collection of symptoms. If you take away the symptoms there is really not much left that can harm you. So, however unpleasant, distressing or temporarily disabling the symptoms, hay fever, in itself, is not a dangerous condition. Since symptoms are such an important part of the disorder, let's take a closer look at them.

Sneezing and itching

The most obvious and common symptom of hay fever is sneezing. Millions of people who suffer mildly from hay fever have no more trouble from it than occasional sneezing. At worst they have a succession of uncontrollable sneezes. Sneezing, of course, is a response to irritation occurring within the nose. Its function is to get rid of any irritant or potentially damaging material that finds its way into the nose, especially particles of matter that might be inhaled. The sneezing is not caused directly by the pollen grains; these are much too small to do so. It is caused by histamine (see Chapter 2), released by the mast cells, and acting directly on nerve endings lying between the cells of the lining membrane of the nose.

When these nerve receptors are stimulated by the histamine, several things happen. First there is an immediate reflex indrawing of a very deep breath. Then the vocal cords in the *larynx* (voice box) are pressed tightly together. Next, the muscles of the chest and the diaphragm tighten sharply so as to compress the air in the lungs. At the same time, the tongue is pressed tightly against the roof of the mouth and the soft palate moved clear to open the way to the nose. Finally, the vocal cords are suddenly pulled apart so that a blast of air rushes up the windpipe and out through the nose. This is a very efficient way of getting rid of fluff or other foreign material. Unfortunately, in the case of hay fever, the only things worth getting rid of — the pollen grains — have already done their harm, so the sneeze serves no useful purpose.

Sneezing is nearly always associated with itching and this may be severe. In children, this persistent itching causes the child repeatedly to rub the nose upwards to try to relieve it. This may happen so often that the child develops an obvious transverse ridge or crease across the skin of the lower part of the nose. This sign is well known to specialists in the subject and is known as the "allergic salute".

Fluid and mucus production

Another distressing and embarrassing feature of hay fever is the watery and mucus discharge. Like other cavities, passages and hollow internal organs of the body the nose is lined with a surface called a mucous membrane. Mucous membrane also lines the inner surfaces of the eyelids and covers the whites of the eyes. In the latter location, the mucous membrane is called the *conjunctiva*. Mucous membranes contain large numbers of goblet-shaped cells, which are actually individual secreting glands, and other small fluid-secreting glands. These normally produce moderate quantities of a watery fluid, to keep the membrane moist, and mucus to keep the surface sticky and trap foreign material. Mucus is a slimy, jelly-like material, chemically known as a *mucopolysaccharide* or *glycoprotein*. It has essential protective and lubricating properties and life would be unpleasant, and perhaps impossible, without it. In the nose, the main function of mucus is to assist in the conditioning of inhaled air and to provide a sticky coating that traps inhaled material.

In hay fever, the histamine and other substances released when the mast cells degranulate are powerfully irritating to the mucous membranes of the nose and eyes. The membranes of the eyes contain large numbers of tiny accessory tear glands and fewer mucus glands. As a result of histamine release, all the glands of the membranes start to work overtime, secreting fluid and mucus, sometimes, seemingly, to the limit of their ability. Again, this excessive secretion serves no useful purpose except, possibly, to dilute the histamine. It can, however, cause severe distress to the sufferer. Running nose and eyes can be temporarily disabling as well as embarrassing and can, occasionally, be dangerously distracting. It doesn't help your driving concentration, for instance.

Nasal congestion

As well as causing overactivity of the secretory glands in the nose and eyes, the effects of histamine are to cause swelling of all the cells of the mucous membrane. In addition, the blood vessels of the mucous membrane and those in the network below it widen, pushing the swollen mucous membrane further away from the underlying cartilages. The resulting swelling can be so severe as to obstruct the nose completely. The increased blood supply also means that increased amounts of watery fluid leak out from these blood vessels to add to the swelling of the membrane. An increase in the blood supply also promotes more rapid secretion of the gland cells. If the nose is blocked, secretions may drip down from the rear openings of the nostrils into the throat. This is called *post-nasal drip*.

Persistent inflammation of this kind actually causes the mucous membrane of the nose to become more sensitive to mast cell granule products. It also increases the sensitivity to other irritants that have nothing to do with pollen or the allergic response. People with hay fever are more sensitive to atmospheric pollution than other people and, as we have seen, some atmospheric pollutants interfere with the ciliary action of the nose lining (see Chapter 1) thus prolonging the action of pollen. Persistence of the symptoms of hay fever after the pollen season may be due to this increase in general sensitivity of the nasal mucous membrane. This is one of the causes of perennial allergic rhinitis.

Nasal obstruction from swelling of the mucous membranes forces the affected person to mouth-breathe and affects the quality of the voice. It can also have a serious effect on the functioning of the mucous-membrane-lined *eustachian tubes* that run from the back of the nose to the cavities of the middle ears. These tubes need to be intermittently open so that the pressure can be equalized on both sides of each ear drum. Eustachian blockage from mucous membrane swelling causes deafness and an unpleasant sense of fullness in the head. Many cases of intermittent eustachian catarrh are caused by allergic swelling of the mucous membrane. Long-term blockage can even lead to infection of the middle ear (*otitis media*). This can do permanent harm (see Chapter 10).

In the case of the nose, only the sufferer is much aware of what is happening. In the case of the eyes, however, the effect is highly conspicuous and sometimes almost alarming to the observer.

Eye symptoms

Irritated mucous membranes become inflamed and red and this is readily visible in the eyes of a victim. Even more striking is oedema of the conjunctivas, which may balloon out between the lids as if they were inflated. The conjunctivas are firmly fixed around the margins of the corneas and are securely attached to the insides of the lids. But over the whites of the eyes they lie loosely on the globes. It is thus possible for considerable quantities of fluid to collect *underneath* the conjunctiva causing the dramatic appearance. Sometimes this conjunctival oedema is so severe that the corneas appear as round discs at the bottom of a gelatinous pit and the eyelids are unable to close over the swollen membrane. Fortunately, this kind of oedema always settles.

Another striking effect of allergy on the conjunctivas is known as *vernal catarrh* or *vernal conjunctivitis*. This condition is rare in temperate climates but is very common in tropical and sub-tropical areas and in the Middle East. In such regions it affects mainly children, boys much more often than girls. In vernal catarrh, the conjunctivas become persistently thickened so that a raised, tyre-shaped, gelatinous ring of permanently swollen conjunctiva forms around each cornea. There is intolerable itching, causing great distress, and a stringy, tenacious discharge from the eyes. Vernal conjunctivitis can also cause gelatinous swellings (like cooked sago grains) to develop on the inner surface of the upper lids, with considerable swelling of the lids and severe itching and discharge. In both of these conditions the conjunctivas are packed with mast cells.

Other symptoms

Hay fever sufferers often experience quite strong itching of the ears, itching that may make scratching irresistible. This is not a histamine effect, however, but a referred sensation due to the fact that the same nerve that provides sensation to the back of the throat also supplies the ear canal and the outer ear. Stimulation of the throat branches of this nerve by histamine and other mast cell granule products can cause a sensation to be passed to the ears.

There is another, and more important, way in which hay fever can affect the ears. The swelling of the mucous membrane at the back of the nose and throat can cause a temporary blockage of one or both of the eustachian tubes. These must be capable of passing air if the ears are to work properly. Any obstruction of the tubes causes an uncomfortable feeling of fullness in the ears and sometimes a degree of deafness or a change in the quality of the hearing. You can read more about this in the chapter on complications (Chapter 10).

It is not widely appreciated that many coughs are caused by the same allergic process that causes hay fever. If you find yourself with an intermittent dry cough that seems to come on for no reason in the spring or summer and then disappears as suddenly as it came, there is a distant possibility that this could be the cause. Most of the allergens that cause hay fever are large enough to be trapped in the nose; some, however, are smaller and are able to get down into the air tubes of the lungs.

Secondary symptoms

The symptoms described above are those caused directly by the immunological process. But anyone affected, to any serious extent, by these symptoms will inevitably have a psychological reaction to them. These reactive psychological symptoms are important and a chapter has been devoted to them. You can read about the emotional dimension in Chapter 8.

CHAPTER
FOUR

How Hay Fever is Diagnosed

Hay fever is a condition you can probably diagnose for yourself with a good deal of certainty. But the matter is not always so easy as you might think. In typical and well-marked cases of hay fever the diagnosis is obvious. Here is a review of the symptoms:

- itching and pricking of the nose, palate, throat and eyes;
- paroxysms of sneezing;
- runny nose and eyes;
- stuffiness of the nose with partial or total blockage;
- irritability;
- depression;
- tiredness;
- a general feeling of being unwell (*malaise*).

If these symptoms are associated with exposure to pollen at the appropriate time of the year, there can be little doubt about the diagnosis. Not all cases, however, are so typical and few show all the features just listed. In fact, the great majority of cases of hay fever are very mild, and many are not recognized for what they are. Millions of people sneeze frequently during the pollen seasons but have no other symptoms and are unaware that they have hay fever.

Another important indication that the trouble is hay fever is the fact that the symptoms are worse at certain times of the day than at others. This occurs in hay fever because of differences in the amount of pollen in the atmosphere (see Chapter 1).

Finally, you must try to distinguish hay fever — which is seasonal, from perennial allergic rhinitis (PAR) — which occurs all the year round. The two conditions are otherwise identical, although caused by different allergens. Both involve IgE and mast cells. If the allergy is perennial, you have to consider the possible causes.

Clinical diagnosis

Not all cases of hay fever are as easy to diagnose as the above account suggests. In some, the cause is less obvious and some present in an unusual way. Such cases really require medical attention. Sometimes, in spite of taking a careful history and enquiring into all the obvious possibilities for allergy, the doctor may still be uncertain about the diagnosis. Here is a case history in which this happened.

Introduction
Barbara seemed to have very typical hay fever but there were features that made it unlikely that hers was a

straightforward case. The effect on her life, however, was serious. Considerable medical investigation was required before the problem was solved.

Personal details
Name Barbara Edelman. Unmarried
Age 33
Occupation Senior executive of a small public relations firm
Family One brother. Both parents alive and well

Medical background
Barbara has always enjoyed excellent health. She is an ambitious young woman who works hard and keeps herself fit by playing tennis in the summer and squash in the winter. She has had no serious illnesses and the only feature of her medical background was a fracture of her right tibia and fibula in a skiing accident when she was 22.

The present complaint
For no apparent reason Barbara has begun to have severe attacks of congestion of the nose, burning in her throat with a choking sensation. There is nasal catarrh with a frequent post-nasal drip. These attacks affect her voice and make it very difficult for her to interview clients comfortably. She is embarrassed by the constant necessity to clear her throat and annoyed at the loss of her usual voice resonance.

The history
The doctor is uncertain of the cause of these symptoms, which are not related to the seasons, but occur at regular

intervals. He asks some more questions and Barbara tells him that the attacks are worst in the mornings, that they occur for a few days only every few weeks. She also admits that during the attacks she also has some slight irritation and watering of her eyes. The doctor then enquires into Barbara's personal and family history. Has she or any close relative ever had hay fever, eczema, asthma or nettle-rash? Barbara is a little surprised at these questions but assures him that there is no such history.

Next, he asks about domestic pets. Does Barbara have a cat or a dog? No. The doctor then asks Barbara how often she vacuum cleans her mattress. Barbara considers this rather impertinent but assures him that this is done regularly. The doctor explains that this question is related to the possibility that the problem could be due to house dust mites or their droppings.

The doctor examines Barbara's throat and then inspects the inside of her nose using a torch and a metal speculum to keep each nostril wide open in turn. He informs Barbara that everything appears to be entirely normal, and that the probability is that she is simply suffering from repeated colds. He prescribes some decongestant nose drops. Barbara is dubious but accepts this advice.

Two months later she is back again, insisting that her attacks are not common colds. The doctor decides to refer her to an allergist.

The management in hospital

In the out-patient department the specialist takes a detailed history and agrees with Barbara that she is not having colds. She tells her that her attacks are almost certainly caused by an allergy and takes a sample of blood for an IgE assessment. At her second visit Barbara is told by the specialist that her IgE levels are unusually high, even for a person with severe hay fever. She explains that IgE is the type of antibody associated with allergic reactions such as hay fever, asthma and urticaria. The problem now is to discover the particular allergen that is causing the attacks. She therefore marks a number of little circles on Barbara's arm with a pen and opposite each writes a word such as "grass", "tree", "fungus", "fur", "dander" and so on. The specialist now brings out a range of small labelled bottles containing extracts of various substances. With the glass rods attached to the stoppers she puts a drop of each in the appropriate circle and then, quite gently, pricks through the drop into the skin with sharp needles. Barbara is then asked to sit in the waiting room for 15 minutes.

The doctor's comments

When Barbara returns with an unchanged arm, the allergist looks a little puzzled. She tells her that none of the common allergens are responsible and that a special test will have to be done. This is called a *radio-allergo-sorbent test*, or RAST for short. This test can actually determine the specific form of IgE that the patient is producing and thus identify the allergen. She takes a blood sample and asks Barbara to come back in two weeks' time. During this period Barbara has another severe attack.

On her next visit the allergist tells Barbara that she

has solved the problem. "Your allergy is due to a rather unexpected cause, a mite called *Lepidoglyphus destructor*. This has been found in farm barns, storage areas generally, building sites, bakeries and in damp houses."

Barbara insists that she has been to no such places. The allergist tells her that it must be somewhere she goes to every few weeks as the attacks occur at such intervals. She also tells her that the mite lives on fungi but that these may not be apparent. Barbara insists that this could not possibly be the cause of her problems.

"Don't you go regularly to a bakery, or perhaps some sort of store?" asks the doctor.

"I get my bread from Sainsbury's . . ." Suddenly, Barbara stops. "The attic!" she says. "Could it possibly be the attic? It is a bit mouldy. And I do have to go up there every few weeks because I haven't room for . . ."

"I suspect we've found the answer," said the allergist.

The follow-up

This was indeed the case. The allergist was interested enough in this unusual case to arrange for samples to be taken from the attic dust and *Lepidoglyphus destructor* was identified by an entomological colleague. Barbara had been thinking about having an attic conversion done and this finding tipped the balance. The place was cleared, a great deal of junk thrown away, the area vacuum cleaned, the wood treated and an architect and builder approached.

From the time the attic was cleared and converted Barbara has had no further attacks.

Other IgE tests

It is not often necessary actually to find out what kind of IgE is being produced in the body of a hay fever sufferer. But when this is the only way to be sure of the diagnosis, the doctor has a choice of methods by which the IgE can be identified. These are clever laboratory tests that were originally worked out to identify immunoglobulins (antibodies) for other purposes but which can equally well be used to investigate IgE. The essential point on which all these tests depend is that any particular antigen — and there are many thousands of these, all different — will result in the production by the body of only its own particular and identifiable protein immunoglobulin (antibody). This antibody will link on only to its own specific antigen. This being so, if you have a sample of the antigen — whether this is on a virus, bacterium, cell, worm parasite, pollen grain or whatever — you can check whether the body of the person concerned has previously been "challenged" by the antigen. In other words, whether the person has had a particular infection or infestation or allergy.

All these special tests depend on checking, in various ways, whether a known antigen combines with its particular specific antibody. This can be done by labelling antigens with a radioactive element, or by linking them with a dye that will fluoresce under ultraviolet light, or in other ways.

The ELISA test

Nowadays, the most popular test of this kind is called the *ELISA test*. ELISA stands for *Enzyme-Linked ImmunoSorbent Assay*. This test is used for so many purposes that it is worth describing in some detail. It is, for instance, currently the standard test for HIV infection. People who are HIV positive will almost certainly have had an ELISA test.

The test detects the antibodies to the particular infection it is intended to look for and requires a known sample of the suspected organism or allergen (which bears the antigen). This sample is stuck onto a hollow in a plastic plate and any unstuck material is washed off. The blood serum is then added to the plate. If the antibody is present it will link firmly to the antigen. A solution is now added containing a substance called a *ligand* that can attach to any kind of antibody and that is chemically linked to a chemical activator (an enzyme) called *peroxidase*. The plate is again washed. The presence of the antibody now means that the enzyme is present. This enzyme, if present, will cause a colour change in a solution, called *chromogen*, which is now added. The enzyme is, of course, retained only if the specific antibody is present and has attached itself to the antigen stuck to the plate. When this is so the *enzyme* operates and the colour changes. This is the indication of a positive result.

The ELISA test can detect antibodies to almost anything. It is capable, for instance, of identifying allergens on all kinds of different pollens, on house and other mites of various species, on mite faeces, on animal skin, scales or fur, on a wide range of fungal spores, and so on. Kits, for pathology laboratories, are produced to identify a very wide range of antibodies. To perform the ELISA test for the diagnosis of AIDS infection, it is necessary to have a sample of the AIDS virus, the human immunodeficiency virus, as the antigen; to perform the test for allergies, samples of the various possible allergens are needed.

Differential diagnosis

This impressive sounding phrase is used by doctors to indicate the process by which a selection is made from the list of possible conditions from which a patient might be suffering. Any given set of symptoms and signs might suggest more than one disease — sometimes several. Accurate diagnosis is essential if the best available treatment is to be provided. This is why doctors are always uneasy if they find themselves trying to treat a disease without knowing precisely what it is.

The differential diagnosis of hay fever is not particularly difficult as there are not many conditions that so closely resemble it as to cause much confusion. This is especially true of seasonal allergic rhinitis (see Chapter 1), but the range widens if the condition is non-seasonal.

Possible causes of confusion, in addition to the common cold, include:

● the condition *vasomotor rhinitis* that features frequent runny nose and nasal congestion for no very obvious reason. This is not an allergic disorder;

- *rhinitis medicamentosa*, a condition caused by various drugs such as aspirin, oral contraceptives, reserpine and hydralazine as well as the "rebound" effect of drugs used locally as drops or sprays to *reduce* nasal congestion (decongestants);
- nasal congestion due to sudden changes of temperature or humidity;
- nasal congestion due to exposure to strong-smelling and irritant vapours;
- runny nose, watering eyes and sweating as a result of taking unduly spicy or physically hot food. This is called *gustatory rhinitis*;
- nasal congestion from alcoholic overindulgence;
- nasal congestion from long-sustained sexual excitement, especially in men.

The last of these is included mainly for interest. It has been widely suggested, possibly on the basis of individual experience, that the nasal mucous membrane is an erectile tissue that may respond in this way to sexual arousal. There is no denying that it has an excellent blood supply, but it seems fanciful to equate it with the spongy erectile tissue of the penis or the clitoris.

CHAPTER
FIVE

Perennial Allergic Rhinitis

Perennial allergic rhinitis (PAR) is not really hay fever, but the symptoms are almost identical. The real difference between PAR and true hay fever is that the former can occur at any time of the year and commonly occurs all the year round. The latter is, of course, seasonal and occurs only when pollens and spores are carried in the atmosphere. In every other respect, including the symptoms (see Chapter 3) and the whole of the immunological process involved (see Chapter 2), the two conditions are the same. PAR can be just as severe as hay fever and, because it can occur at any time, is often more disabling.

The allergens

PAR has many more possible causes than hay fever. If you are prone to allergies, it is important that you should have an idea of the range of allergens that can cause it. The following list is far from complete, because no one knows all the substances that can cause PAR. New allergens are constantly being discovered. The list does, however, contain the commonest and most important of the known allergens:

- household dust mites;
- dust mite excreta;
- cockroach excreta;
- insect parts;
- organic fibres and lint;
- domestic animal skin flakes (dander);
- animal fur;
- fungal spores from mouldy hay;
- weevil-infested wheat flour;
- *Penicillium* spores from mouldy cheese;
- cat saliva;
- silverfish;
- dust lice;
- pyrethrum (used as an insecticide);
- orris root;
- flax seed;
- cotton seed;
- vegetable gums;
- pigeon droppings;
- budgerigar droppings;
- mushroom compost;
- cork dust;
- woodpulp;
- hairdressing chemicals such as ammonium persulphate;
- various drugs in powder form;
- industrial enzymes;
- bee, wasp and other insect stings.

All these allergens are proteins or carry proteins. It is always the proteins that cause the trouble. You will see that some of these allergens are likely to be encountered in the home environment while others are more likely to be picked up at work. In the case of the industrial allergens, the risk to casual visitors, such as customers in a hairdressing salon, is very small. People who work in environments in which PAR allergens are present are, however, in danger of developing an allergic rhinitis, especially if they already have atopy (see Chapter 2).

Domestic mites

The most important human allergens causing PAR are the household mites and their products. This has been proved by a great deal of research. Of the many species of mites, the most important are *Dermatophagoides farinae* and *Dermatophagoides pteronyssinus*. If you know a little Greek you will have worked out that this genus of mite lives by eating skin. *Derma-* is Greek for "skin" and *phagos-* means "eating" (as in *phagocyte*). So far as we know, flakes of human skin are the principal source of nourishment of these tiny creatures. So as to feed most comfortably, house mites live in bedding, mattresses, pillows, soft toys, upholstery and carpets. They appreciate a nice warm atmosphere and reproduce most actively at temperatures between 18°C and 21°C (65°F to 70°F). They also prefer a relative humidity of at least 50 per cent.

Dermatophagoides species are so small that they are barely visible to the naked eye and are seldom seen.

They are about 0.5 millimetres 1/50 inches long. The allergen that causes the most trouble is not carried by the mite itself but occurs on its faeces. These are coated with a thick layer of the protein enzymes they use for digestion and it is one of these proteins that acts mainly as the allergen. Interestingly, the faecal protein allergen that causes most trouble is a digestive enzyme used by the mite to break down the skin protein it has eaten. If mites are present, the allergen is present.

The fact that the main allergen is on the mite faeces is important, because the balls of faeces are relatively heavy and do not readily float in the air as do pollen grains. They do, however, become airborne for half an hour or so if bedding is shaken or during household cleaning. The use of vacuum cleaners (through which these faecal balls can usually pass) also causes a brief airborne episode. These are the main ways in which this particular potent allergen gets into the noses of adults.

It has been found that children's soft toys are commonly heavily infested with *D. pteronyssinus*, so children with PAR may be getting the allergen directly from such toys. The number of mites on a given area of soft toy is likely to be two-and-a-half times as great as on a bed mattress. There is, however, one very effective and safe way of dealing with mites on soft toys such as teddy bears — put the toy in the freezer and leave it there for a few hours. Teddy bears don't have enough water in them to freeze solid and soon recover from the experience. The mites, however, don't.

Studies have shown that mites are more prevalent if a bedroom is occupied by more than one child and if the bedroom is damp. Other research has also shown that children with severe allergic problems are greatly improved if taken to Alpine regions at altitudes above 1,000 metres. At such altitudes, the air is so dry that mites cannot survive. It was, incidentally, the observation of this fact that first drew attention to the significance of house mites in PAR.

Other species of mite incriminated in causing PAR include the storage mites *Tyrophagus longior*, *Acarus farris* and *Lepidoglyphus destructor* and mites from the *Euroglyptus* and *Cheyletus* genera. Almost certainly many others are involved. Scientists recognize some 30,000 different species of mites, and this is probably about one-tenth of all those that exist, so there are plenty to choose from.

Domestic animals

The main cat allergens come from cat saliva and cat skin. Cats deposit large quantities of saliva on their fur in the course of washing. This saliva, which contains a small proportion of protein organic matter, quickly dries and the organic content is released into the domestic atmosphere. Because of this, and because most cats wash frequently, the air of cat loving households is fairly constantly loaded with cat saliva allergens. These protein allergens are very small and light, and remain for long periods in the air. They are an important cause of PAR. Cat skin scales (dander) and hair particles also become readily airborne.

It has been shown that levels of these allergens can

be substantially reduced if the human owners accept the responsibility for cat washing. It is unnecessary to use the same methods as the cat; a weekly wash with a mild baby shampoo, although unpopular with the cat, can solve the PAR problem for some people. Many owners, allergic to animal fur, dander or saliva, will have a fairly shrewd suspicion of the cause but may be reluctant to admit it for fear of being advised to dispose of their pets.

Dog hair does not appear to be a significant allergen. Saliva, dander and dried urine, however, are common causes of PAR. Again, regular washing is recommended.

Other insect allergens

Domestically, the most important of these seem to be cockroach products and parts. Cockroaches are highly successful colonizers of urban environments and are present in most buildings, both in the tropics and in temperate regions. They are especially prevalent where sources of food are available to them and are adept at concealing themselves. Hundreds of cockroaches can hide in a kitchen that appears to be wholly uninhabited. They prefer a warm, humid and dark habitat and live off almost anything organic, especially food scraps, paper, books, clothing and dead insects. Females commonly deposit 50 batches of 16 eggs during a lifetime of 18 months and these hatch after 45 days.

Cockroach excreta and the powdered debris from dead cockroaches and their insect prey can readily become airborne to act as nasal allergens and cause

PAR. If you live exclusively in an urban area and suffer from unexplained perennial allergic rhinitis, you should certainly consider the possibility that your problem is due to this cause. The cockroaches may be present in your home or, perhaps more likely, in your place of work.

Very determined efforts are needed to deal with cockroach infestations and it is unlikely that you will succeed in eradicating the nuisance without professional help. Studies have shown that only spraying by properly trained and well informed pest control specialists is likely to be successful.

Treatment

The most important element in the treatment of PAR involves the removal of the allergen, or, if that is not possible, separation of the sufferer from it. Treatment of the symptoms is also important. Symptomatic treatment is identical to the treatment of seasonal allergic rhinitis (hay fever) and you can read all about that in Chapters 9 and 10.

CHAPTER
SIX

All About Antihistamines

It is probably true to say that antihistamine drugs are the mainstay of the management of hay fever and PAR. Antihistamines are certainly used more widely than any other class of drugs to treat hay fever. And now that many of them are available to you over-the-counter without prescription, there is much you can do for yourself to alleviate your hay fever symptoms.

There is a convention in naming drugs that the "official" or *generic* name is spelled with a lower case initial. Trade names, on the other hand, are capitalized. This convention is followed in this book. For every generic name there are usually several, sometimes scores, of trade names for the same stuff. It is worth checking the generic names of your favourite medications so that if one preparation is unavailable you may possibly be able to obtain an identical substitute under another name.

You already know quite a lot about histamine, but to understand fully how the antihistamine drugs work it is necessary to review the actions of this unpleasant substance and to learn more about how it causes so much trouble to so many people.

More about the effects of histamine

We have seen that histamine has several actions:

- to widen small blood vessels;
- to cause the smallest vessels to leak fluid;
- as a result to lead to waterlogging (oedema) of tissues;
- to narrow air tubes;
- to stimulate sensory nerves so as to cause strong discomfort, irritation and itching;
- to cause glands to secrete.

Histamine has two other effects that have not yet been mentioned. It is a powerful stimulant of stomach acid and it is used by the brain and nervous system to carry messages. The action of histamine on the brain is not fully understood but we do know quite a lot about it. We know that too much histamine causes a severe headache and that smaller quantities are necessary in the brain for normal brain function and the maintenance of full consciousness. The latter effect is best shown by what happens when histamine is prevented from acting in the brain by the action of antihistamines.

The molecules of histamine operate by locking into certain action sites, on the surface of cells, called histamine receptors. These are present on cells all over the body and are of three types. Those we are concerned with here are found especially on cells such as the smooth muscle cells of arteries and air tubes, the cells of the nose lining generally, and on the brain cells.

How antihistamines work

Antihistamine drugs were first discovered as early as 1937. Unfortunately, the first known antihistamine turned out to be much too poisonous to be used as a medicine. By 1944, however, the much safer drug *pyrilamine maleate* had been developed. By the early 1950s many useful and safe antihistamines had been developed. These drugs are chemically similar to histamine in that they fit neatly into the receptor sites, but they differ from histamine in that, although occupying the sites, they do not act on the cells in the way that histamine does. In fact, they do not act on the cells at all. They are just like plugs; they fill the sites but don't activate the cells. The whole point of this is, of course, that if the histamine receptor sites are all already occupied by the antihistamine drug molecules, it really doesn't matter how much histamine is swilling about in the area — it simply cannot get to the receptors to have its usual effects.

Until recently it was believed, and with good reason, that this was all that the antihistamines did. Indeed, until a range of new antihistamines (the "second generation" antihistamines) was developed, this probably was all that they did. Some of the new drugs, however, while acting very efficiently as receptor site blockers, do seem to have another very useful effect. Drugs such as *terfenadine* actually manage to limit the release of histamine from mast cells. All in all, antihistamines are highly effective in controlling the symptoms of hay fever and PAR.

Antihistamines and the brain

Antihistamines that get to the brain, to block the histamine receptor sites there, prevent the normal neurotransmitter action of histamine. This has a good effect and a not-so-good effect. The good news is that blocking histamine action on the brain can cure, or at least greatly alleviate motion sickness. The snag is that the person concerned can become quite sleepy. Sleepiness is probably the principal undesired side-effect of antihistamine drugs. Only certain antihistamines are used in this way; others are not recommended for children. Some antihistamines are so effective in blocking nerve transmission that they can even be used as local anaesthetics.

Because there has been a great demand for antihistamines that did *not* cause sleepiness, research scientists decided to look rather closely at the reason why some drugs seemed to be able to get from the bloodstream into the brain while others did not. Drugs in the blood get to the cells of the body by passing through the walls of the smallest blood vessels — the single-cell-layered capillaries. Studies of the blood capillaries in the brain showed that they were different from capillaries elsewhere. While capillaries in the body generally had quite large pores between their cells, those in the brain had cells fused tightly together. If a drug molecule was large, it could get through the walls of the body capillaries with no trouble but it might be prevented from getting through the walls of the capillaries in the brain.

If you look at the chemical formulae of the second generation antihistamine drugs you will see that most of them have larger and more complex molecules than those of the earlier antihistamines. Most experts believe that the absence of sedating and other nervous system effects of some of these newer antihistamines, especially terfenadine, is due to the fact that they are unable to get through the walls of the brain capillaries, or, as doctors express it, cannot pass through the "blood-brain barrier".

Length of action of antihistamines

Antihistamine drugs are well absorbed when taken by mouth and are not broken down by stomach acid. The peak levels in the blood occur two to three hours after they are taken. The useful effects on symptoms, however, start within an hour and the greatest effects start five to seven hours after taking the dose.

Antihistamines act for much longer than the time they are present in the blood. For example, after a one-week course of some of them, an appreciable effect persists for another seven days. In an emergency, antihistamines can be given by injection directly into the bloodstream. This produces an almost immediate effect. Some of the more recent antihistamines dissolve poorly in water, however, and are not available in injectable form, so the earlier, more soluble drugs are used.

There is no evidence that long-term use of antihistamines in any way reduces their effectiveness or the rate at which they are eliminated from the body. Tolerance to the sedative effects of some antihistamines may, however, develop, so this can become less of a problem with time. Unfortunately, you can't rely on this happening with all of them.

One thing you should note — exceeding the recommended dosage does not increase the effect. Careful trials have shown that even doubling the standard dosage does not produce a significant increase in the relief of symptoms. An increase in dosage could be dangerous, however, so don't try it.

Side-effects of antihistamines

It is important that you should be aware of the possible effects of antihistamines. The commonest and most troublesome of these is sedation. This shows itself by sleepiness, general slowing and lengthened reaction time. Note that this can be greatly worsened by alcohol and that the combination can be dangerous. You might, for instance, find yourself prosecuted for "driving under the influence" after taking only one or two drinks if you are also taking antihistamines. The law will not excuse you on the grounds that the medication is justified. Some antihistamines are so strongly sedative that they are used for this purpose, especially in children. These selected antihistamines are considered the safest sedatives for children.

Some of the more recent second generation antihistamines do not reach the brain as easily as others and so have little or no sedative effect. The antihistamines that are available over-the-counter are said to be non-sedating, but you should be careful all the same.

Other possible side effects of antihistamines that you should be aware of include:

- diminished alertness;
- slowing of mental activity;
- blurring of vision;
- dry mouth;
- difficulty with urination;
- digestive upsets;
- constipation;
- headache;
- impotence;
- disorientation;
- sometimes paradoxical stimulation;
- dizziness;
- weight gain;
- heart irregularities;
- skin rashes.

Apart from the effects on alertness, none of these side effects are particularly common. Note that side-effects may occur with one person but not with another. If they occur in your case you should simply avoid that particular drug. There is no question of treating side-effects.

There are a few other points to note in this context. You should be rather careful with antihistamines if you suffer from angle-closure (narrow-angle) glaucoma or if you have an enlarged prostate gland so that it takes you longer to empty your bladder than it used to. If you are an epileptic or have any form of liver disease you should also be careful. If you do have any of these conditions it would be as well to discuss the matter with your doctor before deciding to treat yourself with antihistamines.

In general, antihistamines are remarkably safe. *Large* overdosage with antihistamines can, however, be very dangerous and can lead to:

- involuntary jerky movements (*dyskinesia*);
- severe muscle spasm (*dystonia*);
- heart irregularities;
- heart block;
- epileptic-type seizures;
- hallucinations;
- psychotic episodes;
- coma;
- death.

Clearly, this is not to be risked. So antihistamines, like other drugs, should be kept out of reach of depressed people and children. Overdosage is treated by inducing vomiting and giving activated charcoal. This helps to reduce the absorption of the drug.

A report published in June 1994 indicated that at that time it was not yet known which of the antihistamines was safest for use during pregnancy. As a general rule, all drugs are to be avoided during the early weeks of pregnancy when the major structures and organs of the fetus are being formed.

Some representative antihistamine drugs

Trade names are capitalized. You can find the generic name of the drug you are using on the packaging.

acrivastine A second generation antihistamine. Used to treat hay fever and nettle rash (*urticaria*). It is taken by mouth. Possible side-effects include drowsiness, but this is rare. A trade name is *Semprex*.

antazoline Used to treat allergic conjunctivitis. It is taken in the form of eye drops. It also has weak local anaesthetic effects. A trade name is *Antistin-Privine*.

astemizole A second generation antihistamine. Used to treat hay fever and allergic skin conditions. It is taken by mouth. Possible side-effects include weight gain and, on very high dosage, heart irregularity. A trade name is *Hismanal*.

Atarax A trade name for *hydroxyzine hydrochloride*.

azatadine A second generation antihistamine. Used to treat hay fever, urticaria, itching and stings. It is taken by mouth. Possible side-effects include drowsiness, slowed reaction time, headache, nausea and either increase of, or loss of, appetite. A trade name is *Optimine*.

azelastine Taken as a metered dose nasal spray for the treatment of hay fever. Possible side-effects include nasal irritation and disturbances of taste sensation. A trade name is *Rhinolast*.

brompheniramine Used to treat hay fever and perennial allergic rhinitis. It is taken by mouth as tablets or a liquid. A trade name is *Dimotane Plus*.

chlorpheniramine Used to treat hay fever, perennial allergic rhinitis and anaphylactic shock. It is taken by mouth or by injection. Trade names are *Aller-chlor, Haymine, Piriton, Phenetron.*

Clarityn A trade name for *loratadine.*

clemastine Used to treat hay fever and perennial allergic rhinitis. It is taken by mouth as tablets or a liquid. A trade name is *Tavegil.*

cyproheptadine Used to treat allergic disorders generally including itchy skin conditions. It is taken by mouth. Possible side-effects include stimulation of appetite, interactions with monoamine oxidase inhibitors (see Chapter 7 — decongestants), drowsiness, etc. A trade name is *Periactin.*

Daneral A trade name for *pheniramine.*

dimethindine maleate Used to treat hay fever, urticaria and other allergic conditions. It is taken by mouth. Possible side-effects include drowsiness and slowed reactions. A trade name is *Vibrocil.*

Dimotane Plus A trade name for *brompheniramine.*

Haymine A trade name for *chlorpheniramine.*

Hismanal A trade name for *astemizole.*

hydroxyzine hydrochloride Used mainly to relieve itching in nettle rash and other skin conditions. It is taken by mouth. A trade name is *Atarax.*

ketotifen A second generation antihistamine. Used to treat allergic rhinitis and allergic conjunctivitis. This drug can stabilize mast cells and reduce histamine release. Possible side-effects include drowsiness, dizziness, dry mouth and, occasionally, jumpiness. A trade name is *Zaditen*.

loratadine A second generation antihistamine. Used to treat hay fever and perennial allergic rhinitis. It is taken by mouth. Possible side-effects include headache, fatigue and nausea. A trade name is *Clarityn*.

mequitazine Used to treat hay fever and perennial allergic rhinitis. It is taken by mouth. A trade name is *Primalan*.

Optimine A trade name for *azatadine*.

oxatomide Used to treat hay fever. It is taken by mouth. A trade name is *Tinset*.

Periactin A trade name for *cyproheptadine*.

Phenergan A trade name for *promethazine*.

phenindamine Used to treat allergic conditions. It is taken by mouth. A trade name is *Thephorin*.

pheniramine Used to control allergic reactions generally. It is taken by mouth. A trade name is *Daneral*.

Piriton A trade name for *chlorpheniramine*.

Primalan A trade name for *mequitazine*.

Pro-Actidil A trade name for *triprolidine*.

promethazine Used for allergies, nausea and vomiting, travel sickness and as a sedative in children. It is taken by mouth as tablet or a liquid. A trade name is *Phenergan*.

Rhinocort A trade name for *budesonide*.

Rhinolast A trade name for *azelastine*.

Semprex A trade name for *acrivastine*.

Sinutab Antihistamine A trade name for a compound of the pain killer *paracetamol*, the decongestant *pseudoephedrine* and *chlorpheniramine*.

Tavegil A trade name for *clemastine*.

terfenadine A second generation antihistamine. Used to treat allergic rhinitis and urticaria. It is taken by mouth. Possible side-effects include digestive upset, skin rashes, sweating, heart irregularity. A trade name is *Triludan*.

Thephorin A trade name for *phenindamine*.

Tinset A trade name for *oxatomide*.

Triludan A trade name for *terfenadine*.

trimeprazine Used to relieve itching in allergic conditions and as a sedative for children. A trade name is *Vallergan*.

triprolidine Used to treat allergy and to relieve the symptoms of colds. It is taken by mouth. Possible side-effects include drowsiness, slowed reaction time and, rarely, skin rashes. Trade names are *Actidil*, *Actifed* and *Pro-Actidil*.

Ucerax A trade name for *hydroxyzine hydrochloride*.

Vallergan A trade name for *trimeprazine*.

Zatiden A trade name for *ketotifen*.

CHAPTER
SEVEN

Other Forms of Treatment

Anthihistamines are by no means the only way of dealing with hay fever and PAR. Some of the other forms of treatment are even more effective than the antihistamines. Unfortunately, the more active a drug or procedure, the more likely it is to have side-effects or other disadvantages, so you have to balance one thing against another. Here are the essential points about the other ways of managing these conditions.

Steroids

Steroids, or, more correctly, *glucocorticoids*, are natural body substances without which we would be in real trouble. They are essential for the normal and safe running of the body, and the amounts produced — by the adrenal glands on top of the kidneys — vary considerably depending on the body's needs.

Many people feel very unhappy at the idea of taking steroids. This is because they have heard alarming tales of the terrible things that steroids, used as drugs, can cause:

- stunting of the growth of children;
- osteoporosis;
- spontaneous fractures;
- breakdown of healed ulcers;
- a shut-down of the body's own steroid production;
- interference with the immune system so that latent infections are reactivated and new infections such as thrush encouraged.

All these things *can* happen and, in people who are receiving large doses of steroids by mouth or injection over long periods of time, sometimes do happen. Treatment of this kind is called *systemic* treatment because high levels of the drugs pass to almost all parts of the body. But in the management of hay fever and PAR there is no question of systemic treatment. If steroids are used, they are used locally (*topically*), nearly always in the form of nasal sprays.

In fact, steroids are the most powerful and effective drugs available for the treatment and control of hay fever and PAR. Used topically, they are every bit as effective as if taken by mouth or injection and are far safer. For years doctors have considered steroids as a kind of fall-back or last resort to be used when everything else fails, but this view is now beginning to change.

One reason for this is the discovery that steroids, used at the beginning of the hay fever season actually prevent the accumulation of mast cells in the nose lining. If you have read Chapter 2 carefully, there will be no need to emphasize how important this is. No mast cells — no hay fever or PAR. Steroids cannot, of course, be relied on to eliminate mast cells completely but, properly used, their effect can be remarkable.

Secondly, steroids are the most powerful anti-inflammatory drugs available and can be relied on to cut down, or even eliminate, the inflammation caused by histamine and other mast cell granule products. Thirdly, steroids interfere with the unfortunate progressive increase in sensitivity to allergens that so often results in hay fever and PAR getting steadily worse.

The steroids most commonly used are *Syntaris* (*flunisolide*), *Aerobec, Beconase* or *Beclazone* (*beclomethasone*) and *Dexarhinaspray* (*dexamethasone*). It is important to use these in exactly the prescribed dosage. A usual instruction might be two sprays (50μg) of flunisolide in each nostril twice a day or one spray (42μg) of beclomethasone in each nostril two to four times a day. You should try to use as little as is necessary to keep the problem under control. It is only fair to say that it is possible to detect slight general effects with normal dosage of dexamethasone nasal sprays. The experts report that no general side-effects have been detected with nasal use of flunisolide and beclomethasone.

These steroids can, however, have certain side-effects within the nose itself. The main problem is a feeling of irritation and burning for a while after using the spray. In some people, perhaps one in fifty, the irritation is severe enough to promote a nosebleed. A very occasional user will even develop a hole in the thin partition between the two sides of the nose (*perforated nasal septum*). This is not particularly serious and will usually eventually heal. Very occasionally a patient might develop a thrush infection of the inside of the nose. This is rare and can be effectively treated.

Decongestants

Congestion (stuffiness) of the nose is an unpleasant feature of hay fever and PAR. It is often so extreme that the nasal air passages are completely closed and you have to resort to mouth breathing. This is not particularly good for health as you are then taking unconditioned air into your lungs. Decongestant drugs are those that act on blood vessels, causing the tiny muscles in their walls to tighten so that they are narrowed and less blood can flow through them. As a result, the vein sinuses under the mucous membrane lining collapse and the lining flattens. If this is not quite clear, read the section on the nose in Chapter 2.

Nasal decongestant drugs are called *alpha-adrenergic blockers*. This name simply means that they prevent an adrenaline-like hormone from acting at certain receptor sites on the muscles in the blood vessel and elsewhere. They have a double effect. As well as shrinking the nose lining they can counteract the sleepiness caused by antihistamines. They work most quickly and effectively when used directly on the nose lining as drops or a spray, such as *Medihaler*, but this method has two great disadvantages. With repeated use, the duration of the effect becomes less; and when the effect wears off there is a strong tendency for the congestion to get at least as bad as it was before, if not worse. This is called *rebound congestion*.

For these reasons decongestants are, on the whole, best taken by mouth in carefully limited dosage. The nasal spray preparation can, however, be useful to let you get off to sleep and to open up the nasal passages briefly so as to let the aerosol from a steroid spray get to the parts it would not otherwise reach. Doctors also use them to permit proper examination of the nose.

If you use decongestants by mouth — usually *pseudoephedrine* or *phenylpropanolamine* in the form of tablets, capsules or mixtures — you may experience certain effects resulting from the action of the drug on other adrenaline receptors in your body. Adrenaline-like or amphetamine-like effects such as jumpiness, irritability, overactivity and insomnia are quite familiar to people taking oral decongestants. You may find these unpleasant.

It is also important for you to appreciate that these effects can actually be dangerous if you have heart disease or high blood pressure or if you are epileptic or have an overactive thyroid gland. They are especially risky if you are being treated for depression or other conditions with a drug of the monoamine oxidase (MAO) inhibitor group. If you are on such a drug your doctor will have warned you to avoid cheese, wine, chocolate, yeasts and other foods. Commonly prescribed monoamine oxidase inhibitor drugs include *Nardil* (*phenelzine*), *Marplan* (*isocarboxazid*), *Parnate* or *Parstelin* (*tranylcypromine*) and *Manerix* (*moclobemide*). While taking these MAO inhibitor drugs, oral decongestants can cause your blood pressure to rise to a dangerous level.

In view of these facts it is best to take medical advice before using oral decongestant drugs.

Cromoglycate

The drug *cromoglycate*, also known as *cromolyn sodium*, has a very useful effect in preventing degranulation of mast cells (see Chapter 2). The way it does this is still uncertain. Most accounts refer to "stabilization of the mast cell membrane" but this idea is no longer so confidently held. From your point of view what matters is that it works. The drug, prescribed most commonly under the trade name of *Intal*, is widely used in inhalers for the control of asthma. Intal is available as a nasal spray and should be used from the beginning of the allergy season, preferably before any symptoms occur.

Some people get an excellent result from cromoglycate; others do not. The drug is very safe and there are hardly any side-effects. The main disadvantage is that it has to be used four to six times a day. Intal is not a steroid or an antihistamine and is certainly worth trying. Note, however, that some preparations, such as *Intal Compound*, also contain an adrenaline-like decongestant. Remember that cromoglycate cannot, and will not, deal with symptoms due to histamine already released from mast cell granules. Its only mode of action is to prevent these unpleasant substances from being released.

If you are greatly troubled by watering and redness of the eyes from hay fever, you can use cromoglycate in the form of eye drops such as *Opticrom* or *Eye-Crom*.

Some representative non-antihistamine drugs

beclomethasone Steroid drug. Used to treat hay fever and PAR. It is taken as a nasal spray. A trade name is *Beconase*.

Beconase A trade name for *beclomethasone*.

budesonide Steroid drug. Used to treat hay fever and PAR. It is taken by nasal spray. A trade name is *Rhinocort*.

cromoglycate An anti-inflammatory drug that prevents the release of histamine from mast cells. It is taken as a nasal spray or drops. A trade name is *Nalcrom*.

Flixonase A trade name for the corticosteroid drug *fluticasone propionate* used as a metered dose spray inhaler to prevent and treat hay fever. May cause irritation to the nose, nosebleeds or may cause upsets of taste and smell.

flunisolide A steroid drug. Used to treat hay fever and PAR. It is taken as a nasal spray. A trade name is *Syntaris*.

Intal A trade name for *sodium chromoglycate*.

Nalcrom A trade name for *cromoglycate*.

pseudoephedrine A powerful decongestant drug. Used to relieve nasal blockage and to facilitate access for other hay fever medication. See precautions mentioned in this chapter. Trade names are *Sudafed*, *Sudafed SA* and *Galpseud*.

Sudafed Plus A trade name for *triprolidine* and the decongestant drug *pseudoephedrine*.

Syntaris A trade name for the steroid *flunisolide*.

Triominic A mixture of the nasal decongestant drug *phenylpropanolamine* and the antihistamine drug *pheniramine*.

Desensitization

Desensitization is a method of treatment designed to boost the effectiveness of the immune system in combating hay fever and PAR. It is done by giving a series of injections of the very allergens that cause these disorders. Since these conditions are caused, in the first place, by a defect in the functioning of the immune system, you can see that any explanation of how desensitization works is likely to be complicated. The fact is that, to date, no one has been able to explain convincingly how it works. Even the latest textbooks of immunology have to admit that the process is not fully understood. We do know, however, that, in cases where it is effective, the levels of IgE eventually drop and those of the commoner antibody type IgG (gamma globulin) rise. IgG is said to be a *blocking antibody* that competes for the allergen, latches on to it and forms a complex that can be removed by phagocytes. IgG, of course, does not trigger degranulation of mast cells.

The first requirement is that there should be a precise diagnosis of the cause of the allergy so that the correct allergen can be given. This must then be made up in a very dilute solution suitable for injection. Injections of gradually increasing amounts of the allergen are given once or twice a week, just under the skin, until the doctor has reached the largest dose short of causing a general reaction. Injections of a substance to which you are known to be allergic can be very dangerous. For this reason, the process is to be undertaken only by someone who really knows what he or she is doing — in other words, a fully qualified scientific allergist. This is no job for self-styled "allergists" or practitioners of alternative therapies.

It takes a long time for the desired effect to be achieved and you should not expect any benefit for at least three months. The injections are usually continued for two or three years. If all goes well, you should begin to become less allergic after the first three or four months and the improvement may then continue to increase progressively for up to two years. For these reasons, the course of injections is best started after the end of the hay fever season and then continued all the year round. They are given very carefully under close medical supervision to avoid severe reactions. If reactions occur they may be immediate or they may be delayed for four to six hours.

The danger of injecting allergens into allergic patients is neither slight nor fanciful. There was an average of one death per year in the UK from this cause over the period from 1959 to 1986. Most of these occurred in people being treated by non-specialists. When these facts became widely known, official disapproval of desensitization was expressed and the practice was largely abandoned. It is only recently that the real experts have again, in the light of increased knowledge, begun to consider the merits of this method of treatment.

A scheme of management

It will be useful to bring all this information together in a brief general account of the best way to manage your hay fever.

The first step is to be sure that you actually have hay fever or PAR. This means making an accurate diagnosis. Check Chapters 3 and 4 which cover symptoms and diagnosis. Next you should try to find out exactly what the allergen is that is causing your trouble. You may be able to do this for yourself simply by observing which particular grasses, tree pollens or fungal spores bring on your allergy. It will not be so easy to identify domestic allergens, but you can make some useful assumptions on the basis of frequency. Check Chapter 5 for details. If you are stuck on this one and simply have no idea of what is causing the allergy, you will have to try to persuade your doctor to arrange a skin prick test (see Chapter 4).

Once the background facts are established, you should do everything you can to avoid the allergen. See Chapter 11. If avoidance fails you are going to have to consider treatment. The first choice is between cromoglycate and an antihistamine. You should certainly use cromoglycate in the form of eye drops if you have much eye irritation with redness and watering. Cromoglycate by nasal spray, such as Rhynacrom, is also a good start but you will have to use it at least four times a day and it is rather expensive. No prescription is necessary.

It is difficult to advise on the choice of antihistamines because there are so many and because you can't really tell which will suit you best until you have tried. It is best to stick to the range recommended for hay fever or PAR rather than those used mainly for other purposes. Many of them are available without prescription.

If nasal congestion is a major feature you will probably need a decongestant. But do remember the possible dangers. Before considering decongestants, read the section above on these drugs. Use decongestants sparingly.

As to the use of steroid nasal sprays, you will have to make up your own mind. They are certainly effective and millions of people have used preparations such as Beconase with great satisfaction and with no indication of dangerous side-effects. You can get Beconase over-the-counter without prescription. Use two sprays in each nostril twice a day. You may find it worth while to read the section on steroids once again.

While on the subject of over-the-counter drugs, you should remember that a great many of these were, until fairly recently, available only on prescription. The fact that you can now buy them directly does not mean that they can safely be used casually or in doses greater than those recommended. To do so could be dangerous. If you need advice on any particular drug you are purchasing, you will usually find that the pharmacist will be glad to answer any of your questions. Pharmaceutical chemists are highly qualified and very well-informed people and often know at least as much about the actions and dangers of drugs as doctors.

The question of possible desensitization, and the management of any persistent complications (see Chapter 10), are matters for your doctor. Complications such as sinusitis or middle ear infection may require antibiotic treatment in addition to routine hay fever treatment. Antibiotics have no place in the management of uncomplicated hay fever or PAR.

CHAPTER
EIGHT

The Emotional
Dimension

Hay fever and perennial allergic rhinitis are not serious illnesses in the sense that cancer of the lung or coronary artery disease are serious. No one has ever died of hay fever. Nevertheless, these conditions are responsible for an enormous amount of distress to millions. This distress arises from interference with many aspects of life, especially human relationships.

It is difficult for those who have never experienced the embarrassments and discomforts of hay fever to understand why sufferers sometimes seem to make such a fuss about what is generally considered to be a minor disorder. Such people may be inclined to respond impatiently to a sufferer's refusal to visit a park or to go for a country walk. But there is nothing minor about a condition that makes it impossible to relate normally to other people.

Social activity

Young people in particular are affected by the emotional dimension in hay fever. Adolescents and young adults, already hypersensitive about their appearance, socially uncertain and easily embarrassed, are liable to become so self-conscious as a result of hay fever that they may prefer to give up social activity altogether rather than risk the humiliation of being seen by those they care about, sporting running red noses and red watery eyes, sneezing at frequent intervals and constantly fumbling with a handkerchief that is quickly becoming soaked. It is easy for others to smile at the social sensitivity of young people; to the sufferer it is all degrading, mortifying and deadly serious.

The purely subjective symptoms of hay fever — those that are not apparent to others such as the persistent soreness of the nose, the itching, pricking and burning in and around the nose and eyes, even severe pain in the face from the sinuses, also make effective socializing very difficult. It is not easy to be bright, lively, amusing or charming when you are feeling rotten, when your nose is blocked and your voice sounds ridiculously nasal to you.

Almost half of the women who suffer significantly from hay fever make the effort to carry on a normal social life. Men, always more sensitive in such matters, tend to opt out more readily. Only a fifth of men try to carry on with normal social relations. When both men and women sufferers are questioned, a fifth of them agree that their relations with others are affected at least to some extent. The sex life is particularly likely to be affected. Many avoid sex when affected. One person in fifty is driven by embarrassment, fastidiousness or even incapacity to a state of total chastity throughout the whole of the pollen season.

Hay fever and work

The same factors that disrupt social and sexual activity can operate to an even more marked extent in relation to work. In a social context you can, at least, excuse yourself and go home. This is more difficult if you are anxious to make the best possible impression on your boss and workmates. Hay fever can also so reduce your mental efficiency that you make silly and embarrassing mistakes. You are likely to believe, and you may well be right, that others are not going to make excuses for you on such trivial grounds as hay fever.

Sometimes the allergen is actually associated with the workplace so that the problems are made worse by going to work. If your job is connected with plants, grass, trees or other sources of allergen, your emotional reaction to your hay fever is likely to be severely exacerbated. If you are an adolescent sufferer and at a stage in your education when exams are of critical importance, you have every justification in feeling hard done by. Unfortunately, annual exams often coincide with the hay fever season. While your luckier colleagues are enjoying the benefits of the cool breezes wafting in from the school or college playing fields through the open windows, you may be sitting there just waiting for what you know will be a really horrible attack that may make it almost impossible for you to carry on writing that all-important paper.

Allergy and sex

The more severe forms of reaction to allergens, in particular asthma (Chapter 9) commonly have a serious effect on the sex life. Hay fever and PAR are less likely to cause major disruption of sexual activity, but they can certainly do so. Severe hay fever, of course, is a real blight on libido and it would be a determined partner who would insist. Aesthetic considerations apart, simple allergic rhinitis is, in itself, no bar to sex. PAR can, however, sometimes cause real problems. Here is a case history that illustrates the point.

Introduction

Walter is an orchestral cellist. He is a shy, lonely man who has never been successful with women. At last, however, he thinks he has found his ideal. Unfortunately, there is an unexpected problem.

Personal details

Name Walter Ainsworth
Age 44
Occupation Professional musician
Family Parents dead. No siblings

Medical background

Walter's general health has been reasonable, with no serious illnesses. He recollects being told that he suffered from eczema as a child, but he now has no skin problems. He finds it difficult to get as much exercise as he should and he is somewhat out of condition. He has always disliked seeing doctors, but his present problem has driven him to it.

The complaint

Walter visits his doctor with a complaint of sudden episodes of sore throat, coughing, sneezing, watering eyes, tightness in the chest and some wheeziness. He finds it particularly difficult to explain this complaint fully to his doctor and at first omits to mention an essential point — that the trouble arises only when he is making love to his fiancée. Fortunately, the doctor's questions are as persistent as they are pertinent and at last the whole story comes out. Walter has been dating Elizabeth for almost two years. Seven months ago they decided to get married. Walter has had no previous sexual experience but for some weeks now Elizabeth has been inviting him to spend the night with her in her flat.

At first, all went well and they had wonderful sex. But on the third or fourth occasion that he stayed overnight with her, he had one of these attacks and this has happened on every occasion since. He has become convinced that this is some kind of psychosomatic response to unconscious guilt. Elizabeth, too, is beginning to wonder whether something is wrong with their relationship. He and Elizabeth are, in fact, very much in love and ideally suited to one another. They are both very unhappy over this strange development.

The doctor asks whether Walter has ever had similar attacks anywhere other than in Elizabeth's flat. Walter assures him that he has not. The doctor then asks where exactly in the flat they make love. Walter shyly tells him that they always go to bed.

"Nowhere else," says Walter.

"Have a go in the lounge," advises the doctor, "and report back to me."

A week later Walter returns. He responds to the doctor's raised eyebrows with a gratified smile.

"All well?" asks the doctor.

"Wonderful," says Walter. "But I'm at a complete loss to understand why the place should make such a difference. Could it be a Freudian thing about bed?"

"Nonsense," says the doctor, and explains that Walter is suffering from a simple allergy to something present in the bedroom. He has a fairly shrewd idea what it is.

The investigation and diagnosis

The doctor then arranges for Walter to have skin prick sensitivity tests and diplomatically suggests that Walter bring Elizabeth with him when he returns for the results. Two weeks later the couple are in attendance.

The doctor explains that the tests have shown that Walter has developed an allergy to house mite faecal protein. It seems, he tells them, that the mites are in the bedding.

Elizabeth is horrified and embarrassed.

The doctor waves this aside and explains that nearly every house has mites. The remarkable thing is that Walter has, until now, escaped the allergy. Walter says he has always slept in nylon sheets. Could this be relevant?

"Certainly," says the doctor, "problem solved."

The treatment

Elizabeth wants to burn all her bedding but the doctor laughs her out of this and advises her about high-temperature washes, miticides and, if necessary, plastic bags. Walter is given a prescription for Beconase and cromoglycate sprays. The doctor has become interested in the case and asks them to keep him posted as to progress.

The follow-up

Walter never has another attack. A month later the doctor receives an eloquent report in the form of a wedding invitation.

CHAPTER
NINE

Hay Fever in Children

Hay fever is not common in very young children. This is because it normally takes years for a sufficient level of IgE to build up (see Chapter 2). Even so, the condition has been described in children as young as one year, and the number of cases rises steadily with increasing age. Children who develop hay fever are nearly always suffering from atopy (see Chapter 2) and commonly also have eczema. They are also prone to develop allergic asthma.

PAR commonly starts before the second year of life and is often associated with asthma. In such cases the allergen is usually the same for both conditions. Long-standing blockage of the nose in such children can lead to disturbances of the growth of the dental arches and irregularities in the way the teeth come together (*malocclusion*). Children suffer more from nasal blockage than adults because their nasal passages are relatively more narrow and can be obstructed by a lesser degree of swelling of the lining than in the case of adults.

Hay fever usually starts after the age of two and tends to become worse with each succeeding pollen season. In children, the most obvious signs are:

- mouth breathing;
- feeding difficulty because of blocked nose;
- snoring during sleep;
- a nasal tone to the voice;
- constant sniffing;
- nose picking;
- nosebleeds;
- nose rubbing;
- frequent sneezing;
- eye watering;
- redness of the eyes and eyelids;
- swelling around the eyes;
- a purplish discoloration around the eyes;
- a crease across the lower part of the nose (the "allergic salute");
- undue tiredness.

Indications such as these should never be simply written off as "a cold". It is important to establish the diagnosis and to ensure that the child has proper treatment. Decongestive drops of pseudoephedrine or ephedrine can be very useful, but should not be used for more than a few days (see Chapter 7). Severe cases will probably need Beconase or cromoglycate nasal sprays.

Hay fever and PAR in children can sometimes have serious consequences.

The effect on the ears

Children affected in this way are more prone than average to the common childhood disorder of middle ear infection (*otitis media*). This is because of the ease with which the tubes running from the back of the nose to the middle ears (the *eustachian tubes*) can get blocked in hay fever. These tubes are important both as a means of equalizing air pressure on both sides of the ear drums and as a means of draining the middle ear of secretions. Failure of drainage makes infection much more likely. Such infection can be very persistent and can lead to hearing defects.

Good hearing is essential if children are to develop normal speech and realize their full mental capacity. One of the most common ways in which hearing is affected in children is by middle ear disease. This can be very insidious, for the child is quite unaware of what is happening and will never complain that he or she cannot hear. Any child who suffers for any length of time from allergic problems of this kind should have an audiogram check of the hearing.

Allergic asthma

Although hay fever is not especially common in children, you will see in Chapter 8 that one important complication of IgE–mediated allergy can be quite serious, especially in the case of children. Here is a case history that illustrates this point.

Introduction

Brook has an allergic tendency which, at first, produces only an allergic rhinitis. Part of the problem is allergy to microscopic particles of household dust. Control of these factors helps considerably but Brook still has fairly frequent attacks. At the age of nine, however, matters take a more serious turn.

Personal details
Name Brook Saunders
Age 9
Occupation Schoolgirl
Family Parents alive and well. Two brothers in good health

Medical background

Brook has had a tendency to eczema from birth but careful management of her skin has kept this under control. She started to have hay fever-like attacks when she was three years old and these have become gradually more severe. Both of Brook's parents are heavy cigarette smokers. Her mother is familiar with the problems of allergy as there is a well-marked family history of hay fever, eczema and asthma on her side, affecting two of Brook's aunts. Mrs Saunders is optimistic, however, as, in both cases, the trouble cleared up completely by early adult life. When Brook is nine, however, a new and alarming manifestation of her allergy occurs.

The first severe attack

The attack started quite unexpectedly with breathlessness, wheezing, and a dry cough. Brook complains of tightness in her chest. In a short time her breathing is increasingly difficult, and she is distressed and anxious. She can breathe in easily but wheezes loudly on expiration. The family doctor is summoned and he gives her an intravenous injection of aminophylline and arranges for her immediate admission to hospital.

The management in hospital

In hospital Brook is given a further intravenous injection of aminophylline and then a corticosteroid drug and another drug to widen the air tubes (a *bronchodilator*). She is also given oxygen by mask. After an hour or two her condition improves dramatically and she is able to breathe easily without assistance.

The doctor's comments

Next morning, the consultant has a talk with Mrs Saunders. He tells her that Brook's allergy to house dust has now developed into a severe form of asthma. The process is essentially the same but now affects the breathing tubes rather than the nose. Her IgE levels have risen substantially. This, he says, is now known to be one of the effects in children of passive smoking. Every effort must be made to prevent further attacks by removing the cause. Bed mattresses must be sealed in polythene and thoroughly vacuum-cleaned every week. And Brook should not be exposed to cigarette smoke.

He explains that asthma is not a trivial condition and that he is going to prescribe medication to be taken by inhaler. The time to stop an asthma attack is at the very beginning and attacks must not be allowed to develop. Brook must be taught to use her inhalers properly, and when to use each kind. Any indication that inhaler treatment is having a reduced effect is a danger sign that must not be ignored. Mrs Saunders is also shown how to use a peak flow meter to check how easily air can get into and out of Brook's lungs. This is to be done every day. Brook must respond to any reduction in respiratory performance by increasing the use of the inhalers.

The follow-up

Mr and Mrs Saunders succeed in giving up smoking. In a short time Brook becomes expert in the use of her inhalers. She knows which one is for routine use to block allergic attacks and which one widens her air tubes. She also knows when to use her third inhaler to control an established attack. Brook can now monitor her breathing ability with her peak flow meter and is able to suggest when a boost in treatment is required.

CHAPTER
TEN

Complications

Sinusitis

The sinuses are cavities in the bone of the skull in the region around the nose. These paired cavities exist below and above the eyes (maxillary and frontal sinuses), between the nose and the eyes (ethmoidal sinuses) and immediately behind and above the nose (sphenoidal sinuses). All these sinuses are lined with the same kind of mucous membrane as the nose, and all of them communicate with the nose by narrow, tube-like openings. These allow the secretions of the mucous membranes to drain out.

When mucous membrane gets swollen, as described in Chapter 3, it is quite common for these narrow openings (which are also lined with mucous membrane) to become closed off. This is a most unfortunate thing to happen. The inflamed mucous membrane continues to oversecrete and pressure builds up in the affected sinuses causing pain that can sometimes be distressingly severe. Fortunately, allergic sinusitis tends to be less persistent and severe than sinusitis from infection, and seldom, if ever, causes fever, general upset and inflammation of the overlying skin. If it goes on too long, however, it may become indistinguishable from infective sinusitis and its allergic origin may not be suspected. Antibiotics, which are the mainstay of the treatment of infective sinusitis, are useless in treating allergic reactions. These have nothing to do with infection.

Eustachian catarrh

Some of the complications of hay fever allergy are quite unexpected. We have already briefly come across problems with the eustachian tubes but as this seems seldom to be recognized as a manifestation of allergic rhinitis it is worth taking a closer look at this unpleasant complication. Here is a case history that covers the essential facts.

Introduction
When his hearing deteriorated Joshua was convinced that his career as a speech therapist was at an end. But his problem turned out to have a simpler solution than he had supposed. An accurate diagnosis and routine treatment were all that were necessary.

Personal details
Name Joshua Engels
Age 52
Occupation Speech therapist
Family Parents alive. Father suffers from asthma. No brothers or sisters

Medical background

Joshua is a private speech therapist who specializes in helping deaf children to articulate clearly. Although his past medical history is unremarkable, he is constantly preoccupied with his health and is inclined to be a bit of a hypochondriac. So when he suddenly realizes that his hearing has changed radically, he is seriously worried. The next day he is in Harley Street anxiously explaining his symptoms to an Ear, Nose and Throat consultant.

The complaint

The most alarming thing about the change in his hearing, he explains to the doctor, is his perception of his own voice. Instead of sounding normal, it reverberates with a horrible kind of distortion in his ears. The actual loss of hearing is comparatively slight and he can make out normal conversation. But he is convinced that if he cannot assess the quality of his own voice, he will not be able to continue with his work.

The investigation

The specialist asks a few questions and Joshua agrees that he has recently been sneezing a good deal and has had unusually watery eyes. The doctor performs an audiogram which shows a slight, general reduction in the acuity of hearing. He then carries out an examination of his ear-drums, with an auriscope, and of his nose with a fine fibre optic endoscope. He also examines Joshua's throat with a head mirror and a tongue depressor and checks the entrance to his larynx with an angled mirror. When he is finished, he asks Joshua to blow his nose and check whether his ears pop. Joshua finds he cannot influence his ears by doing this.

The consultant then explains that he proposes to anaesthetize the inside of Joshua's nose and pass a fine tube called a eustachian catheter to equalize the air pressure on either side of the ear-drums. Joshua finds this unpleasant but not painful. As soon as air is blown through the catheter on both sides, Joshua realizes that his hearing is back to normal.

The diagnosis

The consultant explains that Joshua has eustachian catarrh — an inflammation of the linings of the tubes that run from the back of the nose to the middle ear. This has caused the linings of the tubes to swell and the tubes to close. The air in the middle ears has then been absorbed into the blood vessels of the mucous membrane, so that the ear-drums are forced inwards by atmospheric pressure and are no longer able to move freely. Passing a tube to let the air into the middle ear (*eustachian catheterization*) has temporarily corrected the problem.

Joshua asks what has caused the inflammation and is told that this is usually due to infection of the nose or throat. As there is no sign of this, the trouble is probably an allergy. This also fits in with the sneezing, the eye watering and the time of the year. This is an unusual symptom of hay fever but the specialist has seen several cases like this before.

The treatment

Joshua is greatly relieved to learn that his problem is not permanent. They discuss treatment. Joshua explains that he is not particularly keen to take antihistamines as he fears that this may lower his concentration. The doctor assures him that there are antihistamines that do not have this effect, but prescribes a cromoglycate nasal spray to be used as a preventive (see Chapter 7). Fortunately, this is sufficient to prevent further episodes of eustachian catarrh.

The follow-up

Joshua needs to use the spray only during the pollen seasons, and, on the whole, succeeds in avoiding ear trouble for several years. Gradually, however, his hay fever gets worse and eventually he requires more vigorous treatment. He is now using a combination of cromoglycate drops, a steroid nasal spray and carefully selected antihistamines (see Chapter 6). His doctor is considering referring him to an allergist with a view to possible desensitization treatment.

Urticaria

One of the important effects of histamine released from mast cells is the action it has on the smallest of all blood vessels — the capillaries. These vessels are very thin-walled and normally allow a certain amount of water to pass out from the blood at the high-pressure (arterial) end and in again at the low-pressure (venous) end. Histamine interferes with this effect so that much more water than usual passes out. In areas where histamine is present near the surface of the skin, therefore, there will be local, balloon-like swellings in the skin. This is called *urticaria* or *angioedema*. Urticaria is not necessarily an allergic process and it is not a direct complication of hay fever, but it is commonly an IgE problem so is much more likely to affect people who have hay fever. It may be caused by drugs such as aspirin, some food additives such as tartrazine, certain foods such as yeasts, and plant and insect stings. Mild and moderate urticaria responds well to antihistamine drugs.

Anaphylactic shock

Happily, this serious allergic effect is rare, even in hay fever sufferers. But it is commoner in these than in non-allergic people. As we have seen, histamine is very powerful stuff. When it reaches mucus gland cells and the small glands that produce a watery fluid, it causes them to secrete strongly. When it reaches the blood vessels in the lining of the nose it causes them to widen so that the whole area becomes flooded with blood. When it reaches the smooth muscles surrounding the air tubes of the lungs (*bronchioles*), it causes them to tighten so that the bronchioles are narrowed and there is difficulty in breathing. Fortunately, the action of histamine is mainly confined to the area in which it is released from the mast cells. But if large amounts are released it can get into the bloodstream and have its effect all over the body. This can be very dangerous because the effects are so widespread. A general widening of blood vessels causes a serious drop in the blood pressure, and the effects on the lungs can be devastating. This generalized effect is called anaphylactic shock and it is often fatal. You may have heard of people killed by a single bee sting. This is how it happens. The affected person must, of course, have been previously sensitized by an earlier sting and must have accumulated IgE.

People who readily produce IgE are more prone to this rare condition than others and should know about it. This is especially important if there has been a previous anaphylactic episode. It may be caused by a drug such as penicillin or aspirin, by an insect sting, by injudicious attempts at desensitization (see Chapter 7), or by any circumstance in which an allergen that can trigger off widespread histamine release is introduced into the body. Apart from the catastrophic drop in blood pressure there is an even greater danger. The soft tissues lining the larynx are especially prone to oedema and if this occurs the airway may be cut off completely. This is probably the most acute emergency of all. Anyone with a closed airway has only minutes to live.

Emergency treatment is by an injection of adrenaline and an antihistamine and, in the most severe cases, an intravenous injection of a steroid. Often an emergency opening has to be made into the windpipe in the neck as the only way of saving life. This is called a *tracheostomy*. It may sound drastic, but there are critical circumstances in which it is the only thing to do. The victim's neck is extended and a bold cut is made with a sharp knife or a razor blade vertically downwards immediately below the projection of the Adam's apple. As soon as the windpipe is opened breathing can occur and a small tube of some kind — maybe the barrel of a ball-point pen — is pushed in to keep the hole open. Many lives have been saved by this kind of crude surgery, performed on the spot.

Asthma

About ten per cent of people with hay fever or PAR develop asthma. One child in ten suffers from asthma. So, obviously, this is something you should know about. Asthma is a major subject in its own right and this book is about hay fever, so only a general outline can be given here. Like hay fever, asthma is becoming more common, and badly managed asthma can be dangerous. Unfortunately, people do sometimes die from asthma, often because no one was aware of the danger signs. Asthma is commonest in atopic people (see Chapter 2).

The air tubes leading to the lungs are called *bronchi* and they have muscle rings in their walls which, under the influence of histamine, can tighten up to cause severe narrowing of the airway. The triggers for histamine release are exactly the same as in hay fever and PAR. These are listed in Chapter 2. In general, the smaller the allergen particles, the more likely they are to get down to the lungs. Asthma can also be triggered by colds, coughs or bronchitis, or even by exercise, especially in cold weather. Emotional factors, such as stress or anxiety, may precipitate attacks.

Asthmatic attacks vary greatly in their severity and are most frequent in the early morning. The main symptoms are:

- breathlessness;
- wheezing;
- a dry cough sometimes brought on by exercise;
- a feeling of tightness in the chest.

During a severe attack, breathing becomes increasingly difficult, causing sweating, rapid heart beat, and great distress and anxiety. The sufferer cannot lie down or sleep, may be unable to speak, breathes rapidly, and wheezes loudly. In a very severe attack, the low amount of oxygen in the blood may cause blue-purple discoloration of the face, particularly the lips. This is called *cyanosis* and it is a clear sign of the severity of the attack. In addition, the skin may become pale and clammy. Such attacks may be fatal. In Britain, about 2,000 people die from asthma each year. Twice as many die from asthmatic complications.

Asthma attacks can be prevented or minimized to a large extent. First the allergen must be identified and avoided if possible (see Chapters 5 and 11). More successful in preventing attacks are drugs, such as *cromoglycate* (*cromolyn sodium*) and inhaled steroid drugs. To be effective, they must be taken several times daily from an inhaler.

Once an attack has started, a preventive drug has limited effects and a drug that relaxes and widens the airways (a bronchodilator), such as *Ventolin, Cyclocaps* or *Salbulin* (*salbutamol*), *Bricanyl* (*terbutaline*) or *Duovent* (*fenoterol*), must be used. If you are asthmatic, you must learn the proper way to administer the drug yourself with an inhaler. Most attacks of asthma either pass naturally or can be controlled by use of a bronchodilator. In some cases, however, an attack may be so severe that it fails to respond to the recommended dose of the drug. In this case, you should repeat the dose. If this has no effect, see a doctor or get yourself to hospital without delay. It is essential to understand that if, in spite of treatment, your asthma is going out of control, this is an emergency situation that requires urgent medical attention, day or night.

There is much more to be known about asthma and you should study one of the many popular books on the subject. Above all, you should, at all times, know about the state of your bronchial tubes. Ideally, you should be regularly checking, with a peak flow meter, the rates at which you breath out. You should be keeping a record of the results, and should know at what point the peak flow rate has become dangerously low.

CHAPTER
ELEVEN

Avoiding Hay Fever

Prevention is always better than cure, and in the case of allergic rhinitis this is particularly so. Avoiding contact with the allergen — once you have discovered what it is — is especially important because, as we have seen, *hay fever gets worse with repeated exposure*. The progressive increase in the amount of IgE and in the number of mast cells and basophil cells means that complications and possibly even irreversible disease become more likely.

Never be content simply to know that you have hay fever; it is essential to know precisely what the allergen is that is causing it. Only when you do know this can you intelligently plan an avoidance strategy. If you are very fortunate, you may be able to avoid the allergen altogether, and if you can do this, you might even be able to cure your hay fever. Unfortunately, it is extremely difficult to avoid allergens completely.

Keeping away from the allergen

An obvious measure is to limit your movements so as to avoid areas in which your allergen is prevalent during hay fever seasons. During these periods you can greatly help to reduce trouble by:

- staying indoors;
- keeping windows closed, even upper-floor windows in tall buildings;
- keeping car windows closed during country trips;
- observing reports of high pollen counts;
- avoiding parks and other open spaces with vegetation;
- keep away from barns, grass mowing, haymaking;
- wearing close-fitting sunglasses or even goggles;
- wearing a mask over the nose and mouth.

Unfortunately, simple masks are far from effective in keeping out tiny particles of the size of pollen grains. If you want to do this really effectively, the only way is to use a kind of spherical space helmet, sealed around the shoulders and connected by a wide tube to a portable, battery-powered filter unit on a belt. This unit can eliminate allergens. Very few people are willing to go this far. Most would feel uncomfortably conspicuous. There is another reason for discomfort. In sunny weather, when you are most likely to need such a device, the greenhouse effect leads to an unpleasant rise of temperature within the globe. You may also find the plastic mists up.

Indoors, it is possible to use electrostatic particle precipitators and high-efficiency air-conditioning systems with particle-trapping filters. These are major and expensive items, not to be confused with domestic "ionizers". Note, however, that while such equipment can clear tiny particles such as pollen grains, you will still be in trouble if your problem is caused by heavier particles such as house mite faecal allergens. These pass briefly into the air when mattresses, bedding etc. are disturbed and may be inhaled. But they soon settle again and are not removed by air filters.

If you suffer from straightforward hay fever, you might consider having one room — such as a bedroom — fitted with a high-efficiency particulate air filter. You can even hire equipment of this kind for use during the hay fever seasons.

Some people have found it worthwhile to go to the length of a change of residence.

What to do about mites

Many people believe that a good weekly hoovering of bedrooms is all that is necessary. Unfortunately, this is not so. A thorough vacuum clean can reduce the mite population by 70 per cent but the population will return to the previous level within a week. Mite faeces particles are highly allergenic and you need to inhale only a few to keep the symptoms going. So if you are going to try to rely on the vacuum cleaner, you will have to use it every day. Remember also that vacuuming causes mite faeces to become airborne, so the sufferer should keep out of the room that is being cleaned.

You must also ensure that the vacuum cleaner bag has very small pores. Stout disposable paper bags are likely to be more efficient than the earlier cloth bags that have to be emptied, but neither can be relied on to prevent small particles from passing through. Particles are more likely to be trapped if the bag has already been used for a while so that the air has to pass through a thick layer of fluff and dust. You might even decide to experiment by putting some loose cotton wool in the bag.

Mites can be killed by various chemicals such as tannic acid, crotamiton or benzyl benzoate. Some people treat their carpets with these. Unfortunately, benzyl benzoate, which is a long-established treatment for another mite problem — scabies — can cause severe skin irritation and may be damaging to the eyes. You have to be rather careful you don't overdo the use of these miticide substances.

Probably the most effective measure against mites is to deprive them of the kind of habitat they like best — cotton or linen sheets, pillowslips, duvet covers and mattresses. If you examine an ordinary bedsheet with a strong hand lens you will see that the cloth contains endless convenient little spaces for these creatures to lurk in and quietly munch on, and digest, the protein skin scales you are so kindly donating. So if you enclose your mattresses and pillows in polythene or nylon bags you will make things hard for the mites. If you decide to do this, ensure that there is no possible danger of a plastic bag coming loose and causing suffocation. Frequent washing of bedding at a high temperature setting of the washing machine will also help to keep the mite population down.

Pollen seasons in different countries

If you are a hay fever sufferer you will be thoroughly familiar with the seasons during which you are affected. You have to remember, however, that if you are planning a holiday or a stay abroad, the peak pollen and other allergen seasons may differ from those you are accustomed to. Wherever you go, try to avoid areas of extensive vegetation, especially grass meadows. The general rule in the tropics is that allergens are likely to be most profuse following rainy seasons.

There are too many countries to cover comprehensively, but here is an alphabetical list of some of those likely to be of interest.

Alpine regions
This is a recommended holiday region if you suffer severely, because pollen counts are low everywhere. You may, however, encounter some grass pollen at the end of July and the beginning of August. House mites do not survive above 1,000 metres.

The Bermudas
Like other warm island regions, such as Singapore and the Seychelles, the pollen counts are low and there is little likelihood of trouble from hay fever. The high humidity, however, does greatly encourage fungal growth. If you are susceptible to fungal allergies, these islands may not be for you.

Caribbean
The pollen counts tend to be high for most of the year with a peak during November to January. Pollen counts are lowest between August and October. There may be a year-round problem from nettles with a peak during March to June.

East Africa

The best time for travel, from the point of view of hay fever only, is during the monsoon season, from mid-June to mid-September, when the atmospheric allergen content is low. This, however, can be a very uncomfortable period from other points of view. Pollen counts can be very high between September and November. The best compromise between weather and pollen is probably between mid-February and mid-June.

Egypt

In most tourist areas grass pollens peak around June, but you may encounter nettle and goosefoot (*Chenopodium*) pollens from March to November, with a peak in April. If you are a hay fever victim you would be best to plan to visit Egypt some time between December and February.

France

Along the Mediterranean coast there is a good deal of pollen at most times of the year with a peak between late May and early June. Grass pollens are worst between April and August and nettle pollens occur between late February and September. Cypress tree pollens occur in January and February, and olive tree pollens in April to July. The west coast of France, however, is a good area for hay fever sufferers, and has low pollen counts for most of the year. In Paris, hay fever sufferers are likely to have trouble throughout most of the spring and summer, March to August.

Greece
The worst of the pollen is from March to July with a peak in May and June. Both grass and tree pollens, especially from plane trees, poplars and olive trees, are prominent during this period. Tree pollens are worst in March and April. Nettle pollens can also be a problem around the same time.

India
The situation is similar to that in East Africa. India has a monsoon climate and during the rainy periods you will have no trouble with hay fever as all the atmospheric pollution is washed away. The after-effects of the rain, however, greatly encourage the growth of grasses and other plants, and pollen counts can rise very high in October and November. So the best time to travel, from a hay fever point of view, is from mid-June to mid-September.

Italy
Along the Adriatic coast and in the Po valley the main problem is from grass pollens. The grass pollen season extends from April to June with a peak in May. Tree pollens, especially from Cypress trees, will be encountered from mid-February to mid-March. Olive trees may also cause problems with pollen dispersion at the end of May and the beginning of June.

Scandinavia
Tree pollens are the main problem because of the extensive forests. In particular, you may expect trouble

from birch pollens from the latter part of May until the middle of July, especially in southern Sweden and Finland. In general, allergies from tree pollens are more troublesome in the south of Scandinavia than in the north. There is also a lengthy grass pollen season from late May until about mid-August. Nettle pollen allergens are also encountered, usually worst in June.

Seychelles
See Bermudas.

Singapore
See Bermudas.

Spain and Portugal
This is not the ideal holiday region for hay fever sufferers, especially in central and southern Spain, where you may expect to encounter pollens from February to December. The worst time of the year is May and June. Things are not so bad in the Algarve and the larger inland cities, where grass pollen counts may be quite low. But watch out for pollens from plane trees in May and June. You will find olive trees in most parts of Spain and Portugal. These cause most hay fever trouble between the end of May and the end of June.

United States
The grass pollen season in most places is from May to October, usually worst in June. In Washington, DC tree pollens are worst from February to May; grass pollens from May to June; and fungal spores from July to August.

Watch out for the ragweed season which, in the eastern and midwestern States, lasts from July to October. This is a potent allergen, often called "sneezeweed" and is the most serious offender causing hay fever in the USA. In the south, in places like Florida, tree pollens, especially cedar pollens, peak between January and March. White oak pollens peak between February and May. In Hawaii, tree pollens are most troublesome between January and April. Weed pollens are plentiful for most of the rest of the year. You might be lucky in May. Pollen calendars are available for all the States.

GLOSSARY

This wordlist serves two functions; it provides a convenient reminder of the meanings of words you may come across while reading the book (although all technical words are, of course, defined when they first appear), and it acts as a kind of summary or recapitulation of the medical principles underlying hay fever and perennial allergic rhinitis (PAR). Cross-references to other definitions in this section are shown in **bold**.

acute Short, sharp and quickly over. Acute conditions usually start abruptly, last for a few days and then either settle or become persistent and longlasting (*chronic*). From the Latin *acutus*, sharp.

aeroallergens Airborne particles, especially tree and grass pollens, that can induce allergic responses, such as hay fever (**allergic rhinitis**) in sensitized persons.

allergen Any substance that can provoke an allergic reaction after coming in contact with the body. Allergens are examples of **antigens** — the wider group of all the substances that the body recognizes as foreign and produces antibodies against. This book is largely concerned with allergens and you can read all about them in Chapter 2.

allergic alveolitis Inflammation of the small air sacs in the lungs, usually caused by inhalation of organic dusts. There are various named types, including Bird fancier's lung, Farmer's lung, Mushroom worker's lung, baggasosis, Maltworker's lung and Maple bark disease. Allergic alveolitis is very much less common than hay fever or PAR. It is a form of pneumonia featuring wheezing, breathlessness, dry cough, fever and a feeling of illness (*malaise*).

allergic rhinitis Hay fever. The susceptibility (**atopy**) is often inherited. A specific immunoglobulin (**IgE**) coats the mast cells in the nose and air passages. When the **allergen** — grass or tree pollen etc. — reaches the mast cells it combines with the IgE and this triggers the release of histamine and other highly irritating substances from the mast cells. Allergic rhinitis is what this book is all about.

allergy An abnormal sensitivity to body contact with a foreign substance, known as an **allergen**. The commonest allergens are grass or tree pollens, dust mites and their excreta or certain metals such as nickel. The effect may take several forms, including weals (*urticaria*), dermatitis, asthma or hay fever (**allergic rhinitis**). An allergic response implies that there has been a prior contact with the allergen during which the immunological processes leading to the hypersensitivity have occurred. Susceptibility to allergy is often inherited. *See also* **allergic dermatitis** and **allergic rhinitis**.

anaphylaxis A severe form of allergic reaction most commonly provoked by drugs such as penicillin,

113

intravenous iron or procainamide, but also brought on by allergy to foods, vaccines, insect stings or snake bites. There is always a history of a previous reaction to the **allergen**. The effects are a drop in blood pressure, local swelling of the skin (*angioedema*), narrowing of the air tubes, itching, vomiting and abdominal pain. The sooner the onset after exposure to the allergen, the more severe the reaction. Anaphylactic shock is a serious, widespread allergic attack which may cause death by airway obstruction from swelling of the lining of the voice box in the neck.

antibody A protein substance, called an immunoglobulin, produced by the B group of lymphocytes in response to the presence of an **antigen**. An appropriate B lymphocyte is selected from the existing repertoire. This then produces a clone of plasma cells — little protein factories each capable of making large numbers of specific antibodies to combat the infection. The B cells also produce memory cells. Subsequent infection with the same antigen prompts the memory cells to clone plasma cells and produce the correct antibodies without further delay. This is an important way in which infection results in subsequent immunity. Antibodies are able to neutralize antigens or render them susceptible to destruction by phagocytes in the body. Unfortunately, the production of one type of antibody does more harm than good. You can read about this in Chapter 2.

antigen Any substance that the immune system of the body can recognize as being "foreign". Antigens are chemical groups on the surface of viruses, bacteria, fungi, pollen grains, donor tissue from other individuals, or any other "non-self" material. The immune system can identify antigens and produce custom-built antibodies to attack the foreign invaders that are carrying them.

antihistamine One of a group of drugs which act to prevent histamine — a powerful and highly irritant agent released in the body by mast cells — from causing its unpleasant effects on local cells and tissues. Antihistamine drugs fall into two groups — those used to relieve allergies that block H_1 receptors and act mainly on blood vessels, and those used to reduce the rate of acid production by the stomach that block H_2 receptors. The latter are not usually called antihistamines but are well known as the drugs *cimetidine* (*Tagamet*) and *ranitidine* (*Zantac*). You can read all about antihistamines in Chapter 6.

atopy An underlying allergic tendency which may show itself in a number of different ways. Atopy is associated with immunoglobulin E (**IgE**) production and is an inherited tendency caused by a gene that alters the binding sites for IgE on **mast cells**. Atopy features a proneness to asthma, hay fever and eczema (atopic dermatitis). The term was derived from the Greek *a-*, "not" and *topos*, "a place", on the grounds that the reaction could occur at a different site from that of contact with the causal **allergen**. This is not the case with hay fever but occurs with anaphylactic reactions. *See also* Chapter 2.

atrophic rhinitis An unpleasant condition affecting the inner lining of the nose which becomes dry and crusty and produces a foul odour. There is loss of the sense of smell and frequent nosebleeds. This is a very rare possible late complication of severe **allergic rhinitis**. There is more about nasal problems in Chapter 1.

basophil cells Granular cells, roughly similar in appearance and effect to **mast cells**, that appear in increasing numbers in people with long-term hay fever. Like mast cells, basophils can produce powerfully irritating substances, such as histamine, with unpleasant effects. In general, basophils are less important than mast cells in the hay fever and PAR reactions. You can safely assume that when mast cells are mentioned, as in Chapter 2, basophils are also likely to be involved.

B cells One of the two main classes of lymphocytes — the white cells found in the blood, lymph nodes and tissue which, with other cells, form the immune system of the body. You should really call them "B lymphocytes" but for convenience they are usually called "B cells". They are the cells that actually produce the antibodies (immunoglobulins). To do so they are quickly modified so that they become very active protein factories and, in this form, they are usually called plasma cells. They are, however, still B cells. *See also* **T cells**.

cilia The microscopic hair-like processes extending from the surface of the lining cells of the nose and other parts of the respiratory system. This lining layer is called *ciliated epithelium*. The cilia move in a coordinated rhythmical lashing motion usually described as being like a wind-blown field of corn. The point of this is to carry out of the nose and air tubes particles of dust, fluff, pollen etc. that have been caught by the sticky mucus. Healthy cilia do an excellent job in helping to condition the air passing through the nose and they ensure that pollen grains do their harm for the shortest possible time.

corticosteroid hormones Natural steroid hormones secreted by the outer zone (*cortex*) of the adrenal glands. These hormones are cortisol, corticosterone, aldosterone and androsterone. The first two, or substances chemically similar to them, are commonly used as drugs to treat hay fever, PAR and allergic asthma. They are highly effective and, because they are usually taken by inhalation, are unlikely to produce any general side effects. You can read more about the steroid drugs in Chapter 7.

cromoglycate, sodium A drug used in allergies. It is said to work by stabilizing the membrane of the **mast cells** to prevent the release of histamine and other irritating substances when antibodies (**IgE**) and **allergens** (such as pollen grains) react on their surfaces. You have to use cromoglycate before the allergens arrive. *See also* Chapter 7.

food allergy Sensitivity to one or more of the substances in normal diets. True food allergy is rare — much less common than you would think from reading popular medical books. Proper scientific tests, especially double-blind trials in which neither the tester nor the person tested know what is being given, have shown that food allergy does not cause many of the disorders commonly attributed to it. Monosodium glutamate (MSG) can cause the *Chinese restaurant syndrome*. Tartrazine sensitivity is an established fact. Other additives, such as sulphur dioxide, sulphites, azo-dyes (used in most textiles) and benzoate preservatives also sometimes cause genuine allergic reactions, such as asthma. Allergy to basic foodstuffs seldom occurs. Food intolerance is fairly common but has nothing to do with allergy.

fungi A large group of spore-bearing organisms that derive their nourishment by decomposing non-living organic matter and absorbing nutrients through their surface. The spores from various fungi commonly cause hay fever. Many fungi can infect the body but, in people with healthy immune systems, infection tends to be limited to the outer layer (epidermis) of the skin and the readily accessible mucous membranes. Immune deficiency from any cause (*see* Chapter 2) allows widespread opportunistic fungus infections of all parts of the body. Malnourishment and poor living conditions predispose to deeper fungus infections following penetrating injuries to the feet and other parts.

gamma globulin A protein, one of the five classes of immunoglobulins (antibodies). Gamma globulin, or immunoglobulin G (IgG), is the most prevalent in the blood and elsewhere and provides the body's main antibody defence against infection. For this reason it is produced commercially from human plasma and used for passive protection against many infections, especially hepatitis, measles and poliomyelitis. Hay fever is concerned with a different immunoglobulin, that might be called epsilon globulin — **IgE**.

histamine A powerful hormone synthesized and stored in the granules of **mast cells** from which it is released when antibodies attached to the cells are contracted by **allergens** such as pollens. Free histamine acts on H_1 receptors to cause small blood vessels to widen (dilate) and become more permeable to protein, resulting in the effects known an allergic reactions. Histamine also acts on receptors in the stomach (H_2 receptors) to promote the secretion of acid. H_2 receptor blocker drugs, such as Zantac (ranitidine) are widely used to control acid secretion. *See also* **antihistamines** and Chapter 6.

hypersensitivity An allergic state in which more severe tissue reactions occur on a second or subsequent exposure to an **antigen** than on the first exposure. A particular group of antibodies (**IgE**) is involved in many hypersensitivity reactions. Hay fever, PAR, allergic asthma and urticaria are all hypersensitivity reactions.

hypogammaglobulinaemia Abnormally low levels of the antibody group gamma globulin in the blood. This is a feature of some kinds of immunodeficiency and can be corrected by monthly injections of gamma globulin. *See also* Chapter 2.

Ig The commonly-used abbreviation for *immunoglobulin.*

IgE Immunoglobulin class E, an antibody class concerned with immediate hypersensitivity reactions, such as hay fever (**allergic rhinitis**), PAR and allergic asthma. IgE has an affinity for cell surfaces and is commonly found on **mast cells**, to which it attaches at certain receptor sites. A gene mutation has recently been discovered that affects IgE receptor sites on mast cells in people particularly prone to hay fever. IgE is the immunoglobulin (antibody) type with which this book is concerned.

immune surveillance A constant checking process carried out by the immune system by which cells that have been invaded by viruses and those that are in the early stages of becoming cancers are detected, attacked and, fortunately, usually destroyed. Such cells put out flags (**antigens**) indicating that something is going wrong. These antigens can be recognized by immune system cells. Immune surveillance is carried out by T lymphocytes (T cells). Without it, most of us would already be dead.

immunity The ability to resist most infections or the effects of many toxic or dangerous substances. The word does not mean what it seems to mean — complete protection. Immunity is relative. It may be present from birth or acquired as a result of infections or immunization. Active immunity involves the production of one's own antibodies (*see* Chapter 2). Passive immunity is conferred by antibodies produced by another person or animal and injected or received across the placenta or in the breast milk. Passive immunity does not last as long as active immunity.

immunoglobulins Antibodies. These are protective proteins produced by B lymphocytes (B cells). There are five classes of immunoglobulins, the most prevalent being immunoglobulin G (IgG), or gamma globulin, which provides the body's main defence against bacteria, viruses and toxins. The others are **IgA, IgD, IgE, IgG** and **IgM. IgE** is the immunoglobulin of concern to hay fever sufferers.

inflammation The response of living tissue to injury. Inflammation features widening of blood vessels, with redness, heat, swelling and pain — the cardinal signs "rubor" (redness), "calor" (heat), "tumour" (swelling) and "dolor" (pain) first recorded by the 1st century Roman physician Aulus Cornelius Celsus. Inflammation is the commonest of all the disease processes. Any word ending in *-itis* refers to inflammation of the part mentioned. Inflammation involves release of substances, known as *prostaglandins*, that strongly stimulate pain nerve endings. In hay fever, prostaglandins are released from **mast cells** along with **histamine** and are partly responsible for the symptoms of the disorder.

inhalers Devices for delivering medication in aerosol, vapour or powder form to the nose, bronchial tubes and lungs, especially for the treatment of hay fever, PAR and asthma. Propulsion of the drug may be by gas under pressure or by an inhaled current of air. Drugs commonly taken in this way include steroids, decongestants and cromoglycate (*see* Chapter 7).

mast cell A connective tissue cell found in large numbers in the mucous membranes and skin and in the lymphatic system. Mast cells play a central part in allergic reactions. They contain numerous large granules that are collections of powerfully irritating chemical substances such as histamine, serotonin and prostaglandins. In people with allergies, the antibody **IgE** remains attached to specific receptors on the surface of the mast cells. When the substance causing the allergy (the **allergen**) contacts the IgE, the mast cell is triggered to release these substances and the result is the range of allergic symptoms and signs. Chromoglycate can stabilize the mast cell membrane and prevent the release of the contents.

mucous membrane The lining of most of the body cavities and hollow internal organs such as the mouth, the nose, the eyelids, the intestine and the vagina. Mucous membranes contain large numbers of goblet-shaped cells that secrete mucus which keeps the surface moist and lubricated. Many mucous membranes are also ciliated (*see* **cilia**).

nasal congestion Swelling (**oedema**) of the **mucous membrane** lining the nose, usually as a result of inflammation from histamine released as an allergic response to tree or grass pollen grains or from a common cold virus infection. Nasal congestion can be relieved temporarily by decongestant drugs but these have some major disadvantages and potential dangers (*see* Chapter 10).

nasal discharge Any fluid running from the nose that is watery or has pus (*purulent*) or blood in it. Nasal discharge usually comes from the mucous membrane of the nose or sinuses but after a head injury may come from inside the skull and consist of the cerebrospinal fluid that normally bathes the brain.

nasal obstruction Interference with the free passage of air through either side of the nose from any cause. Causes of obstruction include swelling of the mucous membrane (**nasal congestion**) from hay fever or PAR, nasal polyps, foreign bodies, or, rarely, cancer of the back of the nose.

nasal septum The thin, central partition that divides the interior of the nose into two passages. The septum consists of a thin plate of bone, behind, and a thin plate of cartilage in front. Both are covered with mucous membrane. Deflection of the septum to one side (*deviated septum*) is common and usually harmless.

nitrogen oxides These are poisonous atmospheric pollutants mainly produced by the action of sunlight on the exhaust fumes from cars and other vehicles. Their relevance to hay fever and PAR is that nitrogen oxides can interfere with the action of **cilia** in the nose. As a result, pollen grains remain on the nose lining longer than they otherwise would, thus making the hay fever worse. Nitrogen oxides also cause irritation in their own right, thereby adding to the severity of the symptoms of hay fever.

oedema Excessive accumulation of fluid, mainly water, in the tissue spaces of the body. Oedema may be local, as at the site of an injury, or general. In allergic reactions local oedema, such as urticaria, is caused by the action of histamine on small blood vessels. General oedema may be caused by allergy, injury, starvation, heart failure, kidney disease, liver disease, hormonal changes in the menstrual cycle, varicose veins or poisoning. Persistent general oedema is treated with diuretic drugs to increase the outflow of urine and so remove water from the body.

otitis media Inflammation in the middle ear cavity. This usually results from spread of infection from the nose or throat by way of the eustachian tube but may arise as a result of blockage of the tube so that drainage from the middle ear is prevented. This can be caused by hay fever. In **acute** suppurative otitis media there is rapid production of pus with a pressure rise that causes the eardrum to bulge outwards. In chronic suppurative otitis media, there is a hole (perforation) in the drum and usually a persistent discharge (*otorrhoea*). Otitis media is persistent and insidious and commonly affects children causing unsuspected deafness and educational disadvantage. All forms of otitis media respond well to expert treatment. (*See also* Chapter 8.)

phagocytes Cells of the immune system that respond to contact with foreign objects, such as bacteria, by surrounding, engulfing and digesting them. Phagocytes occur widely throughout the body wherever they are likely to be required. Some wander freely throughout the tissues. Phagocytes act most effectively if their prey has first been inactivated by attachment of **antibody**.

phagocytosis The envelopment and destruction of bacteria or other foreign bodies by phagocytes.

pollenosis A general term for the allergic responses to atmospheric pollen grains from trees, grasses, flowers or weeds.

postnasal drip An intermittent trickle of watery nasal discharge or mucus from the back of the nose into the throat. The excess secretion usually results from inflammation of the mucous membrane of the nose, as in **allergic rhinitis** or **rhinitis** from any cause.

rhinitis Inflammation of the mucous membrane lining of the nose. Rhinitis is one of the most common human complaints and is a major feature of hay fever (**allergic rhinitis**) and of the common cold. The membrane becomes swollen, so that the air flow is partly or wholly obstructed, and its glands become overactive causing excessive mucus production and a watery discharge. Vasomotor rhinitis is the result of a disturbance of the nervous control of blood vessels in the mucous membrane. Hypertrophic rhinitis, with thickening and persistent congestion of the membrane, is the result of long-term inflammation or repeated infection. Atrophic rhinitis features shrinkage and loss of the mucous membrane, with dryness, crusting and loss of the sense of smell. (*See also* Chapter 1.)

rhinorrhea Watery discharge from the nose. This is usually due to **rhinitis,** but following a head injury with a fracture of the base of the skull, a persistent drip from the nose may be due to leakage of cerebrospinal fluid from the brain cavity.

sick building syndrome A varied group of symptoms sometimes experienced by people working in a modern office building and attributed to the building. Symptoms include fatigue, headache, dryness and itching of the eyes, sore throat and dryness of the nose. No convincing explanation has been offered but some cases are undoubtedly due to allergic reactions. Ozone from photocopiers and laser printers can make matters worse by interfering with the action of **cilia**.

sinusitis Inflammation of the mucous membrane linings of one or more bone cavities (sinuses) of the face. This almost always results from infection. There is a feeling of fullness or pain in the forehead, cheeks or between the eyes, fever and general upset. Treatment may involve surgical drainage and antibiotics. (*See also* Chapter 8.)

skin tests Investigations to determine allergic sensitivity to various substances by pricking the skin with a needle through a drop of a solution of small quantities of the substance or by applying the substance under patches (patch tests).

sneezing A protective reflex initiated by irritation of the nose lining and resulting in a blast of air through the nose and mouth that may remove the cause. The vocal cords are firmly pressed together, air in the chest is compressed and the cords then suddenly separated. (*See* Chapter 1.)

spore A single-celled form of a fungus or other simple organism by which it can be spread. Spores are capable of developing into an adult. Fungal spores often become airborne and form common **allergens**, giving rise to hay fever.

steroid drugs Drugs identical or similar to the natural steroid hormones of the outer zone (cortex) of the adrenal glands. Modern synthetic steroids are often many times more powerful than the natural hormones hydrocortisone and corticosterone. (*See also* Chapter 7.)

submucous resection An operation on the nose to relieve **nasal obstruction** by removing displaced cartilage and bone from underneath the mucous membrane of a deviated central partition (septum) of the nose. This is occasionally needed in long-term cases of **allergic rhinitis** that have led to persistent blockage (*See also* Chapter 1.)

T cells The important class of immune system cells complementary to the **B cells**. T cells fall into five distinct groups, the most important of which are the *killer* T cells and the *helper* T cells. Killer cells are aggressive lymphocytes that roam the body searching for, and destroying, abnormal cells that have been invaded by viruses or have developed cancerous tendencies. Helper T cells cooperate with B cells in producing the right kinds of antibodies. It is the helper T cells that are destroyed in AIDS.

vernal conjunctivitis An allergic form of inflammation of the conjuctiva probably caused by contact with spring pollens. It affects mostly young boys in tropical or sub-tropical countries. You can read more about vernal conjunctivitis in Chapter 3.

INDEX

129

steroid drugs, 68, 117, 127;
  functions of, 70;
  side-effects, 68-9
steroid hormones, 115
stuffy nose, 127
submucous resection, 127

T cells, 18, 116, 127
tartrazine, 98
Timothy grass, 9
total allergy syndrome, 15
turbinates, 29
Tyrophagus longior, 53

urticaria, 97

vasomotor rhinitis, 47
vernal catarrh, 36
vernal conjunctivitis, 127

watery nose, 125
weed pollens, 9

Yorkshire fog grass, 9

HEALTH AND SELF HELP

DR ANTHONY CAMPBELL
Getting the Best For Your Bad Back

THEODORE DALRYMPLE
If Symptoms Persist

ANNE DICKSON AND NIKKI HENRIQUES
Menopause: The Woman's View

DR JOAN GOMEZ
Sixtysomething

MARGARET HILLS AND JANET HORWOOD
Curing Arthritis Exercise Book

DR BRICE PITT
Making the Most of Middle Age

DR CAROLINE SHREEVE
High Blood Pressure

DR TOM SMITH
Coping With Bronchitis and Emphysema

STEPHEN TERRAS
Arthritis

NANCY TUFT
Looking Good, Feeling Good

CLAIRE WEEKES
More Help for Your Nerves